Psychometric Assessment, Statistics and Report Writing

An introduction for psychologists, teachers and health professionals

Dr. Barry Johnson and Dr. Gareth Hagger-Johnson

Published by
Pearson
Assessment
80 Strand
London WC2R 0RL

Pearson is a trademark, in the U.S. and/or other countries, of Pearson Education, Inc. or its affiliate(s).

Visit our website at www.pearsonclinical.co.uk

Printed in the United Kingdom

978 0 7491 63 77 8

13 14 15 16 17 A B C D E

Contents

LIST OF FIGURES

This book is designed primarily to support users of psychometric tests. It provides specialist teachers, psychologists and other health professionals with a practical reference book on basic statistical methods to aid them in their diagnostic interpretation of psychometric test scores when assessing children, young people and adults with special educational needs and specific learning difficulties. It offers a complementary resource to published test scoring and reporting software. It acknowledges that assessors often need to have available practical guidance and references on a number of statistical matters, particularly as the range of available tests is now extremely wide.

The level of statistical information provided is suitable for those UK teachers who are either training for their practising certificate in special education or seeking renewal of their certificate in order to be deemed as appropriately trained and safe to practice. It will also be helpful to experienced specialist teachers and psychologists who are practising as diagnosticians but who feel that they need additional help with their understanding and efficient application of a range of statistical concepts and approaches. Trainee and newly qualified educational and clinical psychologists in the UK will also find the book useful as an aid to their induction to fieldwork assessment practices and their CPD requirements for maintaining their HCPC professional registration. The book will be particularly relevant for those professionals involved in providing reports for clients who require assessments for consideration of eligibility for access arrangements for formal examinations such as GCSE/GCE and Disabled Students' Allowance (DSA).

The book includes references to a range of contemporary psychometric tests. The examples are selected predominantly from tests published or distributed by Pearson Assessment. The book draws on the tests' standardisation data and encourages users to adopt a critical stance when selecting tests for diagnostic purposes. It focuses on common mistakes and misunderstandings made by assessors when they attempt to interpret psychometric information for the purposes of providing diagnostic reports for their clients. In doing so, it is likely to be of significant help by ensuring that these professionals can be confident that their conclusions reflect sound principles of statistical interpretation and hypothesis-testing. Case examples and scenarios are given which are of the type commonly experienced by professionals, thereby making it relatively easy for them to be applied within their own contexts of need. Relatively simple *Excel* formulae and table creations are introduced to encourage professionals to establish incrementally a repertoire of reference sources, statistical tools and personal overview data relating to their assessment inputs. Tips are given on how to merge statistical data into reports and how to insert charts directly from data sources, thus making more efficient the report writing process and the gathering of overview data across assessments.

The book's early chapters are arranged to give case examples with related summaries of the statistical issues relevant to the cases being investigated. As the case examples continue, the statistical issues are expanded and gradually covered in more depth, enabling the reader to evolve their understanding and learning in a controlled way, yet still anchoring their acquired knowledge to the practical examples given. Later chapters give information on more complex means of interrogating psychometric information and are suitable for the more advanced and knowledgeable diagnostician.

Above all, it is hoped that the book encourages those involved in the diagnostic process of assessing clients' needs to adopt an inductive stance to their assessment framework. Assessment is not testing and testing is not assessment. The assessor needs to be continuously introducing and refining hypotheses, carefully selecting from a wide range of suitable tests. Each assessment needs to be fit for purpose, individualistic in style, and not pre-determined in such a way that the assessor goes into automatic pilot by administering the same core tests to all clients. Hence having the knowledge and confidence to compare and interpret scores across tests is an essential requirement for today's diagnostic assessor.

It is important to note that as new editions appear of the tests used for illustrative purposes, it is likely that the quoted reference tables and page numbers will not remain accurate. However, it is anticipated that similar tables/formulae will be found in different editions to aid one's understanding of each concept introduced. Where references to older tests occur, this is to illustrate particular concepts with tests that are currently accepted by professional organisations. Similarly, Microsoft Office *Excel* 2010 is used in this book, which is likely to be updated. Examples may differ from the procedures needed in other versions. Current legislation will also change, for example, the statement of special educational needs will be replaced by an Education, Health and Care plan in 2014 (Petersen, 2012).

It should be noted that throughout the book the following convention has been adopted: the feminine personal pronoun is used to denote the assessor and the masculine personal pronoun is used to denote the person being assessed.

Dr. Barry Johnson is Principal Educational Psychologist and Head of Assessment Services for Dyslexia Action, formerly known as The Dyslexia Institute. He is a member of the UK's Specific Learning Difficulties Assessment Standards Committee (SASC) and its sub-committee, the Specific Learning Difficulties Test Evaluation Committee (STEC). Barry has worked as an educational psychologist for 39 years in many settings in the UK and is an approved assessor for the British Psychological Society's qualification 'Test User: Educational Ability/Attainment (CCET)'. He has significant experience in the teaching of psychometrics to teachers and other professionals as well as advising on quality assurance parameters for psychologists' and teachers' diagnostic assessment and report writing needs across a wide area of educational and clinical settings. Barry provides assessment reports for the legal arena, including UK SENDIST hearings, and gives second opinions on borderline and complex cases involving the psychometric assessment of clients with special educational needs.

Dr. Gareth Hagger-Johnson is a psychologist and Senior Research Associate in the Department of Epidemiology and Public Health, University College London. He teaches methodology and statistics to both undergraduate and postgraduate students. His research and specialist areas are cognitive epidemiology, health behaviours, health literacy and personality traits. He is co-author of *Introduction to Research Methods and Data Analysis in Psychology* (Langdridge & Hagger-Johnson, 2009), and has published his research in peer-reviewed journals including Health Psychology, Journal of Epidemiology and Community Health, Psychosomatic Medicine, the Journal of Psychosomatic Research and Quality of Life Research.

Acknowledgement

The authors would like to thank Rick Portsmouth, educational psychologist and Director of Dyslexia North, for his comments and advice on draft sections of this book.

Permissions

Microsoft product screenshot(s) reprinted with permission from Microsoft Corporation.

Section 1:
Statistical Terms and Equations

Chapter 1
Basic Statistical Terms

Introducing basic principles of the concepts of:

- **confidence range**
- **standard deviation**
- **the normal distribution curve**
- **reliability coefficient**
- **standard error of measurement**
- **Type I and Type II errors.**

Diagnostic assessment of the individual invariably involves the comparison and interpretation of scores across tests. Let us look at this simplified, but typical, scenario often experienced by diagnostic assessors.

Case Example 1

You administer to Albert, aged 10 years six months, the Spelling subtest from the *Wechsler Individual Achievement Test: Second UK Edition for Teachers* (WIAT-II^{UK}-T) (Wechsler, 2006) and obtain a standardised score of 86 that is derived from Albert's raw score on the assessment. This standardised score enables you to form a view on Albert's test performance in relation to similar-aged children. Your hypothesis-testing procedure leads you then to administer the *Beery-Buktenica Developmental Test of Visual-Motor Integration, Sixth Edition* (Beery VMI; Beery *et al.*, 2010) where Albert obtains a standardised score of 98. Can you conclude from this evidence that Albert's level of visual-motor integration as measured by the Beery VMI is significantly higher than his level of spelling skills?

Understandably, the two manuals for the tests do not offer information on how scores on these two particular tests can be compared. If you assume that the two scores are significantly different, then this decision may influence every decision that you make from now on. You may conclude that Albert's teaching programme needs to have an emphasis on spelling instruction and even wonder if he has a specific difficulty in spelling. However, before you go any further, you need to know if the difference of 12 standard score points (98 minus 86 – the two test scores reported above) is statistically significant or not. Otherwise, you run the risk of basing your work on unsafe statistics. This simple case exemplifies the importance of being able to understand the platform of statistical principles that your assessment framework stands on. All too often, assessors make judgements about children's scores on tests without applying statistics or based on the incorrect interpretation.

Chapter 1 Basic Statistical Terms

Points to Consider

We all have relative strengths and weaknesses: one person may be a brilliant nuclear physicist but a mediocre speller; another person may be illiterate but an excellent snooker player, and so on. It is not unusual for people to have irregular profiles of such capabilities. Similarly, within education, it is commonplace for children to have irregular profiles of strengths and weaknesses as measured across tests of abilities, aptitudes and skills. We need to be able to acknowledge this normality of irregularity in our diagnostic assessments yet at the same time identify those differences that are clinically significant, i.e. those differences that we would regard to be rarely found. If we do not, then we run the risk of claiming erroneously that differences between scores are unusual and clinically important and thereby indicative of underlying specific learning difficulties, when they are not.

The raw score on a test is of little value because it has no benchmark to aid comparison with the potential range of scores of other similar aged people. If a client obtains a raw score of 15 on a test, one has no means of knowing whether this is a strong or weak score in relation to the potential scores of other people. The assessor will not know if a test score is below average or above average, nor will she know how extreme the score is from the average score for the relevant age. By the application of Classical Test Theory, raw scores can be converted to standardised scores and in doing so, enable such comparisons to be made. Also, standardised scores are more amenable to mathematical processing. Most assessors of clients with special needs generally understand and know how to convert raw scores into standard scores from their training and the instructions available within test manuals. They are also usually aware of references to terms and statistical data such as 'confidence range' and 'level of confidence' among others. However, it is at this point where some assessors start to hesitate, both with regard to their understanding of these terms and how to make use of them. All too often, such concepts are regarded as adding unnecessary detail or irrelevant information and are therefore ignored. Not only is this dangerous but, ironically, the potential for such terms to be of practical help to the assessors is then lost.

Before progressing further with this book, you need to understand fully the terms 'confidence range', 'true score' and 'level of confidence' and some other statistical terms.

The Statistics

Standard Error in the System: True and Observed Scores

All tests have some degree of unreliability but it is important to make them as reliable as possible otherwise they are not useful. Reliability is concerned with consistency or stability.

The degree of a test's reliability is related to people's responses to each of its test items. Every time a response is given to a test item we cannot assume that this reflects a 'true' score. If a client was to repeat a test item, the quality of his response is likely to be different, being influenced by a mass of variables that could be having an effect at any one time on his performance capability. In other words, we have to accept that there is always error in the system when a client attempts a test item. This error may be random or systemic where the latter is caused, for example, by an oddity of a test's construction that may affect the performance of the client. However it may be due to factors such as noise, mood, motivation or illness and therefore it is logical that somehow the 'noise in the system' of assessment and test construction needs to be taken into account. Sometimes, a child's performance will be judged by his teacher as good on one day but disappointing on another. Here, the teacher is making intuitive judgements and instinctively acknowledging the error in the system that randomly could be contributing positively or negatively at any one time to the child's performance.

Therefore, in noting the implications of the above for measurement, it can be suggested that any one obtained score is never considered to be the 'true' score. A client's *true score* is routinely and intrinsically linked with an *error* component. So, any observed score can be seen as being made up of these two components – the true score (reflecting the assumed underlying 'true' ability within the client) and the *error* component that represents chance or random fluctuation. This enables us to represent these assumptions within a simple mathematical formula:

$$X = T + E$$

where X = observed score at any one time, T = true score, and E = error score.

One could judge that the degree of the error over time will be balanced or focused around the true score in such as a way that one can assume that in the end the positive and negative measurement errors would be expected to reflect the shape of a 'standard normal distribution curve'. Scores would cluster towards the mean score (the true score) with extreme and unusual scores (the minority) fading towards both tails of the normal curve, some to the left and an equal number to the right. We will explore this phenomenon in more detail below and such a curve is shown in Figure 1.4. The formula can be made more specific to account for this positive and negative distribution:

$$X = T +/- E$$

Here, the obtained score, X, can be placed either side of the true score, T, within the higher and lower error ranges around the true score.

If we put some numbers in place of these letters to create an imaginary case example, we can see that if a person obtained a standardised score of 105 on a test, and we knew, or could calculate, that the error score value was 5, then the formula could be used to give us:

$$105 = T +/- 5$$

A simple algebraic twisting of this formula by swapping the 105 and T variable to either sides of the equation and reversing their signs in doing so then lets us know that:

$$T = 105 -/+ 5$$

or:

$$= 100 \text{ to } 110$$

i.e. T, the true score, lies somewhere between 100 and 110. This range can be considered for our purposes as a 'confidence range' that is also often referred to as a 'confidence interval' or 'confidence band'. In other words, we are confident that the client's true score lies somewhere within this range. Therefore, confidence ranges enable you to place the obtained score within a range of possible scores to enable you to be confident that the true score lies somewhere within the range stated. The size of this range will be decided by how confident you wish to be with your judgement that the confidence range does include the true score. Most test manuals now provide this information as a means of conveying the important message that when you derive the one standard score from the one raw score from one test administration, this score needs to be placed within a boundary of confidence.

Normal Distribution and Standard Deviation

Before we go on to unpack further the concept of the confidence range, let us firstly understand two other basic concepts, that of standard deviation and the standard normal distribution curve. Consider the small set of 10 scores below in Figure 1.1, from a screen shot from an *Excel* file:

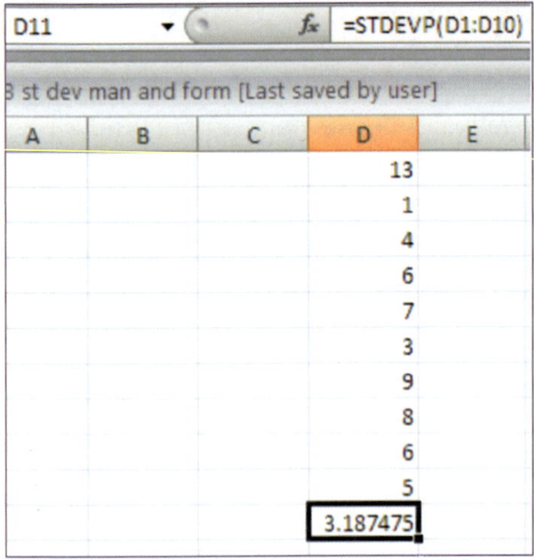

Figure 1.1: Standard Deviation using Excel *(i)*

You can see that there is a range of scores with values ranging from 1 to 13 and the highlighted cell at the bottom of column D gives a number that is the standard deviation for this set of scores. What is this number and how is it calculated?

In essence, the standard deviation value gives us a measure of the spread of these 10 scores. Although one way of judging the spread of scores is to seek out the highest and lowest scores to obtain their range, that is 1-13, this is not a safe or an accurate way of measuring their spread because it ignores the other number values within the range. One needs to have a means of measuring the spread of each of the 10 scores in relation to all of the others. This is performed by calculating the mean (the average) of the scores and seeing how each score deviates from this mean score. The formula is:

$$SD = \sqrt{\frac{\Sigma (X - \bar{X})^2}{N}}$$

where SD = standard deviation, X = an individual score, N = the number of scores, and $\bar{X}$ = the mean of the scores. The Greek sigma sign Σ corresponds to 'the sum of'.

This formula is available in *Excel*, as shown below in the formula bar:

Clicking on fx in the formula bar in *Excel* will enable you to select this formula; you do not have to type it in. Note that this particular formula is slightly different to other formula options available in *Excel 2010*. In *Excel 2010* you will find reference to STDEV.P and STDEV.S (see below) but you will also find reference to and availability of the formulae STDEVP and STDEVS that also work in *Excel 2010* for files in older versions of *Excel*.

In Figure 1.2, the *Excel* formula provides the standard deviation in cell D14 whilst the arithmetical procedure calculated manually is also given in columns E and F to help you understand the process of calculation. In column E there are values for the difference between each score and the mean (cell D12) of the total set of scores. For example, cell E2 gives the difference, 6.8, between the value of 13 in cell D2 and the mean score of 6.2 in cell E12.

	A	B	C	D	E	F	G	H	I
1					X-mean	$(X\text{-mean})^2$			
2				13	6.8	46.24			
3				1	-5.2	27.04			
4				4	-2.2	4.84			
5				6	-0.2	0.04			
6				7	0.8	0.64			
7				3	-3.2	10.24			
8				9	2.8	7.84			
9				8	1.8	3.24			
10				6	-0.2	0.04			
11				5	-1.2	1.44			
12			mean=	6.2		101.6	Sum of $(X\text{-mean})^2$		
13						10.16	Sum of $(X\text{-mean})^2$ divided by 10		
14				3.187475		3.187475	SD		
15									

Figure 1.2: Standard Deviation using Excel *(ii)*

Column F gives the squared values of each of the differences in column D. The reason why each difference score is now squared is to deal with the negative values. If we just summed the difference scores without taking account of negative difference scores then the concept of the 'spread' of differences would be lost. Negative values would tend to cancel out positive values. Squaring a negative value transforms it to a positive value and all positive values can be totalled to give a cumulative sum.

The sum of these squared differences is given in cell F12, which is 101.6, and this value is divided by the number (10) of scores and is given in cell F13. Cell F14 gives the square root of this value and therefore the standard deviation of the set of scores. This value is identical to the value given by the *Excel* formula in cell D14 and thus confirms the accuracy of our manual calculations.

Therefore, the standard derivation is a means of measuring spread of scores. Indeed, if the square root function was removed from the standard deviation formula above, then the formula:

$$\frac{\Sigma(X - \overline{X})^2}{N}$$

gives us what is called the *variance*. The terms standard deviation and variance are very similar and, conceptually, they are both the same in that they are concerned with measuring spread or range of scores. The standard deviation tends to be favoured for use in statistical formula because it lends itself more easily to the arithmetical process of calculation. Variance is in squared units, which are conceptually obscure, whereas standard deviation is in the same units as the original measurement. This is another reason why standard deviation is more intuitively appealing and easy to manage.

One very important area to note now is to do with sampling. Chapter 12 will discuss this further but for the sake of introducing the normal distribution curve, as shown in Figure 1.4, suppose that the set of 10 scores above was considered to be a selection of scores from a wider pool of numbers and not a finite set of numbers. If you were to take another 10 number values from such a pool, then they would most probably be different. Here you could be seen to be sampling - selecting a sample of items from a pool of items. In such a situation, the above formula for the standard deviation is modified as:

$$SD = \sqrt{\frac{\Sigma(X - \overline{X})^2}{N - 1}}$$

The *Excel* formula is shown in Figure 1.3.

D11 | *fx* =STDEV(D1:D10)

	A	B	C	D	E
1				13	
2				1	
3				4	
4				6	
5				7	
6				3	
7				9	
8				8	
9				6	
10				5	
11				3.359894	

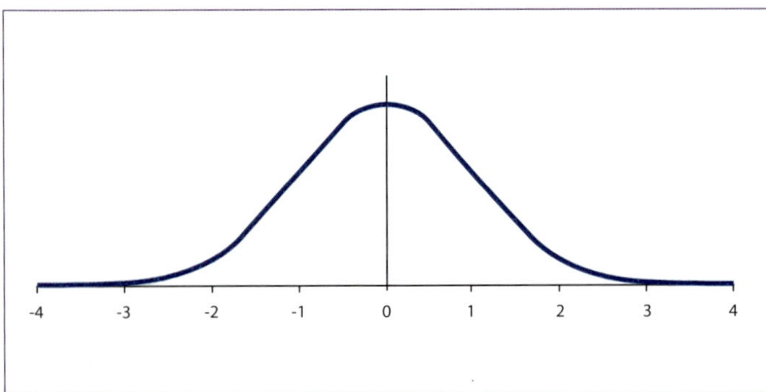

Figure 1.3: Standard Deviation using Excel *(iii)*

The resulting standard deviation is slightly different to the previous one, but not much different, and indeed the higher the number of values sampled, the closer these two types of standard deviation values become. The use of (N-1) instead of N is called 'Bessel's Correction' (Kenney & Keeping, 1951). Therefore, when you are calculating a standard deviation you need to make an early decision as to whether or not the numbers you are processing are considered to be a finite set or a sample from a population of items.

Normal Distribution

Psychometric tests are usually designed to reflect the normal distribution curve's properties of incidence along the dimension of very low scores to very high scores. What is this normal distribution?

In life, people have a range of abilities, aptitudes and skills that combine to make them unique as individuals and create a heterogeneous and rich society. In Classical Test Theory it is assumed that every ability, aptitude or skill that one wishes to assess occurs in people according to the properties of the standard normal distribution, or bell-shaped curve (see Figure 1.4).

Figure 1.4: Standard Normal Distribution

All distributions of capabilities as portrayed by this graph have the same general form with common characteristics and properties. The scores tend to congregate closely around the centre, tapering off from the centre on either side. The height of the curve is highest at its middle and indicates that more scores are recorded here than anywhere else. Very few scores are recorded at either extreme of the tapered ends that are called the left and right tails.

Fixed proportions of test scores lie within sections of this standard, normal curve identified between the numbers -4 to +4. Each section is called a standard deviation. The standard deviations are usually presented along the horizontal axis from -3 to +3 rather than -4 to +4. This reflects the fact that only a very small proportion of cases fall within the two tapered tail-ends of the curve. Figure 1.5 shows the percentage of the standard distribution curve that lies in each of its standard deviations along the horizontal axis and the proportion of scores that always fall within each. If we had drawn the curve to include the range -4 to +4 standard deviations then each of the tails would hold approximately 0.1% each of the curve's area.

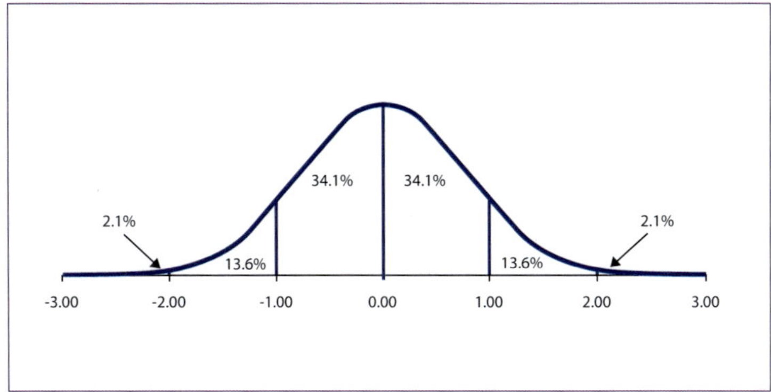

Figure 1.5: Area Percentages within the Standard Deviations of a Standard Normal Distribution Curve

We can see that approximately 68% of scores fall within the standard deviation range of -1 to +1, and approximately 95% of scores fall within the standard deviation range of -2 to +2. Note that these figures are approximations, rounded up from numbers that are more precise. You may sometimes see the range of -1 to +1 standard deviations referred to as having 2 x 34.13 (= 68.26%) and the range -2 to +2 standard deviations as having 2 x 47.72 (= 95.44%). However, it is more common to see the 68 and 95 whole numbers being referred to. Note in Figure 1.5 that the standard deviations are taken to two decimal places. This is to prepare you for the introduction of *z* scores in Chapter 2 which are commonly used as accurate measures of dispersal along the range of the normal distribution curve.

Reliability

We have already noted that test scores need to be placed within a range of confidence because no test can deliver a perfectly reliable test score. Reliability is concerned with consistency. If you want a car that is reliable, you want it to perform in a consistent way. Likewise, when using a psychometric test, you need it to be as reliable as possible with the impact of any noise, or variability, in the system to be reduced as much as possible. If a test has poor reliability then a client's observed score on the test will reflect this, leaving you with a lack of confidence in its meaning.

Test designers have different ways of measuring the reliability of their tests. The four main types are as follows.

1) Test-retest Reliability

This type of reliability measures the consistency of a test over repeated administrations, in other words, over a time period. The greater the consistency, the higher will be the measure of reliability. The main disadvantage of this type of reliability measurement is having to take account of any learning (practice effects) from the first test administration.

Chapter 1 Basic Statistical Terms

2) Parallel Forms Reliability

Publishing companies sometimes create a test providing two or more equivalent means of delivering it by supplying parallel forms of the test. The various test items reflect the same levels of difficulty but the material content (the test items) is different. So, for example, the *Test of Word Reading Efficiency – Second Edition* (TOWRE-2; Torgesen *et al.*, 2011) provides two parallel forms, Form A and Form B, to assess both sight word efficiency and phonemic decoding efficiency. In such cases, the parallel forms are designed to correlate highly with one another, in other words to provide very similar scores regardless of which parallel form test is selected. Therefore, a client's scores on both parallel tests would be very similar. Parallel forms are extremely popular in that they reduce significantly the impact of practice effects over administrations and thus are helpful when tracking clients' real progress over time. If the same test items were given each time, test takers may remember and learn the answers. Most test manuals give advice on the recommended time gap between administrations of parallel tests.

3) Inter-rater Reliability

This form of reliability is concerned with ensuring that when different assessors administer the same test, they obtain similar test scores. A test that is difficult to administer, is vague with its scoring criteria, or has poorly worded instructions, is not likely to have high inter-rater reliability. If a test has low inter-rater reliability, then practical problems follow in those situations where more than one assessor is involved in assessing a client over time. The desire for tests to have high inter-rater reliabilities accounts for the emphasis on establishing precise standardised instructions for the administration of the test items and very clear scoring procedures and pass/fail criteria. This is an important type of reliability and highlights the need for assessors to read and learn the operational instructions given in test manuals. If they do not, then they are likely to compromise the reliability of the results. One very important feature here is the amount of support and guidance that is allowed to be given in the repetition of instructions, modelling, elaboration and answering of queries from clients. It is crucial to have a working knowledge of each test's guidance concerning these points. Otherwise, your administration of the tests will not reflect the standardised, operational procedures and the obtained scores will lack sufficient reliability.

4) Internal Consistency Reliability

This form of reliability is concerned with the extent to which the items of a test are measuring the same underlying concept. Therefore, each item is analysed for its relationship with all of the other test items. If all of the test items correlate highly with one another, then its internal consistency reliability will be high. Internal consistency is often estimated by a split-half reliability index, the Coefficient Alpha Index (Cronbach, 1951), often known simply as Cronbach's alpha (α). The split-half estimate is created by dividing the test into two parts, such as odd/even items or first half/second half, and then administering the two forms to the same group of individuals and correlating the responses. Such a process in the construction of a test allows for individual test items to be selected or rejected as the correlation coefficient is influenced.

It is therefore important to have an understanding of the concept of correlation. Consider the following screen shot from *Excel* (Figure 1.6) where we have two sets of score samples and we want to know to what extent they relate to each other. In *Excel* we can obtain a measure of the correlation between the two sets of scores by applying the formula for the Pearson's Product Moment correlation. The correlation coefficient, Pearson's *r*, is given as +0.88 (to two decimal points) which can be regarded as a high correlation.

B13 | f_x =CORREL(A2:A11,B2:B11)

	A	B	C	D	E	F
1	Set A	Set B				
2	61	70				
3	63	78				
4	78	77				
5	72	70				
6	90	95				
7	110	99				
8	86	90				
9	79	84				
10	59	60				
11	99	87				
12						
13	correlation=	0.882622				
14						

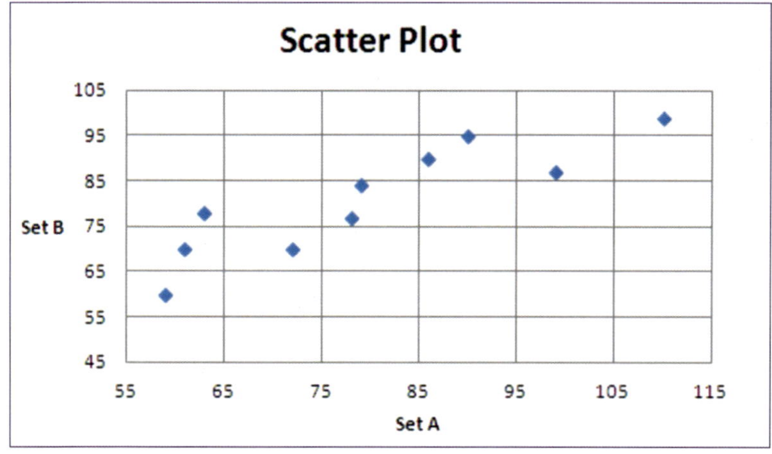

Figure 1.6: Pearson's Product Moment Correlation using Excel

The scores can be presented in the form of a scatter plot in order to obtain a visual representation of the relationship between them. As can be seen in Figure 1.7, one can identify a trend of the scores rising from bottom left to the top right. In other words, if there is a relatively low score in Set A, its corresponding score in Set B will also tend to be low. This reflects a positive correlation. If the chart gave scores that rose from the bottom right to the top left, then this would reflect a negative correlation, i.e. high scores in one set of scores would be correlated with low scores in the other set.

Figure 1.7: Scatter Plot

Selecting the Type of Reliability Coefficient

In noting that there are different types of reliability coefficients that are commonly reported in test manuals, you will find yourself hesitating when needing to select a reliability coefficient from a test manual in order to apply some of the statistical formulae presented in this book. A test can have a range of reliability coefficient values for the types of reliability described above. Unfortunately, the advice on which to select is not clear nor consistently given in the literature. Boyle and Fisher (2007) state that when determining the standard error of measurement (a value used in calculating confidence ranges, see below), the relevant reliability coefficient can either be a measure of internal consistency or a measure of test-retest or alternate forms reliability. Kline (2000) states that the test-retest reliability coefficient is the preferred choice but Anastasi and Urbini (1997) make no recommendation regarding choice of reliability coefficient. Harvill (1991) highlights that the standard error of measurement will vary as a result of choice of type of reliability coefficient, thus intimating that any type can be used. Feldt *et al.* (1985) argue that the test-retest reliability coefficient should be chosen mainly because this coefficient reflects the pragmatics of the main need in the field, that of comparing test scores over time. Bruton *et al.*(2000) distinguish between relative reliability and absolute reliability. Absolute reliability is defined as the degree to which repeated measurements vary for individuals, i.e. the less they vary, the higher the reliability. The standard error of measurement is interpreted as a measure of absolute reliability. It logically follows from their argument that the relevant measure of reliability is test-retest for the purposes of standard error of measurement calculation. Cortina (1993) summarises the views that coefficient alpha, a form of split-half reliability measurement (see above), is the most commonly accepted formulation of reliability and indeed most publishing companies use coefficient alpha when calculating their tests' reliability coefficients. Reynolds (1990) also argues that, for the purposes of judging discrepancy amounts between scores, coefficient alpha is the recommended procedure for estimating reliability, and concludes that internal-consistency reliability (alpha) will almost always be the most appropriate reliability estimate for intelligence and achievement tests because these values best determine the accuracy of the test scores.

Given the lack of consistent guidance, it is for the assessor to decide which type of reliability coefficient to use and consider the most valid for the task to be performed. What is important is to appraise all the reliability coefficients reported in the test manual in order to be aware of any relative weaknesses it may have with any aspect of its reliability. Also, the task to be performed will need to be considered. For example, if the assessor was frequently assessing with a colleague and pooling clients' scores for whatever reason, then inter-rater reliability would be considered to be important for this type of task.

A brief checklist such as the following may be useful to apply when considering a new test for its standards or reliability.

- Does the test's technical manual have a section on its reliability?

- Is more than one type of reliability coefficient given?

- Does the test have parallel forms?

- What type of reliability are you more concerned with, given your particular circumstances? Does the test have a reliability coefficient for this type of reliability?

- Are confidence ranges given? If not, is the standard deviation of the test given so that you can calculate them from the reliability coefficients?

- Are reliability coefficients given for different age ranges of the test's standardisation sample and for the different subtests if it has them?

- Find the lowest and the highest reliability coefficients given in the manual. Are you satisfied with this range?

- Is there an equivalent test that has better reliability coefficients?

Confidence Ranges

Having learned about the properties of the normal, standard distribution curve and the importance of reliability, let us now explore the concept of confidence ranges and how we can quantify them.

Confidence ranges are derived from a test's standard error of measurement, a type of standard deviation as described above and an indicator of error surrounding the 'true score' on a test. There are only two statistical variables to consider when calculating the confidence ranges of a test: its reliability and standard deviation.

The simple formula to calculate the standard error of measurement (SE_m) is:

$$SE_m = SD \sqrt{1-r}$$

where SD = standard deviation of the test (usually, but not always, 15), and r = the reliability coefficient of the test for the age range of the client being assessed.

Confidence Level

We have noted that making judgements about test scores involves taking a risk because of the noise in the system that means you have to assume that your observed score is not the client's true score. You can only estimate where the client's 'true' score lies and in doing so, you set the level of risk that you are prepared to accept. If you were a pharmaceutical company and made a prescription drug whose proportion of ingredients was so critical that any error would be likely to cause death or serious illness, would you be prepared to accept that 68 out of 100 of the drugs' capsules could be guaranteed as safe? Probably not. Would you increase the safety level by accepting that 95 out of 100 would be safe? Again, probably not. In educational and clinical assessment, you have to make similar decisions, although it is often the case that the publishing companies have made this decision for you by giving confidence levels for confidence ranges within the relevant appendices of the test manual. For example, the *Wechsler Individual Achievement Test – Second UK Edition* (WIAT-II[UK]; Wechsler, 2005) gives you a choice of two confidence levels, 0.1 (accurate 90 out of 100 times) and 0.05 (accurate 95 out of 100 times). Other tests may only give you one level of confidence. Some tests steer you to give one level of confidence but which you yourself may consider unsafe given your circumstances, and other tests may not give any confidence intervals. An example of the latter is the *Adult Reading Test* (ART; Brooks *et al.*, 2004) where only percentile scores are given for you to equate with the raw scores that clients obtain on the various subtests. It is therefore important to read the guidance given on choice of confidence ranges and understand how they are derived. For those test manuals that do not offer confidence ranges, you should be able to find the essential information (the standard deviations and reliability coefficients) to calculate them yourself. For those tests whose reliability coefficients are acceptable but for some reason confidence levels and ranges are not included in the manuals, it is worth considering establishing your own set of confidence range tables for the tests. An example is given in Chapter 8.

Having learned above from the properties of normal distribution and how clients' responses tend to fall within this distribution, we can now see how we can be 68% confident that a true score lies within a confidence range of plus or minus ($\pm$) one standard error of measurement. We can be 95% confident that the true test score lies within ±1.96 standard errors of measurements. Therefore, when we see and use the term confidence range we now know that it is based on the properties of the normal distribution curve.

Let us take three imaginary tests (A, B, and C) with the same standard deviation of 15 but with different reliability coefficients of 0.7, 0.8 and 0.9. Their standard errors of measurements can be calculated as shown in Table 1.1.

Table 1.1: Tests and their Standard Errors of Measurements

Test A	Test B	Test C
$SE_m = SD \sqrt{1-r}$	$SE_m = SD \sqrt{1-r}$	$SE_m = SD \sqrt{1-r}$
$SE_m = 15 \sqrt{1-0.7}$	$SE_m = 15 \sqrt{1-0.8}$	$SE_m = 15 \sqrt{1-0.9}$
$SE_m = 8$	$SE_m = 7$	$SE_m = 5$

As can be seen, the three tests' standard errors of measurements are noticeably different with the differences being influenced mainly by the reliability coefficients. The lower the reliability coefficient, the higher the SE_m Given that tests are usually designed to have a standard deviation of 15, then it is the reliability coefficient of the test that is crucial in the formula for the standard error of measurement. This is why publishing companies strive to make their tests as reliable as possible – in order to reduce the standard error of the scores obtained.

Let us now calculate the confidence ranges for these three tests and take as an example, a client with a standardised score of 98 (see Table 1.2).

Table 1.2: Tests and their Confidence Ranges

Test A	Test B	Test C
$SE_m = 8$	$SE_m = 7$	$SE_m = 5$
Confidence ranges at 68% level of confidence =		
98±8	98±7	98±5
= 90–106	= 91–105	= 93–103
Confidence ranges at 95% level of confidence		
98±(1.96x8)	98±(1.96x7)	98± (1.96x5)
= 82–114	= 84–112	= 88–108

Note that the **less** reliable a test, the **wider** its confidence ranges will be. It is important to note that a test's reliability coefficients may be quite different for different ages of clients and for its parallel forms. If you are calculating a test's standard error of measurement in order to obtain the confidence range, then you need to select the reliability coefficient, if available, for the relevant age range within that test. The same is true for the standard deviation for the formula above.

If you try to check your calculation of a test's confidence ranges with the confidence ranges given in the test manual, you will probably observe that they are not quite the same and, for high or low scores in particular, the reported confidence ranges appear to be asymmetrically placed around the observed test scores. This reflects the use of the concept *standard error of the estimate* rather than the *standard error of measurement* that takes into account the phenomenon of regression to the mean. We shall visit these terms in Chapter 8 but for the moment, we will explore briefly regression to the mean. Imagine that a child scores extremely highly on a test of visual memory. If he were to complete the assessment multiple times, for example four times, then, as we have learned above, his scores will not be the same every time because no assessment is 100% reliable. However, where are the next three scores likely to be? He has scored so highly on the first occasion that there is more of a chance that these next three scores will be lower than his first score than they will be higher. In other words, they will be pulled towards the mean or regress to the mean – the centre point of the normal distribution curve shown in Figure 1.4. The same applies to someone scoring for the first time with a very low score. On the next, say, three scores, there is more of a chance of them approaching the mean than being lower than the first score. These examples portray the phenomenon of *regression to the mean*. Therefore, when calculating confidence ranges, publishing companies sometimes take this into account by employing a formula that uses a term called the *standard error of the estimate* (see Chapter 8), not the standard error of measurement. The higher the reliability of the test, the less the impact of regression to the mean will be. Therefore, when using highly reliable tests, the confidence ranges calculated by either method will not be greatly different from one another.

If Albert had completed the WIAT-II^{UK}-T Word Reading subtest and you wanted to compare the obtained score with the WIAT-II^{UK}-T Spelling score of 86, the test manual is designed to provide you with statistical information to guide you easily to compare confidence ranges. This is because when the WIAT-II^{UK}-T was standardised, the sample of children used provided co-normed data; in other words, the children were administered all of the same test items. This enabled the developers of the WIAT-II^{UK}-T to obtain direct statistical information to enable you to compare easily scores across the relevant subtests, in this instance, Word Reading and Spelling. Let us suppose Albert obtained a score of 95 on the WIAT-II^{UK}-T Word Reading subtest. However, the test manual informs you that you now have to take into account your selected level of confidence for the test score of 86 on the WIAT-II^{UK}-T Spelling subtest. This leads you to consider that Albert's so called 'true score' on this spelling test lies somewhere in the range 79-93 at the '.05 level of confidence'. The equivalent confidence range at the .05 level of significance for the Word Reading subtest is given as 91-99.

In effect, because the confidence ranges overlap, as indicated in Figure 1.8, the spelling score is not reliably and significantly lower than the reading score for the level of confidence selected.

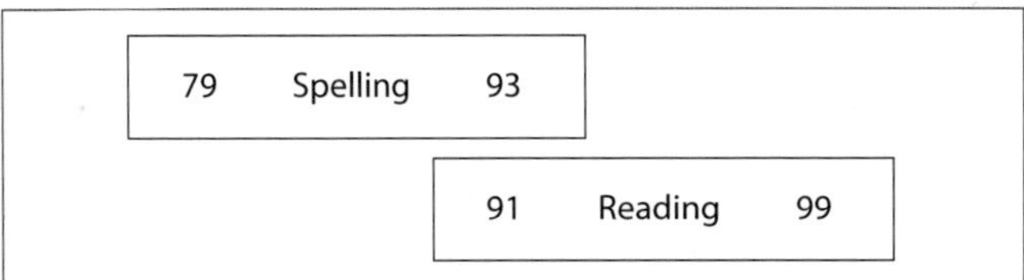

Figure 1.8: Overlapping Confidence Ranges

The rationale is that there is a chance that Albert's true score on the WIAT-II^{UK}-T Spelling subtest could be equal to, or even greater than, his true score on the WIAT-II^{UK}-T Word Reading subtest. You cannot therefore make a statement in your final report that, based on these scores, Albert's level of spelling skills is significantly lower than the level of his reading skills.

Finally, therefore, let us now go back to Case Example 1 and calculate and compare the confidence ranges for the two test scores. The Beery VMI manual informs you in Table 7, on page 106 that the standard error of measurement for a child aged 10 years is 6. Therefore, the 95% confidence range for the obtained score of 98 has a range of $\pm$ (1.96 $\times$ 6), which is approximately 86 -110.

Now, the 95% confidence range for Albert's WIAT-II^{UK}-T spelling score of 86 is 86 $\pm$ 7. This is derived from Table D.1, page 154 from the WIAT-II^{UK}-T. Note that in this table the numbers given are for confidence interval magnitudes and so multiplying by 2 is not necessary as you did for the Beery VMI's standard error of measurement. The multiplication has already been performed for you. However, you do have to compute the $\pm$ factor. Therefore, the spelling score has a 95% confidence range of 79-93. This overlaps with the Beery VMI confidence range of 86-110 and so you cannot conclude that the spelling and VMI scores are statistically different from one another.

(Note that in the *Raven's Educational UK Standard Progressive Matrices – Plus Version and Mill Hill Vocabulary Scale* (SPM+ and MHV; Raven, 2008), Table 6.1, page 54, the method of calculating and selecting the confidence ranges for these two subtests is unusual in that the confidence ranges are derived directly from the raw scores, not the standard scores. As a result of this method being used, the three options for the selection of degree of confidence are actually 85.6%, 94.2%, and 99.8%.)

This conclusion may leave the assessor in a state of some confusion because, intuitively, it may seem obvious that a score of 86 on the Spelling subtest must be significantly below the Beery VMI score of 98. This is where the application of psychometric statistics is helpful and yet at the same time unnerving. One needs to know the limitations as well as the strengths of one's tools and use those statistical resources that can lead one to make valid conclusions about the evidence obtained. Confidence ranges can be compared and scores in certain situations can validly be interpreted as significantly different from one another. As stated earlier, it is common for children to have irregular scores, and the use of confidence ranges is a powerful and simple means of reminding the assessor of this phenomenon. Clearly, the assessor needs to understand the processes involved and thereby not make mistakes and avoid over-identification of specific learning difficulties. We should emphasise that if you find that two scores are not significantly different from one another, this is just as important as finding a significant difference.

The assessor may also ask, 'Why not simply administer three tests and take the mean or median (the middle-value score) of the three scores in order to reduce error.' However, each test must be different (if one wishes to avoid practice effects), there may not be time, and the metric of the scales may be different (requiring conversion, which takes additional time). Such an approach would not be realistic, given the overall number of areas to assess in a typical diagnostic assessment. Crucially, the tests may measure different skills because of having different construct validities.

Type I and Type II Errors

Interpreting test score differences as significant when they are really due to measurement error is known as a Type I error: a *false positive*. Interpreting score differences as due to chance measurement error when such differences are actually real is known as a Type II error: a *false negative*. The higher your selected level of confidence the less chance you will make Type I errors, i.e. you will increase the chance of identifying differences that are validly different and of clinical importance. Conversely though, if your selected level of confidence is low, then you run the risk of identifying too many clients as having irregular profiles of scores. One way of remembering this feature is to see level of confidence as the mesh in a fishing net. If your mesh is too fine (Type I error), you catch more of the fish you want to catch but also too many fish of the wrong sort. If your mesh is too coarse (Type II error), you'll catch some but not most of the fish you want to catch.

The statistical concepts of sensitivity and specificity are closely related to Type I and Type II errors (*Clinical Evaluation of Language Fundamentals – Fourth Edition UK* (CELF-4[UK]; Semel *et al.*, 2006), pages 260-261). These terms tend to be used in those psychometric test manuals that are concerned with clinical conditions such as language and communication disorders that span the medical and educational arenas. Sensitivity measures the proportion of positives that are correctly identified (e.g. the number of children who have a language disorder) and specificity measures the proportion of negatives that are correctly identified (e.g. the number of children who do not have a language disorder). The classification will vary as a function of the cut score selected (e.g. a total language score of 1 SD or more below the mean)

Therefore, If 'a' = a true positive (correctly identified), 'd' = a true negative (correctly rejected), 'b' = a false positive (incorrectly identified) and 'c' = a false negative (incorrectly rejected), then:

Sensitivity of the test = a/(a+c) and Specificity of the test = d/(b+d).

See for example the *Diagnostic Evaluation of Articulation and Phonology* (DEAP; Dodd *et al.,* 2002), Manual, page 43-47, which reports the sensitivity and specificity from one random and two clinical samples.

There is usually a trade-off between these two measures and the predictor test will also possess some degree of error. Sensitivity and specificity can therefore provide overall summary statistics of how well a test can identify a disorder, although this overall summary can be misleading because of the need to take into account the estimated base rate of the particular clinical disorder being considered. Such estimates of the base rates of clinical disorders – the prevalence of the disorder in the population- may vary depending on the context being investigated. If one assumes a base rate is relatively high or relatively low, then these assumptions will influence both the 'positive predictive power' (PPP), i.e. the likelihood that a person with a positive test result actually has the disorder, and the 'negative predictive power' (NPP), i.e. the likelihood that someone with a negative test result actually does not have the disorder, of your test (see Table 8.1.8 of the CELF-4[UK] Manual, page 261). Deciding on the base rate/prevalence of a disorder may be influenced by research findings and/or the degree of safety or confidence that the assessor requires when applying the test.

If the base rate, sensitivity, and specificity of a test are known, PPP can be calculated using the following formula:

$$\text{PPP} = (a \times br) \text{ divided by } [(a \times br) + (1 - br) \times b]$$

where a = a true positive, c = a false negative, and br = base rate, and NPP can be calculated using the following formula:

$$\text{NPP} = [d \times (1 - br)] \text{ divided by } [(d \times (1 - br) + (c \times br)]$$

where d = a true negative. (*Preschool Language Scales, Fifth Edition* (PLS-5; Zimmerman *et al.*, 2011), Examiner's Manual, page 91).

In books on statistics and research methods, you will see reference to the 'null hypothesis'. The practice of research methodology involves formulating and testing hypotheses that are statements that need to be confirmed or rejected in order for you to advance your investigations. The null hypothesis can be seen as a default position, i.e. where you start by saying (your null hypothesis) that there is no relationship between the variables that you are measuring. So, in Albert's case above, you would start with the null hypothesis of assuming that there is no relationship between Albert's degree of visual motor integration and his spelling skills and perform an investigation to reject or accept this hypothesis. Type I and Type II errors relate to this null hypothesis, as shown in Table 1.3).

Table 1.3: The Null Hypothesis

	Null Hypothesis (H0) is True	Alternative Hypothesis (H1) is True
Failure to Reject Null Hypothesis	(a) Correct decision	(b) Incorrect decision Type II error 'False Negative'
Reject Null Hypothesis	(c) Incorrect decision Type I error 'False Positive'	(d) Correct decision

In Albert's case, consideration of confidence ranges has led to the correct decision, cell (a), where you have concluded not to reject your null hypothesis. Look upon the use of the null hypothesis as enabling you to obtain clear information before you can make any claims about relationships or differences between variables that you are measuring. Remember, however, that the conclusion is based upon your pre-determined level of confidence.

As mentioned previously, the benchmark percentage level of confidence within the general area of statistics is 95%. However, there is a view for educational and some clinical purposes that this is unnecessarily high. As long ago as 1959, a persuasive argument was made by Davis (1959) to accept the 85% level of confidence in the educational arena. He argued that this would balance the undesirable effects of both Type I and Type II errors when comparing test scores. The main argument was that the consequence of making a Type II error is not disastrous. The implication is that it is assumed that any observed mistake could be rectified as a result of continued monitoring and consequent educational intervention. Any resulting negative impact could be considered to be relatively minor, compared to, for example the medical arena, where diagnostic decisions may not be reversible and where people's lives may literally be at risk, or where additional treatments could be expensive, intrusive or even too late. Hence the reason why a few current tests in the education and allied health fields still recommend the 68% or the 90% level.

As time progressed, such leniency (Davis, 1959) was generally revoked in favour of higher levels of confidence, arguably driven by the increasing availability of more reliable tests that gave narrower confidence bands in comparison to earlier tests. Also, as special educational and health policies evolved, so did the awareness that referrals of proportions of students into expensive provision needed to be carefully filtered according to availability of budget and resources. Selection of clients with learning or clinical profiles reflective of relative infrequency in the normal population led decision makers to accept cut-off points of $\pm$ two standard deviations and this statistical reference point permeated application of a range of statistical formulae when assessors were involved with test score comparisons (Reynolds, 1990).

The way forward in choosing a confidence level is for you to realise that you are responsible for the decision on level of risk and that in settings where you initially use relatively low confidence levels, it is always wise to assess, monitor and review. Being able to set your own confidence level gives you more control over deciding on the level of risk involved. It also enables you to report a consistent level of confidence across tests that you have used. If you do not, then the reader of your report could quite rightly query why you are using different levels of confidence across tests for the particular purpose for the assessment. The reader will have identified a degree of inconsistency about your hypothesis-testing procedures (Chapter 4 will examine this area in more detail). If this approach is combined with the use of very reliable tests, the overall reliability of the process of test score comparison will be improved considerably.

Standard Deviation and Normal Distribution Curves that are not 'Standard'

Some tests do not accurately reflect the standard, normal distribution – one test's standardisation sample and derived scores may have a 'flattened-out' distribution, another may have a 'squashed-in' shape. They both have the same number of standard deviations (6 or sometimes 8) but the size (width) of these deviations will be different in these two cases. Figures 1.9 to 1.11 portray this feature.

Curve A

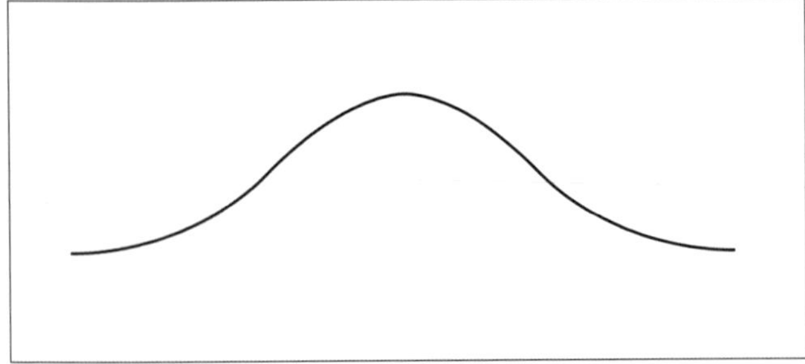

Figure 1.9: Moderately Large Standard Deviation

Curve B

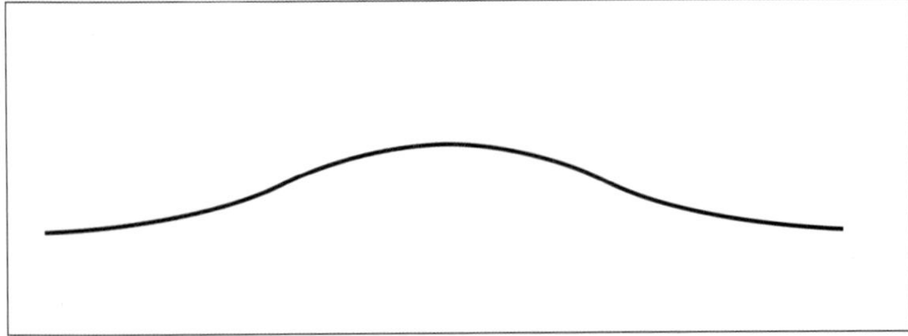

Figure 1.10: Large Standard Deviation

Curve C

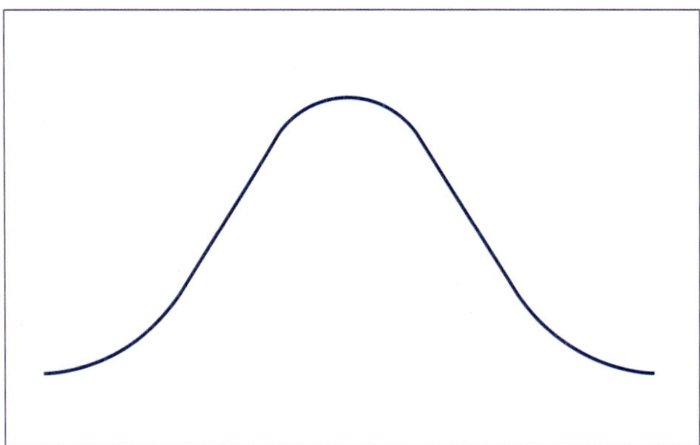

Figure 1.11: Standard Deviation of a Standard Normal Distribution Curve

What is different across the three curves is that for each of their standard deviations, the length of the spread of scores along the horizontal axis will be different. For example, the spread of scores with each of Curve B's standard deviations will be wider than those of Curve C. It is useful to experiment by creating different types of normal distribution curves using *Excel* in order to understand this difficult area that is often conceptually confusing. Figure 1.12 shows a screenshot of a standard normal distribution curve derived by creating a range of standard scores from 50 to 150 in column A with the formula for the normal distribution in the formula bar that gives the distribution values at each standard score in column B. A scatter plot of the scores gives the chart showing the standard normal distribution curve with a mean of 100 and a standard deviation of 15. Cell B2 is highlighted for the formula in the formula bar:

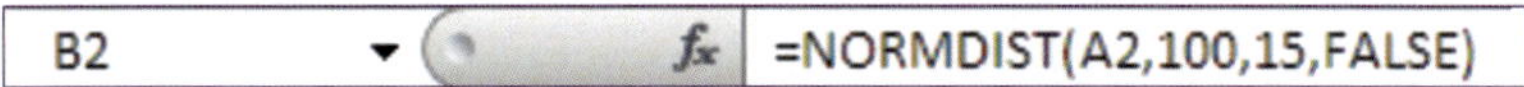

In the formula, A2 is the cell value of a standard score of 50. We have selected 100 as the mean score for normal distribution and 15 refers to the standard deviation value.

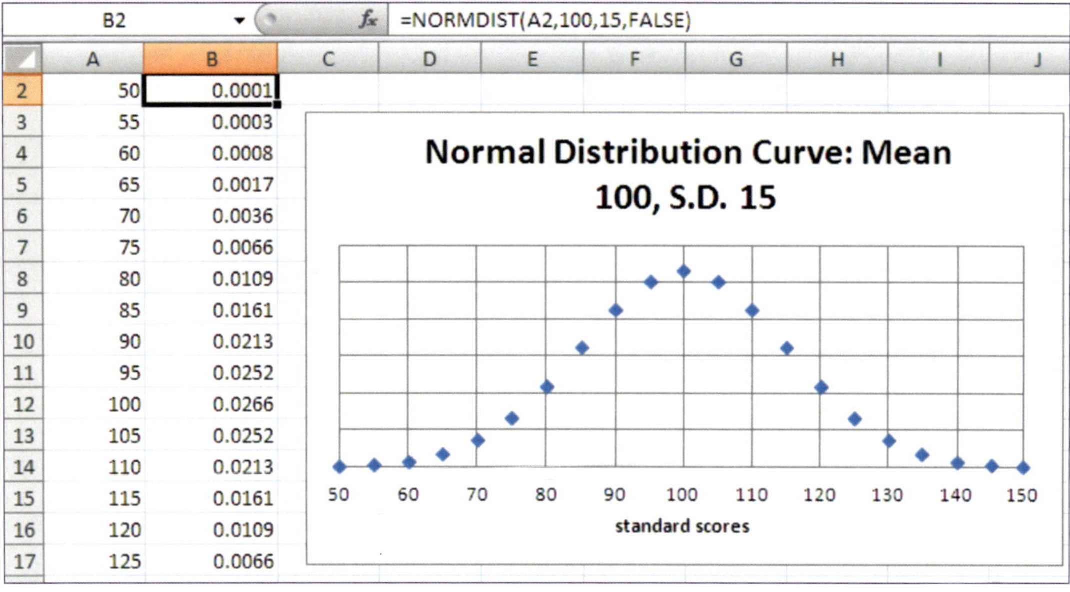

Figure 1.12: Normal Distribution Curve in Excel *– SD 15*

Now, let us change the standard deviation to values of 20 (Figure 1.13) and 10 (Figure 1.14) in the formula bar and see how the normal distribution curves are different to that of the above standard normal distribution curve:

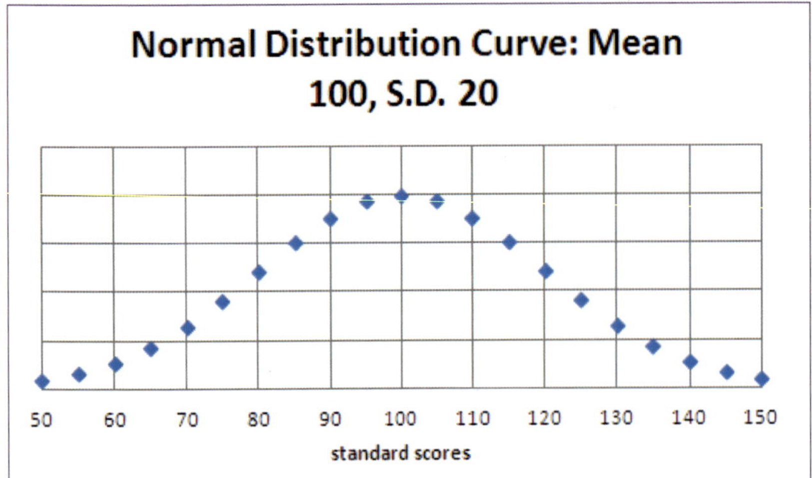

Figure 1.13 Normal Distribution Curve in Excel – SD 20

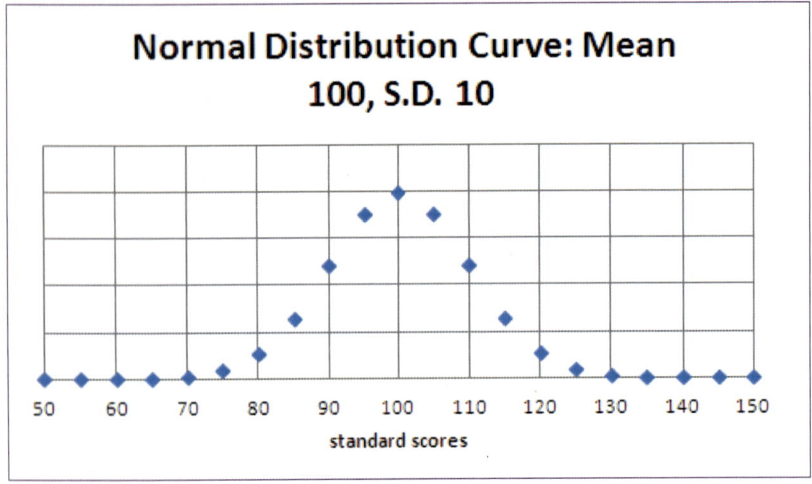

Figure 1.14 Normal Distribution Curve in Excel – SD 10

Most published tests have a standard deviation of 15 with a mean of 100 and this reflects the need to have a balance of spread of scores to distinguish between clients' capabilities but at the same time to minimise the standard error of measurement of the test concerned. Remember, this value, 15, refers to the width of each of the standard deviations, not their quantity.

The most important feature to remember about normal distribution curves is that regardless of whether or not a curve is a standard normal distribution curve, approximately 68% of any curve falls within two standard deviations (one either side of the mean), 95% falls within four standard deviations, and 99.7% falls within six standard deviations (see Figure 1.5). This feature enables each normal distribution to be perceived as a probability distribution. Thus, any score at any point along a curve's distribution can be interpreted as a form of probability; in other words, how likely or common the obtained score is. The next chapter investigates further this very important area.

Chapter 2
Types of Standard Scores

Introducing:

- **types of standardised scores: *T*, *z*, percentiles**
- **properties of the standard normal distribution curve**
- **creating look-up tables.**

Case Example 2

You are a specialist teacher and want to compare Julie's scores on a range of tests performed by both you and your school's educational psychologist. The psychologist administered to Julie two subtests from the *Wechsler Abbreviated Scale of Intelligence – Second Edition* (WASI-II; Wechsler, 2011) where T scores of 55 and 35 were obtained on the Block Design and Similarities subtests, respectively. T scores are a form of standardised score. Your tests results are in standard scores where a score of 110 was obtained for the WIAT-II[UK]-T Word Reading subtest and a score of 80 was scored for the WIAT-II[UK]-T Comprehension subtest. Such scores are commonly referred to as standard scores when they have a mean of 100 and a standard deviation of 15. You want to be able to compare the T scores from the psychologist's tests with the standard scores from your tests. You also want to present your assessment scores in the appendix of your report in such a way that the report's readability is maximised for the client. Therefore, your first task is to convert all of the scores into a common metric, enabling you to complete the empty cells in the columns in Table 2.1 with your preferred type of standardised score.

Table 2.1: Types of Standardised Scores (i)

	T Score	Standard Score
WASI-II Block Design	55	
WASI-II Similarities	35	
WIAT-II[UK]-T Word Reading		110
WIAT-II[UK]-T Comprehension		80

Points to Consider

T scores are only one form of standardised score. A standardised score is a score that is derived from a raw score but where this raw score has been converted to the standardised score to enable a comparison to be made with the scores obtained by other people. The only oddity about them is that, unlike most tests that use standard scores and which have a mean of 100 and a standard deviation of 15, T scores have a mean of 50 and a standard deviation of 10. All you need is a simple formula that helps you convert from one to the other, just as you would with converting imperial measurements into metric measurements. Once you have all scores converted to the same metric, then you can compare them easily in a valid way.

Chapter 2 Types of Standard Scores

Be aware that although high scores on tests are often indicative of above-average performance, some tests that involve measures of social/personality factors may highlight high scores as being indicative of undesirable performance. High and low scores do not necessarily mean desirable and undesirable attributes, respectively. It all depends on what the tests are measuring. For example, a very high score on a test of anxiety is probably not a desirable, 'good' score.

The Statistics

Using Z Scores to Convert Different Types of Standardised Scores to a Common Metric

At this point, we are going to make the task of conversion appear at first sight to look unnecessarily complicated by converting both T scores and standard scores into another form of standardised score called the z score. The formula to obtain z scores is:

$$z = \frac{X - M_x}{\sigma_x}$$

where X = the actual score recorded, M_x = the mean score of the test used, and σ_x = the test's standard deviation.

Note that when considering the standard normal distribution curve it is common for the z scores range to be reported from −3.0 to +3.0, reflecting the number of standard deviations across the normal distribution curve (3 below the mean z score of 0 and 3 above the mean). Sometimes, as noted in Chapter 1, you find that the range is increased from −4 to +4 in order to accommodate the very few scores at both tails of the normal distribution curve (see Figure 1.4). Note also that z scores are one of the few types of standardised scores that can have negative values. This feature is useful in that you know instantly if score is below the mean, because of its negative value.

Z scores are important as a means of converting different types of standardised scores to a common metric. Z scores can therefore be considered the gold standard of statistical measurement. You can look upon z scores as a means of measuring the distance one score is away from the mean of the distribution of scores that you are concerned with. Z scores are also extremely useful as a means of placing a child's score precisely along the standard normal distribution curve, within any of the curve's 6 (or sometimes 8) standard deviations. Always remember that z scores below the mean are given a minus status (−1 to −3).

Once you have the z score, you can change this z score into any other type of standardised score – the formula is:

$$\text{Score on new scale} = (z \times SD_{new\ scale}) + \overline{X}_{new\ scale}$$

where $\overline{X}_{new\ scale}$ refers to the mean of the new scale.

Therefore, if you take Julie's T score on the WASI-II Block Design subtest, you know that the test has a mean of 50 and a standard deviation of 10. You can convert it to a z score by applying the first formula,

$$z = \frac{X - M_x}{\sigma_x}$$

$$= \frac{55 - 50}{10} = \frac{5}{10} = +0.5$$

Then, to convert this z score into a standard score on a new scale for a test that has a mean of 100 and standard deviation of 15, the second formula is:

$$\text{Standard score} = (z \times SD_{new\ scale}) + \overline{X}_{new\ scale}$$

$$= +0.5 \times 15 + 100 = +7.5 + 100 = 107.5$$

which you can round up to 108. Therefore, a T score of 55 is equivalent to a standard score of 108 on a scale where the mean is 100 and the standard deviation is 15.

Now, take the WASI-II Similarities subtest, where a T score of 35 was obtained. Convert this to a z score using the same formula:

$$z = \frac{X - M_x}{\sigma_x}$$

$$= \frac{35 - 50}{10} = \frac{15}{10} = -1.5$$

Then again apply the second formula:

$$\text{Score on standard score scale} = (z \times SD_{new\ scale}) + \overline{X}_{new\ scale}$$

$$= (-1.5 \times 15) + 100 = -22.5 + 100 = 77.5$$

which you can round up to 78.

The WIAT-II[UK]-T Word Reading subtest standard score of 110 can now be converted to a z score, using our formula:

$$z = \frac{X - M_x}{\sigma_x}$$

$$= \frac{110 - 100}{15} = \frac{10}{15} = +0.666$$

which you can round up to +0.67.

The calculations can be repeated to enable you to complete Table 2.2, giving you the T, z, and standard scores for the four tests.

Table 2.2: Types of Standardised Scores (ii)

	T Score	Z Score	Standard Score
WASI-II Block Design	55	+0.50	108
WASI-II Similarities	35	-1.50	78
WIAT-II[UK]-T Word Reading	57	+0.67	110
WIAT-II[UK]-T Comprehension	37	-1.33	80

Chapter 2 Types of Standard Scores

These calculations then allow you to appraise the total set of scores that now have a common metric – indeed you have a choice of three, but the standard scores with a mean of 100 is the most common one to use. All of these types of scores are interchangeable – if you start with T scores, you can convert to standard scores. If you start with z scores, you can convert to T scores, and so on.

Note that the same conversion process can also be applied to scaled scores that have a mean of 10, a range of 1-19, and a standard deviation of 3. Many tests that are used by psychologists and speech and language therapists and some that are used by specialist teachers use such a metric and so it is useful to be able to convert these types of standardised scores.

The CELF-4^{UK} is an example of a test used by speech and language therapists that provides raw score conversion to scaled scores that range from 1 to 19. So, for example, if a child had a scaled score of 15 on the CELF-4^{UK} Semantic Relationships subtest then to convert the scaled score to a standardised score the same formula could be used as follows:

$$z = \frac{X - M_x}{\sigma_x}$$

$$= \frac{15 - 10}{3}$$

$$= \frac{5}{3}$$

$$= 1.67$$

Again, applying the second formula above:

$$\text{Score on new scale} = (z \times SD_{new\ scale}) + \overline{X}_{new\ scale}$$

$$= (1.67 \times 15) + 100$$

$$= 25.05 + 100$$

$$= 125 \text{ (approximately)}$$

The *Detailed Assessment of Speed of Handwriting* (DASH; Barnett *et al.*, 2007) and its version for students in further and higher education, the *Detailed Assessment of Speed of Handwriting 17+* (DASH 17+; Barnett *et al.*, 2010) are examples of tests available to specialist teachers that provide scaled scores on subtests.

You will find conversion charts in most books on statistics or on the Internet. You may notice that not all such tables give exactly the same scores within the conversion table and this mainly reflects choice of decimal place for the z scores and, where percentiles are given, the type of definition of percentile used (see below on this particular issue). Another potential confusion is the lack of consistency of the use of the terms 'standard score' and 'standardised score'. Often these are used interchangeably but, for the purpose of this book's instructions, a standard score is defined as a form of standardised score with a mean of 100 and a standard deviation of 15.

It is simple to create your own look-up table using the formula in Table 2.3.

Table 2.3: Creating a Look-Up Table

Z Score	T Score (SD = 10, mean = 50)	Standard Score (SD = 15, mean = 100)	Scaled Score (SD = 3, mean = 10)
z	10z + 50	15z + 100	3z + 10

Therefore, an *Excel* table such as the one in Appendix A can be derived by deciding on your z score range (either -3 to +3, or -4 to +4) as shown in Figure 2.1.

C4			f_x	=15*A4+ 100	

	A	B	C	D
1	**Conversion Table for Standardised Scores**			
2	**z Score**	**T Score**	**Standard Score**	**Scaled Score**
3			**(SD 15: mean 100)**	**(SD 3: mean 10)**
4	-3.0	20	55	1
5	-2.9	21	57	1
6	-2.8	22	58	2
7	-2.7	23	60	2
8	-2.6	24	61	2
9	-2.5	25	63	3
10	-2.4	26	64	3

Figure 2.1: Excel Conversion Table for Standardised Scores

Cell C4 is highlighted and its corresponding formula is shown as an example in the formula bar.

Another example of making use of *Excel* is as follows for converting scaled scores (column A) into standardised scores with a mean of 100 and standard deviation of 15. The formula bar gives the *Excel* formula for a standard score of 115 (cell B8) equating to a scaled score of 13 (cell A8) in Figure 2.2.

B8			f_x	=(((A8-10)/3)*15)+100	

	A	B	C	D	E	F
1						
2	19	145				
3	18	140				
4	17	135				
5	16	130				
6	15	125				
7	14	120				
8	13	115				
9	12	110				
10	11	105				
11	10	100				
12	9	95				
13	8	90				
14	7	85				
15	6	80				
16	5	75				
17	4	70				
18	3	65				
19	2	60				
20	1	55				

Figure 2.2: Excel Conversion Table for Scaled Scores

Probability and the Normal Distribution Curve

Using *P* Values to Obtain Percentiles

Because z scores are directly linked to the standard normal distribution of scores in this way, they can also be used to give us a measure of probability of any one z score being obtained as well as defining what proportion of scores would lie below and above this particular z score. If a z score has a large value, then the proportion of scores up to the value of this z within the normal distribution curve will also be correspondingly large. The proportion remaining will be correspondingly smaller. In Figure 2.3, the z score is 1.5. The corresponding proportion of the normal distribution curve below (and above) this score will be 'set' by the value of this z score.

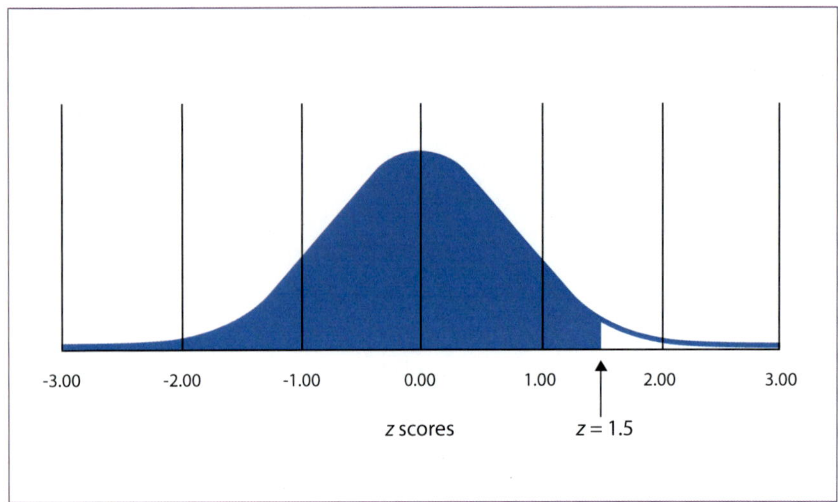

Figure 2.3: Z Score of 1.5 on the Standard Normal Distribution Curve

Therefore, z scores potentially enable us to obtain a corresponding measure of what the likelihood or chance of a score achieved on a test will be.

Table 2.4 shows a sample from the table given in Appendix B. Such tables have a number of names, but those that start from the extreme left hand tail with negative z scores tend to be called *cumulative* distribution z or p tables. Ones that start with a zero z score are often called *partial z* or *p* tables. The table given in Appendix B lists positive z scores down the vertical and further decimal parts along the horizontal. If one has a z score of +0.4, then one can find the area of the standard normal distribution covered by looking first in the first column for a score of .4 and tracking along to the second column (headed 0) to see the number 0.6554. Note that in such a partial table, a z score of 0 has a p of 0.5 – in other words 50% of the distribution beneath the standard normal distribution curve. Appendix C gives the left hand side of the negative values for our z scores along the standard normal distribution.

The value of 0.6554 also represents the probability of this z score occurring: we can say that the cumulative probability of a z score of +0.4 is approximately 0.66 or in percentage terms, 66%. For our z score of 1.5 in Figure 2.3 the p can be seen as 0.9332, or in percentage terms 93%.

Table 2.4: Extract from a Z-P Table

Positive z Scores									
z	0	0.01	0.02	0.03	0.04	0.05	0.06	0.07	0.08	0.09
0	0.5000	0.504	0.5080	0.5120	0.516	0.5199	0.5239	0.5279	0.5319	0.5359
0.1	0.5398	0.5438	0.5478	0.5517	0.5557	0.5596	0.5636	0.5675	0.5714	0.5753
0.2	0.5793	0.5832	0.5871	0.5910	0.5948	0.5987	0.6026	0.6064	0.6103	0.6141
0.3	0.6179	0.6217	0.6255	0.6293	0.6331	0.6368	0.6406	0.6443	0.6480	0.6517
0.4	0.6554	0.6591	0.6628	0.6664	0.6700	0.6736	0.6772	0.6808	0.6844	0.6879
0.5	0.6915	0.6950	0.6985	0.7019	0.7054	0.7088	0.7123	0.7157	0.7190	0.7224
0.6	0.7257	0.7291	0.7324	0.7357	0.7389	0.7422	0.7454	0.7486	0.7517	0.7549
0.7	0.7580	0.7611	0.7642	0.7673	0.7704	0.7734	0.7764	0.7794	0.7823	0.7852
0.8	0.7881	0.7910	0.7939	0.7967	0.7995	0.8023	0.8051	0.8078	0.8106	0.8133
0.9	0.8159	0.8186	0.8212	0.8238	0.8264	0.8289	0.8315	0.8340	0.8365	0.8389
1.0	0.8413	0.8438	0.8461	0.8485	0.8508	0.8531	0.8554	0.8577	0.8599	0.8621
1.1	0.8643	0.8665	0.8686	0.8708	0.8729	0.8749	0.8770	0.8790	0.8810	0.8830
1.2	0.8849	0.8869	0.8888	0.8907	0.8925	0.8944	0.8962	0.8980	0.8997	0.9015
1.3	0.9032	0.9049	0.9066	0.9082	0.9099	0.9115	0.9131	0.9147	0.9162	0.9177
1.4	0.9192	0.9207	0.9222	0.9236	0.9251	0.9265	0.9279	0.9292	0.9306	0.9319
1.5	0.9332	0.9345	0.9357	0.9370	0.9382	0.9394	0.9406	0.9418	0.9429	0.9441
1.6	0.9452	0.9463	0.9474	0.9484	0.9495	0.9505	0.9515	0.9525	0.9535	0.9545
1.7	0.9554	0.9564	0.9573	0.9582	0.9591	0.9599	0.9608	0.9616	0.9625	0.9633
1.8	0.9641	0.9649	0.9656	0.9664	0.9671	0.9678	0.9686	0.9693	0.9699	0.9706
1.9	0.9713	0.9719	0.9726	0.9732	0.9738	0.9744	0.9750	0.9756	0.9761	0.9767
2.0	0.9772	0.9778	0.9783	0.9788	0.9793	0.9798	0.9803	0.9808	0.9812	0.9817

An example site of the above table is at: http://www.sjsu.edu/faculty/gerstman/EpiInfo/z-table.htm

(Source: Dr. B. Gerstman, San Jose State University, San Jose, California, United States 95192-0052. Used with permission from the author.)

For z scores that are negative, i.e. to the left side of the standard normal distribution curve, look at Table 2.5, a sample from Appendix C. Note that Table 2.5 starts with negative z scores. To find a p for a z score of -2.55, first find the row that starts with -2.5 then go to the sixth column that is headed 0 .05 to find 0.0054, in the same way as with positive z scores for the previous table.

Table 2.5: Extract from a Negative Z-P Table

Negative Z Scores									
z	0.09	0.08	0.07	0.06	0.05	0.04	0.03	0.02	0.01	0
-3.0	0.0010	0.0010	0.0011	0.0011	0.0011	0.0012	0.0012	0.0013	0.0013	0.0013
-2.9	0.0014	0.0014	0.0015	0.0015	0.0016	0.0016	0.0017	0.0018	0.0018	0.0019
-2.8	0.0019	0.0020	0.0021	0.0021	0.0022	0.0023	0.0023	0.0024	0.0025	0.0026
-2.7	0.0026	0.0027	0.0028	0.0029	0.0030	0.0031	0.0032	0.0033	0.0034	0.0035
-2.6	0.0036	0.0037	0.0038	0.0039	0.0040	0.0041	0.0043	0.0044	0.0045	0.0047
-2.5	0.0048	0.0049	0.0051	0.0052	0.0054	0.0055	0.0057	0.0059	0.0060	0.0062
-2.4	0.0064	0.0066	0.0068	0.0069	0.0071	0.0073	0.0075	0.0078	0.0080	0.0082
-2.3	0.0084	0.0087	0.0089	0.0091	0.0094	0.0096	0.0099	0.0102	0.0104	0.0107
-2.2	0.0110	0.0113	0.0116	0.0119	0.0122	0.0125	0.0129	0.0132	0.0136	0.0139
-2.1	0.0143	0.0146	0.0150	0.0154	0.0158	0.0162	0.0166	0.0170	0.0174	0.0179
-2.0	0.0183	0.0188	0.0192	0.0197	0.0202	0.0207	0.0212	0.0217	0.0222	0.0228
-1.9	0.0233	0.0239	0.0244	0.0250	0.0256	0.0262	0.0268	0.0274	0.0281	0.0287
-1.8	0.0294	0.0301	0.0307	0.0314	0.0322	0.0329	0.0336	0.0344	0.0351	0.0359
-1.7	0.0367	0.0375	0.0384	0.0392	0.0401	0.0409	0.0418	0.0427	0.0436	0.0446
-1.6	0.0455	0.0465	0.0475	0.0485	0.0495	0.0505	0.0516	0.0526	0.0537	0.0548
-1.5	0.0559	0.0571	0.0582	0.0594	0.0606	0.0618	0.0630	0.0643	0.0655	0.0668
-1.4	0.0681	0.0694	0.0708	0.0721	0.0735	0.0749	0.0764	0.0778	0.0793	0.0808
-1.3	0.0823	0.0838	0.0853	0.0869	0.0885	0.0901	0.0918	0.0934	0.0951	0.0968
-1.2	0.0985	0.1003	0.1020	0.1038	0.1056	0.1075	0.1093	0.1112	0.1131	0.1151
-1.1	0.1170	0.119	0.1210	0.1230	0.1251	0.1271	0.1292	0.1314	0.1335	0.1357
-1.0	0.1379	0.1401	0.1423	0.1446	0.1469	0.1492	0.1515	0.1539	0.1562	0.1587

To summarise, some z-p tables only give you the z scores to the right hand side of the normal distribution curve, i.e. only the positive z scores. With these partial z-p tables you can still obtain the p values of negative z scores because with the standard normal distribution curve being symmetrical around the mean, or zero z score, then you just have to subtract your obtained p score from 1 when starting with a negative z score. So for example, with a z score of -2 .0 you could look up a positive z score of 2.0 to get a p of 0.9772. The p for the negative z score of -2.0 would then be (1 – 0.9772), which is 0.0228. Table 2.5 shows that a z score of -2.0 does indeed give a p score of 0.0228.

Now that we know that a z score can identify a score at a precise point on the normal distribution curve of all scores and we can calculate the proportion of scores below (and logically, above) it, then it is possible to change the z score into another type of standardised score, the percentile rank. Percentile rank scores are scores that rank, in percentage terms, the scores that are lower than the percentile rank score that you are concerned with. Therefore, for example, if a child has scored at the 75th percentile rank, then we know that his score was higher than that obtained by 74% of the population of other children taking the same test.

To convert a z score into a percentile rank, you simply multiply by 100 the obtained *p* score that equates to the z score. Therefore, taking the above examples we can complete another conversion table, Table 2.6, as follows.

Table 2.6: Converting Z Scores to Percentiles

Z	P	Percentile Rank
0.40	.6554	65.54
1.85	.9678	96.78

It is conventional to round percentile ranks to the nearest whole number. This gives us a percentile rank of 66 for a z score of +0.4, and a percentile rank of 97 for a z score of +1.85. Appendix D gives a table of z and percentile equivalent scores.

It is important to note that percentile ranks are a form of standardised score that is only concerned with ranking scores along a line of measurement. They do not enable you to obtain a measure of by how much one person's score differs from another person's score. Percentile scores are not graded equally along the width of the normal distributions of scores. They cluster together towards the centre of the curve and span out at the tail ends. Towards the end of this chapter we will explore the meaning of percentiles in more depth and see how they can be calculated from information on ranking of scores.

Therefore, we can now add a further column to give us percentile ranks, by applying the above process to convert the z scores and rounding up our numbers (see Table 2.7).

Table 2.7: Tests of Standardised Scores (iii)

	T Score	Z Score	Standard Score	Percentile
WASI-II Block Design	55	+0.50	108	69
WASI-II Similarities	35	-1.50	78	7
WIAT-II[UK]-T Word Reading	57	+0.67	110	75
WIAT-II[UK]-T Comprehension	37	-1.33	80	9

Chapter 2 Types of Standard Scores

Percentile Ranks

As already noted in this chapter, there are different definitions of the term 'percentile'. This leads to some confusion when comparing and using look-up tables when one wants to report both standard scores and percentiles across test manuals. The first definition of percentile is that it is *a measure that tells us what percent of the total frequency of measures score at or below a score*. A percentile rank is therefore the percentage of scores that fall **at or below** a given score. A second definition is that a percentile is *a measure that tells us what percent of the total frequency of measures scored below a score*. According to this definition, a percentile rank is therefore the percentage of scores that fall **below** a given score.

Below are two examples of how percentile ranks are calculated by applying these two slightly different definitions.

Definition 1

For a score of X out of a set of n scores

$$\text{Percentile rank} = \left(\frac{A + 0.5B}{n}\right) \times 100$$

where A = number of scores below X, B = the number of scores equal to X, n = number scores.

So, if a child scored 40th on a test out of a group of 150 children (and did not 'tie' with any other children (i.e. 110 children scored lower than this child, and none had the same score as this child), then applying this formula:

$$\text{Percentile rank} = \left(\frac{110 + .5 \times 1}{150}\right) \times 100 = \frac{110.5}{150} \times 100 = 74$$

Definition 2

For a score of X out of a set of n scores:

$$\text{Percentile rank} = \left(\frac{number\ of\ scores\ below\ X}{n}\right) \times 100$$

$$= \left(\frac{110}{150}\right) \times 100 = 73$$

One can see that there is a difference of percentile ranking of approximately one with these two examples (the actual difference before rounding is 0.3). Our z score conversion tables in Appendices B and C using p values can be equated with Definition 2.

Case Example 3

You use the ART, but are concerned that it only provides centile (i.e. percentile) scores for conversion of raw scores and does not provide statistical information on confidence ranges. You wish to establish your own look-up tables of standard scores to reflect the standard normal distributions with a mean of 100 and a standard deviation of 15.

Points to Consider

The ART is a frequently used test when assessing students in further and higher education (FHE). It has subtests to assess reading accuracy, reading rate, reading comprehension and writing speed and is one of only a few tests that is UK-standardised on these important areas. ART is an approved test for assessment in the UK for Disabled Students' Allowance (DSA). For these reasons, you are keen to use it. However, as this test only provides centile scores converted from raw scores the assessor does not have sufficient statistical information to apply confidence ranges, nor easily compare ART subtest scores with other test scores. You have available reliability coefficients (alpha coefficients) for the ART's subtests on page 19 of the manual that span the .81 to .97 range but with no information on reliability for the writing speed subtest. How do you proceed to design your look-up tables for standard scores and confidence limits?

The Statistics

You are aware that percentiles are a form of standardised score and that they equate to fixed positions on the standard normal distribution curve. It is therefore possible with the use of established look-up tables to convert the percentiles into their corresponding *z* scores on the standard normal distribution.

Looking at Table A10 on page 23 of the ART manual, you have a source of how raw scores are linked to centile scores for FHE students' reading accuracy, reading rate, reading comprehension, and writing speed. Firstly, open an *Excel* file to create a table for the total set of scores given in this table. Create three columns: *centile, reading accuracy* and *z score*. Insert the numbers for the centiles, 1 through to 100, by typing the first two or three numbers, selecting these cells and extending the number series by pulling down the fill handle (the add symbol as shown in Figure 2.4) at the bottom right of the relevant cell, until you fill the column's cells up to the 100th centile .

1	centile
2	1
3	2
4	3
5	
6	
7	
8	
9	
10	

Figure 2.4: Filling Cells in Excel

Alongside the centile scores in the next column for the reading accuracy scores, insert the appropriate reading accuracy raw scores as given in Table A7 on page 22 of the manual. Then for the third column insert the *z* scores for each of the percentile numbers given using the table found in Appendix D of this book, as shown in Figure 2.5. There is no need to go beyond two decimal points for this exercise.

centile	reading accuracy	z score
1	10.00	-2.33
2	16.00	-2.05
3	19.00	-1.88
4	24.00	-1.75
5		-1.64
6	27.00	-1.55
7	33.00	-1.48
8	36.00	-1.41

Figure 2.5: Deriving Z Scores from Raw Scores via Percentiles

It is important to be aware that percentiles only rank scores in order, so the distance between them along a distribution curve will vary according to the values of scores, the standard deviations and the scores' points on each curve. You want your z scores to be converted to a common metric of standardised scores, i.e. have a standard deviation of 15 and a mean of 100. To do this you employ the formula:

$$\text{Standardised score} = (z \times 15) + 100$$

You therefore need to insert a new column in your table, headed *standard score*, and using the formula bar for the above formula, insert the standardised scores for the equivalent z scores as in Figure 2.6.

D3				f_x =(C3*15)+100	
	A	B	C	D	E
1		reading		standard	
2	centile	accuracy	z score	score	SEm
3	1	10.00	-2.33	65	6
4	2	16.00	-2.05	69	6
5	3	19.00	-1.88	72	6
6	4	24.00	-1.75	74	6
7	5		-1.64	75	6
8	6	27.00	-1.55	77	6
9	7	33.00	-1.48	78	6
10	8	36.00	-1.41	79	6

Figure 2.6: Deriving Standard Scores from Z Scores

You can now equate each raw score with its centile, its equivalent z score, and finally, its equivalent standard score.

Having calculated the standard scores, you can proceed to calculate the confidence ranges because you now have the reliability coefficients for all the subtests (except writing speed).

Create a new column, SE_m, and in the formula bar, insert the formula:

$$SE_m = SD\sqrt{1-r}$$

where for reading accuracy the reliability coefficient, r, = 0.81, and the SD = 15, therefore:

$$SE_m = 15\sqrt{1-0.81}$$

$$= 6$$

The screen now looks like Figure 2.7.

E3				f_x	=15*SQRT(1-0.85)	
	A	B	C	D	E	
1		reading		standard		
2	centile	accuracy	z score	score	SEm	
3	1	10.00	-2.33	65	6	
4	2	16.00	-2.05	69	6	
5	3	19.00	-1.88	72	6	
6	4	24.00	-1.75	74	6	
7	5		-1.64	75	6	
8	6	27.00	-1.55	77	6	
9	7	33.00	-1.48	78	6	
10	8	36.00	-1.41	79	6	

Figure 2.7: Deriving the Standard Error of Measurement

You can now calculate the confidence ranges for all of the scores. If you then wish to accept a 95% confidence level for your range descriptors, then the SE_m should be multiplied by 1.96 and this figure subtracted from, and added to, each of the standard scores. Create two new columns in your table and use the formula bar to help you calculate the two sets of numbers, as in Figure 2.8.

F3					f_x	=D3-1.96*E3	
	A	B	C	D	E	F	G
1		reading		standard		95% confidence	
2	centile	accuracy	z score	score	SEm	range	
3	1	10.00	-2.33	65	6	54	76
4	2	16.00	-2.05	69	6	58	81
5	3	19.00	-1.88	72	6	60	83
6	4	24.00	-1.75	74	6	62	85
7	5		-1.64	75	6	64	87
8	6	27.00	-1.55	77	6	65	88
9	7	33.00	-1.48	78	6	66	89
10	8	36.00	-1.41	79	6	67	90

Figure 2.8: Deriving Confidence Ranges

You can now create new files or extend this table for the different percentile scores for male, female, and FHE students given in the separate tables of the ART manual on pages 22-23.

Stanines

An alternative to the concept of percentiles is the stanine. A stanine (STAndard NINE) is a type of scale that provides a range of 0–9 points with a mean of 5 and a standard deviation of 2.

Scores on an assessment can be converted to stanines by following these stages:

1. Rank the clients' test scores from lowest to highest

2. Give the lowest 4% of these scores a stanine of 1, the next 7% of scores a stanine of 2, etc, according to Table 2.8.

Table 2.8: Stanines and Ranking

Ranking	4%	7%	12%	17%	20%	17%	12%	7%	4%
Score	1	2	3	4	5	6	7	8	9

Except for 1 and 9, stanines divide the baseline of the standard normal distribution curve into equal amounts of the characteristic being measured. Stanine 8 is as far above average (5) as stanine 2 is below average. The proportions within each of the stanines is given in Figure 2.9, as is their relationship to percentiles.

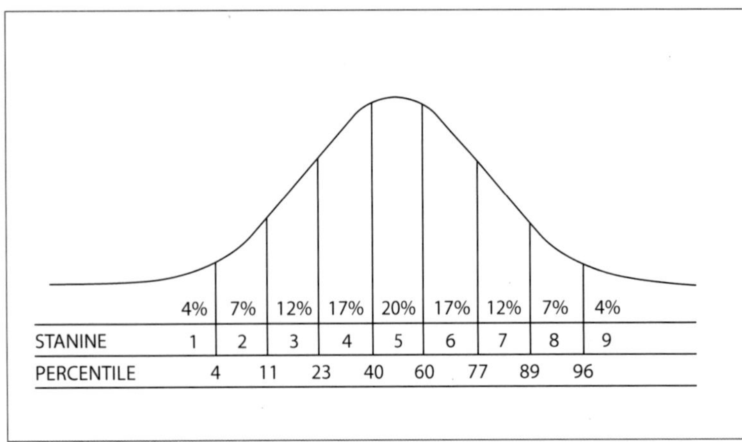

Figure 2.9: Stanines and Percentiles

Stanines are not commonly referred to in contemporary test manuals. This is because there is no great need in educational and clinical arenas to categorise clients' scores into such particular score ranges. However, quartiles are referred to in tests such as the WIAT-II[UK]. The main use of quartiles is to obtain overview measures of, for example, how many children in a year group fall into the bottom 25% of the population of children as a whole.

As mentioned above, look-up tables to convert across various types of standardised scores are readily available in books and on the Internet. You may find it useful to print off one of these examples from the public domain to keep for reference purposes. Their numbers may differ slightly, mainly because of how they round up their numbers, and the definition used for percentiles. However, this is acceptable and so do not worry about which reference you choose. Also, note that if you are using a test manual with its own table of standardised score comparisons such as standard scores and percentiles, that this table can be used with other tests' data and vice versa. In other words, if you have a standard score on, for example, the Spelling test from the WIAT-II[UK] and for some reason you have temporarily mislaid the test manual, you can use an equivalent table from another available test to convert the standard score to a percentile.

Another way of appreciating the equivalence of these scores and having a visual aid of their placement on the normal distribution curve is to obtain an illustration such as Figure 2.10, which gives z, T, percentiles, stanines, scaled and standard scores along the span of the standard normal curve.

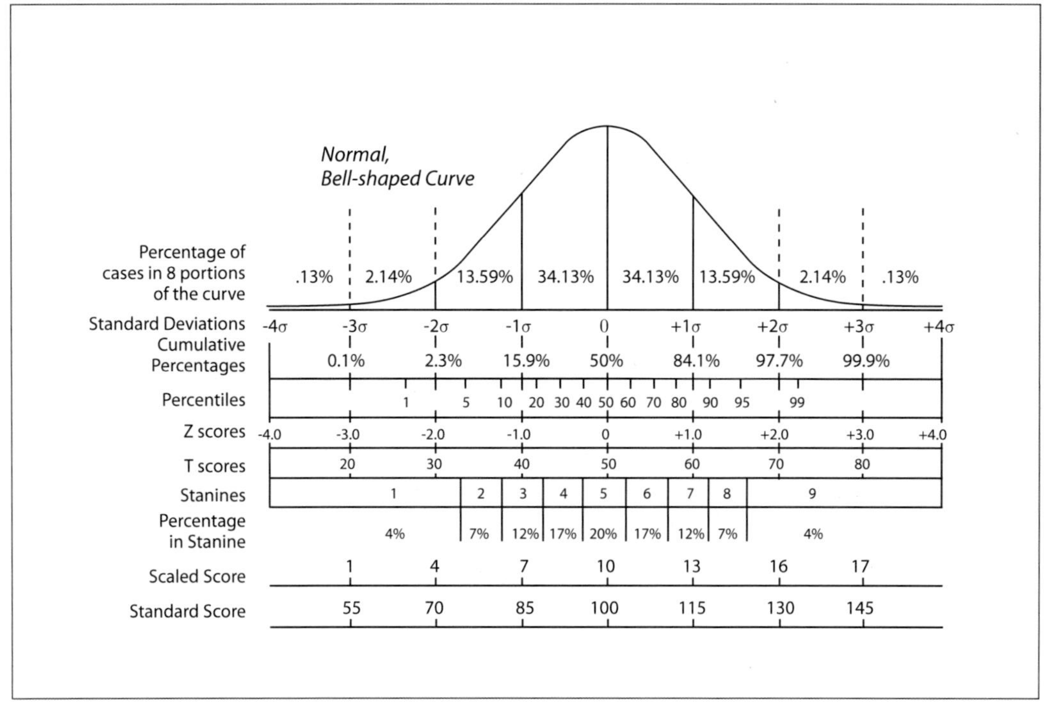

Figure 2.10: Standard Normal Distribution Curve and Standardised Scores

Many test manuals and record forms have this type of figure placed within them in order to help the assessor obtain a visual format to appraise their scores and help with the conversion of scores when required. An example is the WIAT-II^{UK}-T, where the figure is displayed on the record form.

Therefore, you are at the point of being able to start comparing scores from different tests that initially used different types of standardised scores. Additionally, you are now able to represent this total set of scores in a report in a way that is comprehensible to the reader in that all test scores can be compared with one another at a glance. In addition, the use of a common metric across tests promotes the application of using charts to help the reader understand the meaning of the final assessment report. This area will be covered in Chapter 17.

Converting a Range of Scores when Scores are not Normally Distributed

Distributions of raw scores can be converted to percentiles, and having obtained these you can normalise the distribution of scores to conform to a standard normal distribution curve. This can be very useful if you want to obtain a set of norms for a particular reference group where the scores are not normally distributed. For example, you may have evolved your own diagnostic test that you consider to be sensitive to your reference group, having incrementally built up a range of test items that you regard to be both diagnostic and discriminatory for the range of clients that you tend to see. Similarly, you may wish to evolve contemporary norms for a particular reference group (with permission from the owner of the intellectual property).

Supposing you obtained the following scores and the frequencies of these scores as given in Table 2.9.

Table 2.9: Frequency of Raw Scores

Raw Score	Frequency
63	3
61	2
56	6
48	5
46	2
42	1
30	2

The distribution is not normally distributed but you would like to reconstruct it to obtain percentile scores and thereby standard scores. As they stand, the distribution of scores can be seen in Figure 2.11.

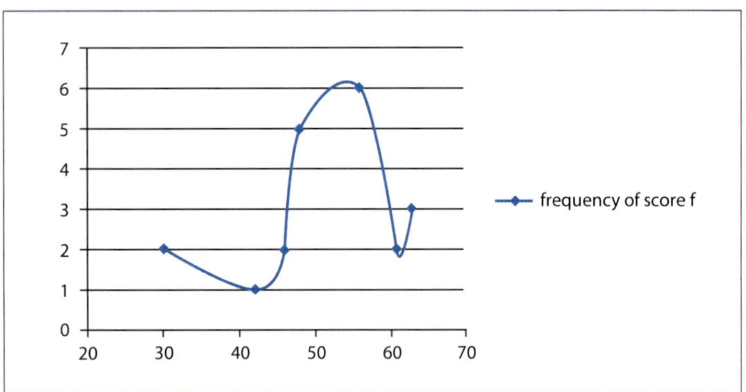

Figure 2.11: Distribution of Raw Scores and their Frequencies

The steps are as follows:

1. Create a table, such as Table 2.10, list in the first column the obtained scores from your group.

2. Create a second column with the frequencies with which each of the scores in the first column occur. Note that the frequencies of the scores are deliberately low for the purposes of this example; in reality significantly more scores would be needed.

3. Create a third column and, starting from the bottom cell and finishing at the top, list the **cumulative** frequencies for the frequency scores in the second column. For example, the cumulative frequency for the score of 30 is 2, because two people scored with a score of 30. For the score of 42, the cumulative frequency is 3 (2 +1) because one person scored with a score of 42 and two people scored with a score of 30, and so on.

4. You then need to modify the third column of observed cumulative frequencies in order to balance these across the range of above and below average scores in preparation for creating percentile scores. Therefore, a fourth column is created and, for each cell, take the cell value for the **previous** cumulative frequency value plus half the value of the frequency number for that particular score. So, for example, for the cumulative frequency cell of 18, add half of 3, so 1.5, which gives 19.5. Then record 19.5 in the row for the score 63 giving a modified cumulative frequency score.

5. With these modified cumulative frequencies you convert them to percentiles by dividing each of them by the total number of observations, which here is 21 (the cumulative frequency noted in the top cell of the cumulative frequency column) and multiplying by 100, and approximating to the nearest whole number. Table 2.10 shows the final set of data.

Table 2.10: Converting Raw Scores to Percentile Ranks

Score	Frequency of score f	Cumulative frequency cf	Cumulative frequency below +.5 f	Percentile rank
63	3	21	19.5	93
61	2	18	17.0	81
56	6	16	13.0	62
48	5	10	7.5	36
46	2	5	4.0	19
42	1	3	2.5	12
30	2	2	1.0	5

The redistribution of scores for their percentile ranks can now be seen in Figure 2.12.

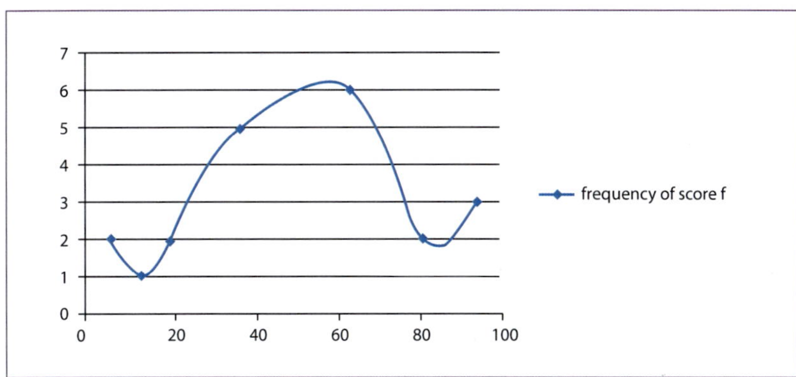

Figure 2.12: Score Frequencies and Percentile Ranks

Note how the scores are now distributed. In comparison to Figure 2.9, the shape of the distribution is now approaching that of a normal distribution. As more scores are added, the more normally distributed they become.

Therefore, you now know that a client with a score of, for example, 46 on your test scores has a percentile of 19. Having a percentile score now allows you to look up in any conversion table or to calculate the equivalent scaled, standard, T, or z score equivalent to this percentile score.

Note that directly converting the raw scores to z scores by use of the formula:

$$z = \frac{X - M_x}{\sigma_x}$$

will not distribute your sample of raw scores into a normal distribution, so be careful not to make this mistake.

One-tailed and Two-tailed Tests of Significance

You have learned about z scores and their relationship with the concepts of *probability* and *chance*. These properties are going to be of great use to you in later chapters of this book, so it is important to have an understanding and working knowledge of the concepts involved. It is helpful therefore to remind you again how to apply the *z-p* tables in Appendix B. For example, for a z score of 2.5 the *p* value is 0.9938. This means that the probability of scores below this z score is 99.38 and the *p* value of scores above this z score is 0.0062 with a probability of 0.62.

Another example of how to use the table in Appendix B is to find the area for a z score of 1.96 that helps you understand how to process such scores with values including second decimal points. Find the value of 1.9 in the leftmost column, then find the hundredth figure from the column heading for 0.06, and read the area below that column, e.g. 0.9750. The area to the *right* of this proportion in our curve would be 1- 0.9750, which is 0.0250. Now consider a z score of -1.96. When we use the table in Appendix C, we can see that this again gives us a proportion or probability of 0.0250. In other words, we can deduce that the probability any z score to the *left* of -1.96 in our normal curve and to the *right* of a z score of +1.96 in our normal curve is 2 x 0.025, which is 0.05. This example of calculating z scores' equivalent proportions/probabilities of -1.96 and +1.96 was not randomly selected. This is because the proportion of 0.05 obtained from the above calculation is a commonly used amount for statisticians and researchers to select as a figure to represent the unlikely occurrence of scores at either ends of the tails of the standard normal distribution – the scores that do not often occur and hence the proportion of scores within the standard normal distribution that are rarely found. The proportion, or probability, of 0.05 is often, but not always, taken as a benchmark of risk, as we observed in Chapter 1 when considering confidence intervals. Figure 2.13 highlights this risk feature.

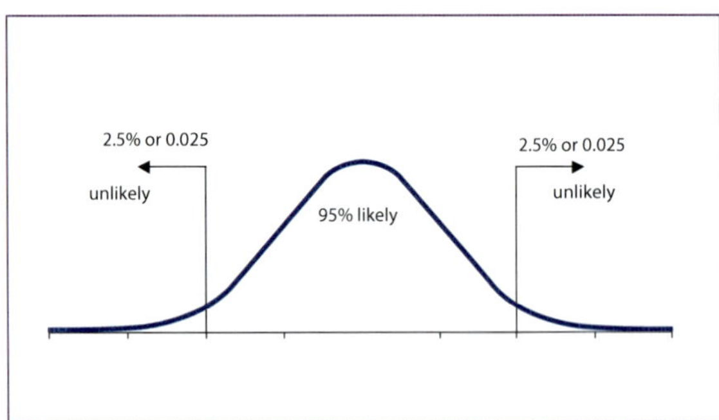

Figure 2.13: Proportion of Unlikely Scores in the Normal Distribution Curve

This now leads us to consider the terms *one-tailed and two-tailed tests of significance*.

First, let us start with the meaning of a two-tailed test. If you have decided on a risk level of being wrong 5% of the time when testing your null hypothesis, i.e. you are using a significance level of 0.05, a two-tailed test allots half of what is called *alpha*, α, to testing the statistical significance in one direction of the normal distribution curve and half of your *alpha* to testing statistical significance in the other direction. But, what is this term *alpha*?

Alpha, α, is the probability that, according to your null hypothesis, a statistical test or result will generate a false-positive error – a Type I error. It should not be confused with Cronbach's alpha (α), a measure of internal consistency reliability that was mentioned in Chapter 1. Conventional methodology for statistical testing is, in advance of undertaking the test, to set what is called a *nominal alpha criterion level* (often $\alpha = 0.05$). This means that .025 is in each tail (dark blue sections in Figure 2.14) of the distribution of your test statistic. When using a two-tailed test, regardless of the direction of the relationship you hypothesise, you are testing for the possibility of the relationship in both directions, as shown in Figure 2.14.

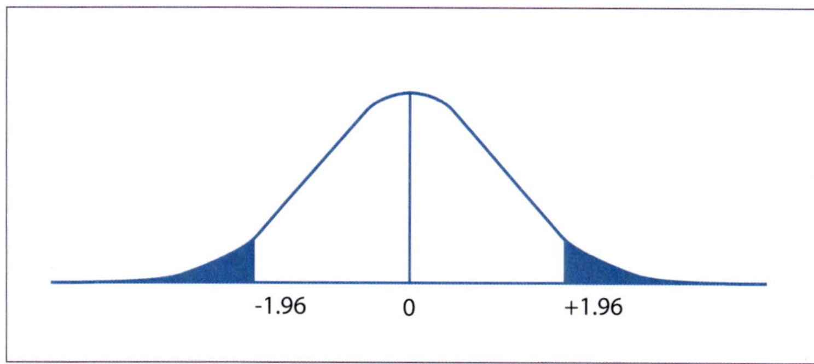

Figure 2.14: Z Scores and Two-Tailed Test

A one-tailed hypothesis is simply one that specifies the direction of a difference, while a two-tailed hypothesis is one that does not. What is the meaning of a one-tailed test? If you are using a significance level of .05, a one-tailed test allots all of *alpha*, α, to testing the statistical significance in the one direction of interest. This means that .05 is in one tail of the distribution of your test statistic. When using a one-tailed test, you are testing for the possibility of the relationship in one direction and completely disregarding the possibility of a relationship in the other direction. Therefore, if you again refer to Appendix B, and look for the z score that is equivalent to a probability of 0.95 (obtained by subtracting .05 from 1.0) you will see that it lies between a z score of 1.64 and a z score of 1.65 – this table does not cover z scores of more than two decimal places. However, logically, it follows that the z score will be 1.645 if we wish to advance to using the third decimal place (see Figure 2.15).

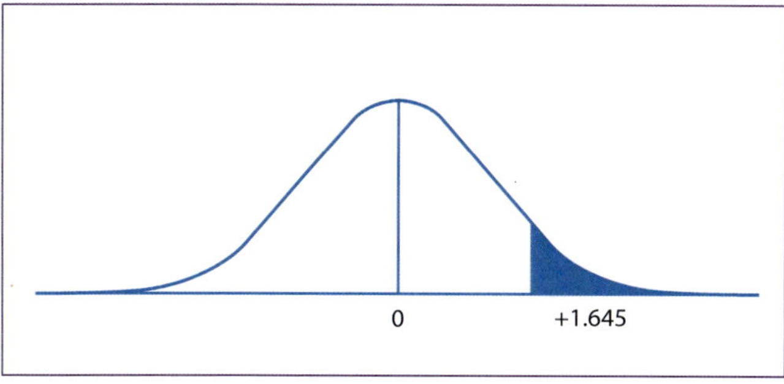

Figure 2.15: Z Score and One-Tailed Test

It is useful to keep a note of the commonly used z values and their equivalent level of confidences, as given in Table 2.11. This is because many formulae require you to select and apply a value of z that reflects your level of confidence.

Table 2.11: Z Scores and Levels of Confidence

	% Level of Confidence
Z value (two-tailed)	
1.645	90
1.96	95
2.56	99
Z value (one-tailed)	
1.28	90
1.645	95

Chapter 3
Standard Error of Measurement of the Difference

Introducing:

- **standardisation of measurement of the difference**

- **comparing test scores with tests of different and same standard deviations.**

Case Example 4

Sally is assessed at age 12 years and 1 month on Form A of the Listening Comprehension subtest of the *Kaufman Test of Educational Achievement, Second Edition* (KTEA-II; Kaufman & Kaufman, 2004c) where her standard score is 115. You then decide to administer the WIAT-II[UK]-T Word Reading subtest where a standard score of 105 is obtained. You again want to know how to compare the two scores in such a way that you can determine whether or not the difference of 10 is statistically significant.

Points to Consider

This query can be approached in the same way as in Chapter 1. However, a different formula can be used to achieve the same goal. We will use the standard error of measurement of the difference formula for comparing two scores. This term takes into account the standard errors of measurements of the two tests, and the formula from Anastasi and Urbini (1997) is:

$$SE_{mdiff} = \sqrt{SE_m a^2 + SE_m b^2}$$

where:

- SE_{mdiff} = the standard error of the difference

- $SE_m a$ = the standard error of measurement for Test a, in this case the Listening Comprehension subtest of the KTEA-II. This value is 6.54 and can be found in the test's manual in Table 7.7, page 96, using the SE_m for Form A.

- $SE_m b$ = the standard error of measurement for Test b, which in this case is the WIAT-II[UK]-T Word Reading subtest. This is 2.60 and can be found in the test's manual in Table 6.3, page 55.

When the formula is applied, the calculation is:

$$SE_{mdiff} = \sqrt{SE_m a^2 + SE_m b^2}$$

$$= \sqrt{6.54^2 + 2.60^2}$$

$$= \sqrt{42.646 + 6.76}$$

$$= \sqrt{49.406}$$

$$= 7 \text{ (to the nearest whole number)}$$

You then need to determine how large this difference could be obtained by chance at the pre-determined level of significance of .05.

To do this, we multiply the SE_{mdiff} of 7 by 1.96, which = 13.72 (the value 1.96 is obtained from Table 2.11, and derived from the z score proportion of scores that lie outside and either side of 95% of the total number of scores within the normal distribution). In other words, for the scores on the two subtests above to be statistically different at the pre-selected significance level of .05, the difference observed must be greater than 13.72. The difference is only 10. So, the null hypothesis that the two scores are not different is not rejected: we conclude that Sally's two scores are not significantly different from one another at the .05 level of significance.

Note that the above formula can be rewritten to calculate more directly (Reynolds, 1990) the z score that reflects the probability of the size of the difference occurring between the two scores:

$$z_{diff} = \frac{z_a - z_b}{\sqrt{2 - (r_x + r_y)}}$$

where:

z_a = the z score on the KTEA-II Listening Comprehension subtest

z_b = the z score on the WIAT-II[UK]-T Word Reading subtest

r_x = the reliability coefficient for the KTEA-II Listening Comprehension subtest

r_y = the reliability coefficient for the WIAT-II[UK]-T Word Reading subtest.

The obtained z score can be linked back to the p table to obtain a measure of how rare or probable the z score is. Again, keeping a summary table of key p values for reference purposes is advisable, such as in Table 3.1. Thus, a high z score difference would give a low p value. In other words, the higher the z score value the less likely, or probable it is to occur by chance. The p value is the probability of the data, if the null hypothesis were true.

Table 3.1: P and Z Scores for One- and Two-Tailed Tests of Significance

Probability *p*	Z	
	One-Tailed	Two-Tailed
0.025	1.96	2.24
0.01	2.33	2.58
0.005	2.58	2.81
0.001	3.08	3.31

There are two advantages to using the formula for the standard error of measurement of the difference when one wants to obtain a view on the importance of a difference between two test scores. Firstly, one can set the level of confidence. Only you know of the circumstances that you are working with at any one time and the degree of your required confidence could vary.

Secondly, this formula allows you to compare tests that have different standard deviations – in the example above they are the same, 15, but they could have been different.

The above formula for the SE_{mdiff} can be rewritten when the standard deviations for the two tests are the same. It becomes:

$$SE_{mdiff} = SD \times \sqrt{2 - r_x - r_y}$$

This variation to the formula for the SE_{mdiff} is particularly useful when one or more of the tests you are using does not publish the standard errors of measurement obtained when the tests were standardised. An example is the ART (Brooks *et al.*, 2004). As the ART's reliability coefficients are given on page 19 it is possible to calculate the SE_{mdiff} for any particular subtests selected. Using the ART's Reading Comprehension subtest as an example, we note that its reliability coefficient is 0.81. Therefore if we were for example to compare a 17-year-old student's scores obtained on the KTEA-II Nonsense Word Decoding subtest and the ART Reading Comprehension subtest we then obtain the reliability coefficient for the Nonsense Word Decoding subtest for this age from Table 7.2, page 91 and note that it is 0.95.

Applying the formula:

$$SE_{mdiff} = SD \times \sqrt{2 - r_a - r_b}$$

$$= 15 \times \sqrt{2 - 0.81 - 0.95}$$

$$= 15 \times \sqrt{0.24}$$

$$= 15 \times 0.49$$

$$= 7 \quad \text{(to the nearest whole number)}$$

Having now obtained the SE_{mdiff} you can now proceed as you did with Sally's case by deciding on your confidence level, multiplying the equivalent *z* value (1.96) by the obtained SE_{mdiff} of 7, and comparing the obtained score with the difference of the two observed scores from the subtests being used:

$$1.96 \times 7 = 13.73$$

Note, however, that in this particular example the ART manual only gives percentile score equivalents for raw scores. Therefore, before the two scores from the KTEA-II Nonsense Word Decoding and the ART Reading

Chapter 3 The Standard Error of Measurement of the Difference

Comprehension can be compared, we would need to convert the percentile scores given for the Reading Comprehension subtest into standard scores, as previously described in Chapter 2.

The standard error of measurement of the difference is frequently employed in test manuals to analyse differences between subtest scores. For example, in the CELF-4[UK], it is used to compare results for scores on its Receptive and Language Index scores in Table 3.5, page 111.

Sometimes, it is difficult to ascertain from a test manual if the test score has a standard deviation of 15. In the absence of such evidence, however, it is possible to work this out by calculating a test's standard deviation from the SE_m. For example, the *Preschool Language Scale – Fourth Edition* (PLS-4) (Zimmerman, *et al.*, 2001), provides a table of SE_ms for its Auditory and Expressive subtests and an overall Composite score in Chapter 7, page 189. If we apply the SE_m formula:

$$SE_m = SD \sqrt{1 - r}$$

and randomly sample a SE_m for a particular age range and identify the reliability coefficient given for one of the subtests, then we can work backwards to check the size of the standard deviation. So, if we select, for example, the age range 5:06-5:11 we find that the reliability coefficient is 0.83 and the SE_m is 6.18. We now have all the information to fill in the SE_m equation above in order to confirm that the standard deviation has indeed a value of 15:

$$6.18 = SD \sqrt{1 - 0.83}$$

$$= SD \sqrt{0.17}$$

$$= SD \times 0.4123$$

$$SD = \frac{6.18}{0.4123}$$

$$= 14.989 = 15 \text{ (nearest whole number)}$$

An important principle to remember is that the standard error of the difference between two test scores is greater than the two individual test scores' standard errors. This is because a *difference* score contains two sources of measurement error that interact with one another, thus compounding the error tendency.

Notwithstanding the popularity of this type of 'simple-difference' approach, it has a weakness. The calculation does not take into account the fact that it is highly likely that the two tests used correlate with one other and this correlation, it is argued, needs to be accounted for especially when attempting to predict an attainment skill level from a cognitive ability level and where you are concerned to determine if any discrepancy found is significant. The feature of correlation brings into play the need to account for *regression*, otherwise the simple-difference approach as outlined above would over-identify clients as having significant score differences. Very high or very low scores on one test would not lead to equivalent very high or very low scores on a second test: the expected scores on the second test will tend to regress towards the mean if the correlation between the two tests is less than 1, which it usually is. The lower the correlation between two tests, the higher will be the effect of such regression. In other words, one would expect the scores on the two tests to be different purely as a product of this statistical phenomenon. Therefore, when attempting to determine if the difference between two test scores is significantly different, first you need to account for the effect of the regression. Extreme scores at either end of the normal distribution curve are more prone to the effect of regression. Chapter 5 will explore this feature in more detail.

Chapter 4
Statistical and Clinical Differences Between Test Scores

Further discussion of the distinction between clinical and statistical differences between scores and an approach to the analysis of groups of test scores from one individual.

It has been established that it is not uncommon for two test scores to be statistically significantly different from one another. Although such findings are important to note and act on, it is even more important to make a judgement about the clinical relevance of such a difference. Let us enlarge on the issues and options available within these two areas.

Levels of Confidence and One- Versus Two-Tailed Hypothesis

We have already noted in Chapter 1 that test manuals differ in their approach to giving information about confidence ranges. Some offer you a range of confidence ranges to select. For example the KTEA-II offers confidence levels of 85, 90, or 95 (Table N.6, page 301-303 in the Norms Book), the *Kaufman Assessment Battery for Children, Second Edition* (KABC-II; Kaufman & Kaufman, 2004a) (Table D2, pages 174-201) and the *Bayley Scales of Infant and Toddler Development – Third Edition* (Bayley-III; Bayley, 2006) (Motor Scale Manual, Table A3 p139, Motor Composite score) give confidence ranges of 90 and 95. Others offer only one, for example the *Kaufman Brief Intelligence Test, Second Edition* (KBIT-2; Kaufman & Kaufman, 2004b) gives a confidence range of 90% (Appendix, Table B1, pages 78-127).

Although nearly all publishing companies now provide confidence ranges, ideally, it should be for the assessor to decide on the confidence levels of the tests selected for the particular task and risk level involved. For the tests selected, the various test manuals will probably lead the assessor to be working at different levels of confidence when working across tests and forming a diagnostic conclusion. This scenario promotes the need for assessors to have the knowledge to establish their own levels of confidence by having the information and statistical knowledge available to convert all tests used to a common level of confidence. Publishing companies now provide sufficient information (the standard deviation of the test and reliability coefficients) to enable assessors to calculate the standard error of measurement relevant to any standardised score and thereby obtain a common level of confidence. Any test that does not provide such basic information should be used with extreme caution as it cannot be deemed sufficiently reliable and any obtained score will not be able to be compared with others to a sufficient level of safety.

The decision to select a p value that reflects a one-tailed hypothesis test is tempting because it provides increased power to reject the null hypothesis if it is false. An example here could be that of a very intelligent student who has been diagnosed as having dyslexia and your aim is to ascertain the degree of his delay in literacy skills. If you chose to use a one-tail test, your position is one of already accepting that you have knowledge that you have no need to take into account differences in test scores in either direction across the tests, as explained in Chapter 2 and in Figure 2.7. In other words, you have a *priori* knowledge to shape your null hypothesis. However, if your aim is to ascertain **whether or not** there is a delay and then, if so, to establish the degree of delay, then you should not select a one-tailed hypothesis. Many assessors, when faced with a cognitively able student with dyslexia, may have some evidence that the student's literacy skills are delayed but often this evidence is weak, often ignoring statistical features such as regression to the mean.

One-tailed tests and acceptance of their *z-p* levels requires the specialist assessor to understand the statistical premise this decision is based on.

Figure 4.1 gives an example of how you can store and use the relevant statistical formula for the purposes of calculating and applying confidence ranges and choice of confidence levels. To have a choice of confidence ranges available enables you to form a view about the clinical nature of any observed differences between scores. Increasing the confidence level to a high value and still finding significant differences between scores, will lead to the conclusion that such an observed difference is very rarely found. The clinical worth and implication of this difference is therefore highlighted.

The *Excel* file uses reliability coefficients within the range .85 to .97 and levels of confidence of 68, 85, 90, 95, and 99. The values of the cells reflect the calculation:

$$z(SE_m)$$

where this value can be placed around the obtained standard score. The *z* score reflects the levels of confidence as shown in Table 4.1.

Table 4.1: Z Values and Levels of Confidence

Z	% Level of Confidence
1.00	68
1.44	85
1.65	90
1.96	95
2.58	99

For example, for any test with a reliability coefficient of 0.88, the cell E4 in *Excel* gives a value of 9 for $z(SE_m)$ at the 90% level of confidence. The formula bar shows the formula:

E4	f_x =1.65*(15*SQRT(1-E1))

which for one side of the relevant score's confidence range is the formula:

$$z \times 15 \sqrt{(1 - r)}$$

A complete *Excel* table can be obtained with the levels of confidence in the first column and the range of reliability coefficients for your range of tests in the first row as shown in Figure 4.1.

E4				f_x =1.65*(15*SQRT(1-E1))										
	A	B	C	D	E	F	G	H	I	J	K	L	M	N	O
1		0.85	0.86	0.87	0.88	0.89	0.9	0.91	0.92	0.93	0.94	0.95	0.96	0.97	
2	99%	15	14	14	13	13	12	12	11	10	9	9	8	7	99%
3	95%	11	11	11	10	10	9	9	8	8	7	7	6	5	95%
4	90%	10	9	9	9	8	8	7	7	7	6	6	5	4	90%
5	85%	8	8	8	7	7	7	6	6	6	5	5	4	4	85%
6	68%	6	6	5	5	5	5	5	4	4	4	3	3	3	68%

Figure 4.1: Confidence Ranges – Levels of Confidence and Reliability Coefficients of Tests

Having created this source, if you frequently applied a range of favoured tests then the next step could be to create a worksheet in the same file where the cells for the confidence ranges would automatically fill in each row for the test scores. An example is shown in Figure 4.2, where the previous table is now named 'z(SEm)' on the tab at the bottom of a separate worksheet.

You can see that in Figure 4.2, a range of standard scores is given (Column B) for the 10 tests administered. Confidence ranges are given alongside each of the test scores by using the formula bar to either subtract (Column C) or add (Column D) the relevant values for the $z(SE_m)$ from the worksheet 'zSE_m'. Thus, the score for Test 6 of 85 in Cell B8 is given in the shaded cells on its right as having a confidence range of 78-92 at the 90% level of confidence.

C8				f_x	=B8-zSEm!I4	
	A	B	C	D		E
1		standard	90% confidence			
2		score	range			
3	Test 1	78	72	84		
4	Test 2	87	77	97		
5	Test 3	102	94	110		
6	Test 4	120	111	129		
7	Test 5	105	99	111		
8	Test 6	85	78	92		
9	Test 7	111	106	116		
10	Test 8	130	121	139		
11	Test 9	100	94	106		
12	Test 10	70	60	80		
13						
14						
15						
16						

zSEm | confid. ranges | Sheet3

Figure 4.2: Tests' Confidence Ranges

The final product would be a source of information on confidence ranges for your preferred tests and, crucially, where now the level of chosen confidence would be the same across all of these tests. Clearly, when constructing such a table, some attention will be needed for those tests where there is evidence that the reliability coefficients differ significantly across certain age ranges. It is convention that the median (the middle score) reliability coefficient for all tests is satisfactory, but you may wish to set your own standards, particularly if you always work with a relatively narrow age range of clients such as, for example, students in college.

Multiple Assessments

The assessor needs to be aware of the pitfalls of approaching diagnostic assessment with no reference to the hypothesis-testing approach. If a client is administered many unnecessary diagnostic tests then the assessor is very likely to observe some statistical differences across a number of pairs of scores. These differences may well be a product of random error, reflecting in part much of the normal statistical properties of sampling and standard error of measurement within Classical Test Theory. Such a problem reinforces the need for the diagnostic assessment to follow the hypothesis-testing approach but at the same time be inductive and individualistic for each client. Tests need to be carefully selected according to the manifesting reason for referral but also readily available across a number of dimensions of need in order to expect the unexpected. The assessor always needs to be objective and enquiring as she engages with the client yet be reflective and able to stand away from the intimacy of the situation to maintain the rigour of the scientific approach. This stance is far different to that of administering a pre-determined battery of tests that may have little relevance to each client's personal needs and circumstances.

Relatedly, the assessor should not select from a range of obtained test scores only those scores that meet a pragmatic need to confirm the presence of a statistical difference without giving due thought to the range of other scores also obtained. Selecting only the two scores that give the most disparate score difference is a common error of psychometric assessment and leads to over-identification of needs for whatever purpose. It is not unknown for an assessor to administer, for example, more than one, single word reading test, select the lowest test score obtained, and use only this for comparison with a score of cognitive ability that also may have been carefully selected as the highest score from a set of other ability scores. Notwithstanding this example of what could be deemed dubious professional practice, an argument can be made that a-posteriori observation of unexpected differences is important to alert the assessor to serendipitous features and for these to be investigated accordingly. In essence, it follows that the assessor needs to adopt a measured stance that is sensitive to the risks and consequences of making both Type I and Type II errors.

It is to be expected that the diagnostic assessor will, as a result of the above considerations, administer a significant number of tests and thus needs to have a statistically safe way of dealing with multiple comparisons. What is the way forward?

Multiple Comparisons

It can be surprising how many pairs of test scores can be permutated from a relatively small number of tests. The formula for the total number N of possible pair comparisons in X tests is:

$$N = \frac{X(X-1)}{2}$$

Therefore, if you gave 10 tests from a battery of subtests, you would have:

$$N = \frac{10(10-1)}{2}$$

$$= 45$$

It follows that the probability of finding a spurious significant difference is high. The formula (Knight, R.G. 1997) for determining how likely it is that the null hypothesis will be rejected incorrectly is:

$$p = 1 - (1 - \alpha)^k$$

where if α is set, for example, at 0.15 (85% confidence level) and k = number of comparisons = 45:

$$p = 1 - (1 - 0.15)^{45}$$

then p becomes close to 1 well before k = 45.

One classic and perhaps over-cautious way of acknowledging this tendency to make Type I errors as a product of multiple comparisons is to apply what is called a 'simple Bonferroni correction' (Abdi, 2007). All this requires is to divide the alpha value for statistical significance by the number of possible pair comparisons. For the above example of six tests, the number of pair permutations is:

$$N = \frac{6(6-1)}{2}$$

$$= 15$$

Therefore, if you normally worked at a confidence level of 95%, a p of .05, then for 15 comparisons the p of .05 would need to be divided by 15, which is .0033. It follows that for such a low p, the size of the necessary difference between any two scores for it to be statistically significant would have to be extremely large. One is then left with the dilemma of having to expect Type II errors with such a procedure, i.e. inappropriately rejecting differences which may be relevant and important for your investigations.

Davis (1959) and Silverstein (1982) have suggested a 'third way' out of this dilemma. It is to: compute the standard error of the measurement of the difference between an average score of test scores and one of the scores making up this average; then readjust the selected .05 or .01 level of significance by dividing by k (or refined equivalent formula involving k) where k is the number of pair-comparisons involved.

A contemporary formula that is a product of what is called the 'Dunn-Šidák Correction' (Abdi, 2007), which looks somewhat daunting at first, is,

$$Difference\ Score = Z\sqrt{\frac{(SE_{mt})^2}{K^2} + \left[\frac{K-2}{K}\right](SE_{mi})^2}$$

where K = number of subtests in the comparison, $(SE_{mt})^2$ = sum of the squared standard errors of measurement for all tests in the comparison, and $(SE_{mi})^2$ = squared standard error of measurement for the particular subtest selected. This formula is given in the WIAT-II[UK] Supplement for Adults in Table H.3, page 154, where significance levels are given for such comparisons between the nine subtests in the WIAT-II[UK].

A variation of this formula is given in the *Wechsler Adult Intelligence Scale – Fourth UK Edition* (WAIS-IV[UK]; Wechsler, 2010) manual in Table B.5, page 239, as:

$$Difference\ Score = Z\sqrt{\frac{(\sum_j^i (SE_a^2))}{K^2} + \left[\frac{K-2}{K}\right](SEm_i^2)}$$

Note that the sigma reference term in the formula $\dfrac{(\sum_j^i (SE_a^2))}{K^2}$ is no different to the term referred to in the above formula provided by Abdi (2007). It refers to the sum of the squared standard errors of measurement for all the subtests in the comparison.

The advantage of such an elegant approach is that it reinforces the *ipsative* dimension of considering the individual client's profile; in other words, it focuses on the amount of differences between the client's **own** standard scores yet retains the test's standardisation principles of comparing each test score with the test's standardisation sample via the normative approach.

We can implement this formula on an incremental basis in order to obtain a procedure for comparing multiple scores across our diagnostic tests. Figure 4.3 shows a screenshot of an *Excel* file where 10 tests have been used, all with the same standard deviation and type of standardised score.

F3			f_x	=1.96*SQRT($D$13/10^2+((10-2)/10)*C3^2)				
	A	B	C	D	E	F	G	H
1		r	SEm	$(SEm)^2$	(K-2)/K	.05 diff		
2								
3	test 1	0.95	3.4	11	0.80	7	test 1	
4	test 2	0.93	4.0	16	0.80	8	test 2	
5	test 3	0.56	9.9	99	0.80	18	test 3	
6	test 4	0.67	8.6	74	0.80	16	test 4	
7	test 5	0.75	7.5	56	0.80	14	test 5	
8	test 6	0.84	6.0	36	0.80	11	test 6	
9	test 7	0.89	5.0	25	0.80	10	test 7	
10	test 8	0.9	4.7	23	0.80	9	test 8	
11	test 9	0.64	9.0	81	0.80	16	test 9	
12	test 10	0.79	6.9	47	0.80	13	test 10	
13				468				

Figure 4.3: Comparison of Multiple Test Scores

The tests, 1-10, are labelled in columns A and G. Column B gives their reliability coefficients, and column C gives the standard error of measurements (SEm) for these tests at the relevant age for the client.

Column D gives the square of each of the tests' SE_m and column E gives the result of the simple fraction:

$$\left[\frac{K-2}{K}\right]$$

which in this case for $K = 10$, is 0.8.

Note cell D13 that is the sum of the squared SE_ms of all of the tests.

Now, column F gives the result of the above formula for the Dunn-Šidák Correction and the *Excel* formula can be seen in the formula bar: the example given is for the highlighted cell, F3.

Note that the last function in the formula refers to:

$$*C3^2$$

which refers to the square of the SE_m in cell C3. We could have selected the cell D3 which gives us the square (the hat symbol followed by '2') of the SE_m, in which case the function,

$$*C3^2$$

would not be required, only the multiple (*) cell D3.

The final value given, which in our example for Test 1 is 7. This is the number that needs to be exceeded for any difference observed in the score on Test 1 compared to the mean of the 10 tests (i.e. including the Test 1 score) when the 10 tests are used in an assessment. If exceeded, this indicates that the Test 1 score is statistically different from the mean of the 10 tests at the .05 level of significance.

Note the magnitude of the relatively large difference of 18 required for Test 3. Tracking back along the *Excel* row 5 for this test, it is not surprising, given the relatively low reliability coefficient of this particular test. This figure drives the size of the standard error of measurement for the test and thus influences significantly the final value when the formula is computed for the difference score for the 10 tests. Again, this highlights the need to select and use only those tests that of are sufficiently high reliability. Whenever you become aware that your statistical analyses are compromised by such reliability failings then always consider abandoning the test in favour of a more reliable one.

You can continue to elaborate your *Excel* table in such a way that significant scores can be highlighted without having to perform a visual search. Consider the table now, with an extra column of test scores in column B. Note that the tables of numbers are pushed one column to the right and so the column heading letters have changed.

H2			f_x =IF(ABS(B2-$B$12) >G2, "signif.","not sig.")					
	A	B	C	D	E	F	G	H	I
1			r	SEm	$(SEm)^2$	(K-2)/K	.05 diff		
2	test 1	114	0.95	3.4	11	0.80	7	signif.	test 1
3	test 2	98	0.93	4.0	16	0.80	8	not sig.	test 2
4	test 3	102	0.56	9.9	99	0.80	18	not sig.	test 3
5	test 4	95	0.67	8.6	74	0.80	16	not sig.	test 4
6	test 5	90	0.75	7.5	56	0.80	14	not sig.	test 5
7	test 6	85	0.84	6.0	36	0.80	11	signif.	test 6
8	test 7	105	0.89	5.0	25	0.80	10	not sig.	test 7
9	test 8	99	0.9	4.7	23	0.80	9	not sig.	test 8
10	test 9	101	0.64	9.0	81	0.80	16	not sig.	test 9
11	test 10	80	0.79	6.9	47	0.80	13	signif.	test 10
12		96.9			468				

Figure 4.4: Highlighting Siginficant Test Scores

The useful 'IF' function in the formula bar can enable you to fill a cell with either 'significant' or 'not significant' according to the size of the difference required for statistical difference between one test score and the mean of the 10 tests' scores. Therefore, in the example highlighted, cell H2 records 'signif.' as a result of the formula:

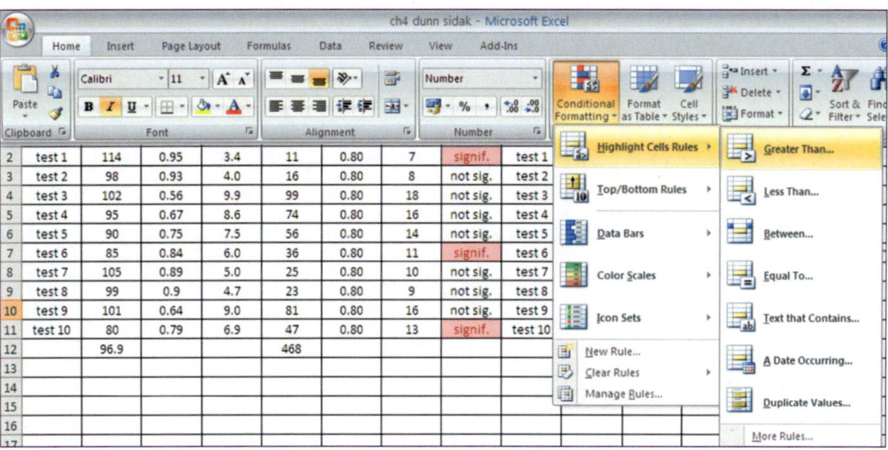

Let us inspect this formula. 'ABS' enables a numerical value to be recorded/computed without reference to it having a negative or positive value. The need for this is driven by the fact that when comparing one test's score with another's, we do not know which score is going to be the highest. So, for example, $110 - 100 = +10$, whilst $100 - 110 = -10$. We need the final number to be an absolute number, i.e. without consideration of its negative or positive sign. It is the size of the difference either way that matters.

Also, note that the cells that give you the 'signif.' return, are shaded in red. This is actioned by selecting the Home tab in *Excel*, and selecting *Conditional Formatting/Highlight Cell Rules/Greater Than*.

2	test 1	114	0.95	3.4	11	0.80	7	signif.	test 1
3	test 2	98	0.93	4.0	16	0.80	8	not sig.	test 2
4	test 3	102	0.56	9.9	99	0.80	18	not sig.	test 3
5	test 4	95	0.67	8.6	74	0.80	16	not sig.	test 4
6	test 5	90	0.75	7.5	56	0.80	14	not sig.	test 5
7	test 6	85	0.84	6.0	36	0.80	11	signif.	test 6
8	test 7	105	0.89	5.0	25	0.80	10	not sig.	test 7
9	test 8	99	0.9	4.7	23	0.80	9	not sig.	test 8
10	test 9	101	0.64	9.0	81	0.80	16	not sig.	test 9
11	test 10	80	0.79	6.9	47	0.80	13	signif.	test 10
12		96.9			468				
13									
14									
15									
16									
17									

Figure 4.5: *Options for Highlighting Significant Test Scores*

You then get the instruction to insert the number to be exceeded in the empty box (Figure 4.6).

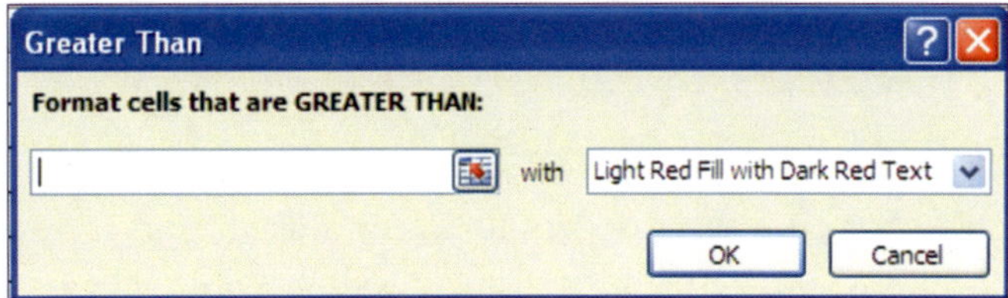

Figure 4.6: *'Greater Than' Option in* Excel

The best way of doing this is to insert the cell reference, such as G2. This is because you can fill each cell within H by conditionally filling the whole column for the red colour conditional request. Other colour options are given in the pull-down menu on the right.

Some test manuals do not apply Bonferroni-type corrections when making multiple comparisons. For example, the WIAT-II[UK]-T Tables E.1. and E.2., page 158, gives differences between the three subtest standard scores required for statistical significance for the age ranges 6:0-16:11 and 17:0-85:11 for two levels of significance, 0.05 and 0.15. The straightforward formula for the standard error of the difference (see Chapter 3) between pairs of tests is applied:

$$Difference\ Score = z \sqrt{(SE_{Ma}^{2} + SE_{Mb}^{2})}$$

Although not stated, the argument here for not applying a correction would be that the number of subtests is not great and so any accusation of 'hunting' for test-pair comparisons could be defended.

Note also that the WIAT-II[UK]-T uses the average standard errors of measurement across all of the two age ranges for application of the formula. This is considered safe when a test can be demonstrated to give high reliability coefficients across the relevant age range. If you were working regularly or solely within one relatively narrow age range, for example with 15-16 year olds then it is logical for you to use within your *Excel* table the standard errors of measurement stated in the manual for this age range. These are given in Tables 6.3-6.4 on page 55 of the WIAT-II[UK]-T manual.

Let us now continue to extend the workings of the above *Excel* file in order to obtain a table of data that also uses the standard error of measurement difference across our 10 tests referred to above in the previous example. The screen shot below extends the *Excel* table to give new columns of data from column J to S. The values of the italic numbers in the cells **above** the diagonal line are the difference scores required at the 0.85 level of significance for any pair of tests selected where $z = 1.44$. The values of the numbers in the cells **below** the diagonal line are the difference scores required at the .05 level of significance for any pair of tests selected where $z = 1.96$. The formula bar:

S10	▾	f_x	=1.44*SQRT($E$11+E10)

gives the formula for the standard error of measurement of the difference using the calculations on column D for the squared values of each of the tests' standard error of measurements. The cell example highlighted is cell S10, which gives the difference required for significance at the .85 level of confidence between Test 9 and Test 10.

	S10		f_x	=1.44*SQRT($E$11+E10)										
	E	F	G	H	I	J	K	L	M	N	O	P	Q	R	S
1	(SEm)^2	(K-2)/K	.05 diff			test 1	test 2	test 3	test 4	test 5	test 6	test 7	test 8	test 9	test 10
2	11	0.80	7	signif.	test 1		7	15	13	12	10	9	8	14	11
3	16	0.80	8	not sig.	test 2	10		15	14	12	10	9	9	14	11
4	99	0.80	18	not sig.	test 3	21	21		19	18	17	16	16	19	17
5	74	0.80	16	not sig.	test 4	18	19	26		16	15	14	14	18	16
6	56	0.80	14	not sig.	test 5	16	17	24	22		14	13	13	17	15
7	36	0.80	11	signif.	test 6	13	14	23	21	19		11	11	16	13
8	25	0.80	10	not sig.	test 7	12	12	22	20	18	15		10	15	12
9	23	0.80	9	not sig.	test 8	11	12	22	19	17	15	13		15	12
10	81	0.80	16	not sig.	test 9	19	19	26	24	23	21	20	20		16
11	47	0.80	13	signif.	test 10	15	16	24	22	20	18	17	16	22	
12	468														

Figure 4.7: Reference Table for Significant Differences between Test Scores

Such a reference table would enable the assessor to have an overview check of test pairs' difference comparisons to maintain a critical, enquiring stance after obtaining a set of scores following a diagnostic assessment. The use of the Dunn-Šidák Correction provides a complementary strategy to take with such multiple comparisons and thereby helps balance the risks of Type I and Type II errors. In so doing, the assessor is helped both ways – to be alert to unforeseen test-pair score differences but also not to identify invalidly test-pair differences as a result of multiple comparisons.

Remember from Chapter 3 that for tests with the same standard deviations, the SE_{mdiff} formula can be re-written as:

$$\text{Difference Score} = SD \times z \sqrt{2 - r_1 - r_2}$$

where r_1 = reliability coefficient of the first test and r_2 = reliability coefficient of the second test, z = the statistical level of confidence, and SD = (same) standard deviation of the tests. Note that the SD is necessary for this formula. In the previous formula for the standard error of measurement of the difference, the standard deviations of the tests are acknowledged within the standard error of measurements.

Chapter 4 Statistical and Clinical Differences Between Test Scores

Certain tests such as the *Gray Oral Reading Tests – Fourth Edition* (GORT-4; Wiederholt & Bryant, 2001), page 39, and the *Comprehensive Test of Phonological Processing* (CTOPP; Wagner *et al.*, 1999), Table 4.6 (page 53), give the assessor a simple formula to advance past confirmation of statistical difference between test scores and to investigate the *severity* of the difference. The formula is:

$$\text{Severe Discrepency} = SD \times z \sqrt{2 - 2r_{xy}}$$

where z = the amount of the normal distribution associated with the relevant p (for example $p < 0.05$, $z = 1.96$), and r_{xy} = correlation coefficient between the two test scores.

Figure 4.8 shows six tests with their respective correlation coefficients ranging from 0.3 (tests 2/4, 4/5) to 0.9 (tests 1/2, 2/5, 4/6).

	test 1	test2	test 3	test 4	test 5	test 6
test 1						
test 2	0.9					
test 3	0.8	0.4				
test 4	0.7	0.3	0.7			
test 5	0.6	0.9	0.6	0.3		
test 6	0.5	0.8	0.4	0.9	0.8	

Figure 4.8: Table of Correlation Coefficients for Tests

Application of the severe discrepancy formula given above would give the severe discrepancy values for the respective pairs shown in Figure 4.9.

	test 1	test 2	test 3	test 4	test 5	test 6
test 1						
test 2	13					
test 3	19	32				
test 4	23	35	23			
test 5	26	13	26	35		
test 6	29	19	32	13	19	

Figure 4.9: Table of Severe Discrepancy Values Between Tests

As can be seen, as the correlation coefficients decrease, then so does the magnitude of the discrepancy for the difference increase for it to be deemed to be severe.

Even after obtaining such a quantitative measure of severe discrepancy, there still needs to be a qualitative view on what the implication is for such a discrepancy. If two tests' standard scores of, for example, 100 and 125 were obtained giving a difference of 25, then this difference may be considered to be different to the case where two scores of 95 and 70 were obtained even though the difference observed is still 25. For the latter two scores, the score of 70 is two standard deviations below the mean score of 100. For the former, both scores lie within the average range or above. This indicates that for the former, there is no observed impairment or below-average normative score indicative of an absolute weakness, whereas this cannot be said for the score of 70. We will discuss the concept of normative and relative weaknesses in more detail in Chapter 18.

In the educational arena, when would the assessor use such a derived measure of severe discrepancy as compared with normal statistical differences between test scores? Notwithstanding the issues highlighted in the previous paragraph, such information may be of use to confirm the unusual nature of a child's circumstances, highlight areas for further diagnostic assessment, or lead to a decision to monitor the particular client carefully over the forthcoming months. Remember though, the major failing of simple difference type comparisons – particularly when ability and attainment scores are being compared - is that they take no account of regression to the mean.

Note that the simple difference formula given above as:

$$Severe\ Discrepency = SD \times z \sqrt{2 - 2r_{xy}}$$

can be modified to take account of regression to the mean when considering ability-attainment comparison of scores (Reynolds, 1990) where the two tests have a common metric, and where X = ability score and Y = attainment score. Chapter 7 will cover the rationale and give an operational example of the use of this formula but it is introduced at this point to stress its relevance to the influence of regression. The formula is,

$$\hat{Y} - Y_i > SD_y \times z_a \sqrt{1 - r^2_{xy}}$$

where $\hat{Y}$ = mean attainment score of all children with IQ = X_i (i.e. the estimated, regressed attainment score), Y_i = the child's attainment score, SD_y = standard deviation of Y, r^2_{xy} = the square of the correlation coefficient between the ability and attainment test. Again, z_a= the point on the normal distribution curve corresponding to the relative frequency needed to denote 'severity' which you could take to be, for example, 1.96. The area of prediction of estimated scores will be covered in Chapter 7.

It is very useful to note that when there is no source of correlation coefficients, these can be estimated by the formula:

$$r_{xy} = \sqrt{0.5} \times \sqrt{r_{xx} \times r_{yy}}$$

where r_{xy} = estimated correlation coefficient, r_{xx} and r_{yy} are the reliability coefficients for the ability and attainment tests in question (Reynolds, 1990). Again, this particular feature will be expanded in Chapter 7.

Chapter 5
Simple Regression to the Mean

Introducing:

- **simple regression to the mean**
- **its relevance to ability-attainment prediction.**

Case Example 5

You have administered the *Woodcock-Johnson III Tests of Cognitive Abilities* (WJ III; Woodcock *et al.*, 2001) to Jane, aged 9 years and 6 months. You obtain a measure of her general cognitive ability with a standard score of 125. You then administer a KTEA-II Spelling subtest and obtain a standard score of 114 and want to know if the difference of 11 is below expectation for a child of this level of cognitive ability.

Points to Consider

Comparing a cognitive ability score with an observed literacy score for the purpose of making predictive judgements about the presence and degree of any discrepancy is a professional minefield if one does not understand the statistical principles and theoretical arguments involved (Reynolds, 1990; Kavale, 1987). Although it has been a core feature of assessment practices for some time (Rust & Golombok, 1999), it is in this area that most teachers and psychologists can easily make mistakes. Notwithstanding the arguments that surround the validity of ability-attainment procedures to aid the diagnosis of specific learning difficulties (British Psychological Society, 1999), there is a need to ensure that professionals apply sound statistics if they wish to adopt an ability-attainment comparison model as part of their diagnostic procedures.

The concept of regression to the mean has already been mentioned briefly in Chapter 4. This term now needs further explanation before we can advance the case example above. The term is defined as:

> *Regression to the mean: the phenomenon that if a variable is extreme on its first measurement, on the second measurement it will tend to be closer to the average of all the future other measurements.*

There are two main phenomena to consider and understand. Firstly, we need to note that scores at the extreme tails (very high or very low scores) of the normal distribution curve are more prone to variability than scores near the average. We can understand this better by considering for example the width of spread of scores in the tails as expressed in percentiles where the gaps between very low or very high percentiles scores within these tails are large, compared to those centralised around the centre of the distribution. Figure 2.10 shows how wide these gaps are between the extreme percentile score ranges. In addition, intuitively, we can imagine ourselves scoring surprisingly extremely poorly or extremely well on a test but realising with some validity of prediction that if we were to take the same test again, then it would be likely that our repeated score would be somewhat different to the first score. The amount of change would be greater compared to the situation where on the first test we performed at a reasonable level. Relatedly, if we scored at either end of the normal distribution curve for our first test, then with future attempts, the obtained scores would be more likely to be nearer the centre of the normal distribution curve. The scores would 'regress to the mean'.

Chapter 5 Simple Regression to the Mean

An example of this regression is as follows. Suppose you take two dice and you throw a six and a five, giving a total of 11. You then throw the dice a number of times. Do you have an equal chance of your future scores being generally greater than 11 or less than 11? Of course, you do not. The future throws are generally likely to be less than 11 – they will regress to the mean (mode = 7) of all scores that can potentially be obtained by all permutations of the dice throws. The 'pull' of a regressed score can be likened to the movement of a pendulum in that there is always an intrinsic force that is pulling the pendulum from either side to the centre point of its range of movement. An example not using quantitative measurement is that of the child who displays undesirable behaviour to a point when in one week his behaviour is so bad that his parents place him on a gluten-free diet, believing that the undesirable behaviour is triggered by an allergy to gluten. The child's behaviour improves over the next weeks leading the parents to believe that indeed it was the gluten that triggered the undesirable behaviour. Another hypothesis could be that the child's behaviour improved solely because of the statistical phenomenon of regression to the mean over time.

Secondly, when one is comparing a child's score on a cognitive ability test with that of an attainment test, ideally the two tests used should be co-normed, i.e. standardised at the same time on the same population sample. An example of this is seen in the co-norming of the *Wechsler Intelligence Scale for Children – Fourth UK Edition* (WISC-IV[UK]; Wechsler, 2004) and the WIAT-II[UK]. Co-norming would give information on the actual differences across the two tests within the standardisation process for you to make judgements about the individual child that you are assessing. You would be able to know the degree to which the two tests differed at differing ages for test scores for the groups used when constructing the tests.

However, it is often the case that assessors select ability and attainment tests that are not co-normed. This may reflect the pragmatics of life, economic constraints, personal preferences, entrenched habits, or the routine expectancies of the organisation that they work in. It will also reflect the diagnostic process whereby the assessor will be continuously hypothesis testing as she assesses and engages with the client concerned, dipping into her range of available tests as the client progressively gives clues about the nature of his difficulties. In addition, publishing companies do not always construct co-normed ability and attainment tests, often preferring to create specialised tests as standalone resources to serve specific requirements of their customers.

It is always advisable to purchase co-normed tests, or at least tests that give information on the relationship between ability and attainment measures in the form of look-up tables. However, publishing companies produce revisions of their tests or create new ones without always co-norming the revisions. Most assessors realise that they are professionally obliged to discontinue their use of old tests and keep their test repertoire up-to-date. However they need to know how to compare ability test score A with attainment test score B, because it is likely that there will be instances when this process is either not explained sufficiently well or given within the respective test manuals they are using.

The Statistics

Let us now see how to correct for regression to the mean when comparing two scores from tests of ability and attainment that have not been co-normed and where you are trying to predict the attainment score from the ability score. Let us consider the example of a child who scores with an IQ composite standard score of 130 on the KBIT-2. If you were able to use a test of spelling that you knew correlated perfectly with the KBIT-2 you would be able to predict that the child should also score with a standardised score of 130 on this spelling test. Of course, no two tests of ability and attainment have such perfect correlation because they do not measure the same abilities. A child may be able to score reasonably well on the IQ test, not so well on the spelling test, and vice versa: this could be in line with expectations. The *less* two tests correlate, the *greater* will be the differences of scores across them by individuals. A more practical example could be that of piano playing and playing darts. Although both activities require finger manipulation and eye-hand co-ordination, you would expect that there would be some people who are good at piano playing but not good at playing darts. The competencies required for both activities are not exactly the same. You would not be able to predict that all good piano players would be good darts players. This feature graphically highlights the problem that some assessors create for themselves when they wish to screen groups of children for learning difficulties. Their procedural argument is that of needing to take into account a child's cognitive ability, then comparing this score with his or her attainment score, and thereby selecting those children whose score differences appear to be significant. If they do not take into account regression to the mean, then they may over-identify a group of children as apparent under-achievers. They may then become puzzled when certain low-cognitive ability children later appear to be 'over-achieving' by displaying unexpectedly high levels of attainment scores. The problem is often exacerbated when a cognitive ability test is selected that correlates far less with the attainment test than compared to other cognitive ability tests. This phenomenon often reflects the decision to use a group test of cognitive ability and/or a belief that the cognitive ability test somehow needs to be some sort of 'pure' form of cognitive ability, untainted by the impact of any possible learning difficulties. Invariably, the latter is thought to be a test of visual (fluid reasoning) cognitive ability. However, the difficulty is that such tests often tend to correlate far less with attainment scores for literacy than do tests of verbal ability. Therefore, the degree of the regression that would need to be taken into account for such tests of visual cognitive ability would be very high and again, without this correction, the identification process would be exceedingly prone to error.

The formula used to correct for the effect of regression to the mean is:

$$y' = r_{xy}(X - 100) + 100$$

where y' = the predicted achievement score, r_{xy} = the correlation coefficient for the two ability and attainment tests, and X = the cognitive ability score obtained.

So, as an example for working through the formula above, if a client's ability score, X, is 125 and the correlation coefficient for the two tests of ability and spelling is 0.60, then the predicted achievement for spelling, y', is:

$$y' = 0.60 \times (125 - 100) + 100 = 115$$

In other words, for a child with an IQ of 125, it would be expected that the spelling score would be *around* 115, a difference of 10 points (our next case example will explore the relevance of this choice of word *around* in more detail). If you obtained a score within the range 115-125 for spelling then you can conclude that the difference observed is not significantly low for this level of cognitive ability, i.e. not extreme or unusual in any way and therefore showing no evidence of delay of spelling skills in relation to expectation of general cognitive ability. This example highlights the need to be aware of the dangers of over-identification when assessing for specific learning difficulties, particularly if the correlation coefficient for the two tests of cognitive ability and academic attainment is relatively low.

Let us now return to our case example of Jane and apply the regression formula above.

One quickly realises that for the formula to be applied you need to have a source that gives you the correlation coefficient for the *WJ III* (Woodcock *et al.*, 2001) and the KTEA-II Spelling subtest. A very good tip to remember when tracking down such correlations is to search the relevant test manuals' chapters on their validity data. These chapters give, as a matter of routine, correlation data with other tests in order to show that the tests were constructed to a sufficiently high level of validity.

Indeed, in Table 7.27, page 112, of the KTEA-II manual, the correlation between the KTEA-II Spelling subtest and the WJ III General Intellectual Ability scores is given as 0.47.

The formula,

$$y' = r_{xy}(X - 100) + 100$$

can now be y', expected spelling score, $= 0.47 \times (125 - 100) + 100$

$$= 111.75 = 112 \text{ (to nearest whole figure)}$$

So, given that Jane scored 114 on the KTEA-II Spelling subtest, this is only two standard score points above the expected spelling score of 112. We are aware that the standard deviations for these tests of ability and attainment are both 15. Therefore, the presence of only two standard score points difference is a negligible difference. We can quickly and safely conclude that the difference of 11 between Jane's scores on the *WJ III* and the KTEA-II Spelling subtest is not unusual, being within the boundary of expectation.

If we use *Excel* to apply the above formula with a correlation coefficient of 0.52 between a test of cognitive ability and a test of attainment to a range of standard scores from 70 to 100, then we can see how regression to the mean has a greater influence on scores that are at the extreme of the normal distribution curve.

For a selected cell, B2, the simple regression formula within the formula bar is:

In Figure 5.1, examine the difference between the expected scores for the cognitive ability standard scores of 70 and 95. For a standard cognitive ability score of 70, the expected attainment score is 84, a difference of 14 points. For a cognitive ability score of 95, the expected attainment score is 97, a difference of only 2 points. Scores do not regress as much when they lie towards the mean of a distribution of scores.

	A	B	C	D	E	
1	score	predicted		score	predicted	
2	70	84		86	93	
3	71	85		87	93	
4	72	85		88	94	
5	73	86		89	94	
6	74	86		90	95	
7	75	87		91	95	
8	76	88		92	96	
9	77	88		93	96	
10	78	89		94	97	
11	79	89		95	97	
12	80	90		96	98	
13	81	90		97	98	
14	82	91		98	99	
15	83	91		99	99	
16	84	92		100	100	

Figure 5.1: Table of Predicted Scores Using the Simple Regression Formula

This type of trend can be observed in chart format in Figure 5.2 where plots are made of predicted scores from ability measures ranging from 130 to 100 down the vertical axis for two tests of attainment, one of relatively low correlation (0.30) with the ability test and the other of relatively high correlation (0.90). Two features can be noted. Firstly, as ability measures approach the mean of 100, the regression effect is not very significant. Expected scores for the two attainment measures also lie towards the mean in the lower right hand sector of the chart. Secondly, the degree of the regression is more marked for the attainment test with relatively low correlation with ability compared with that for the attainment test with a relatively high correlation with ability.

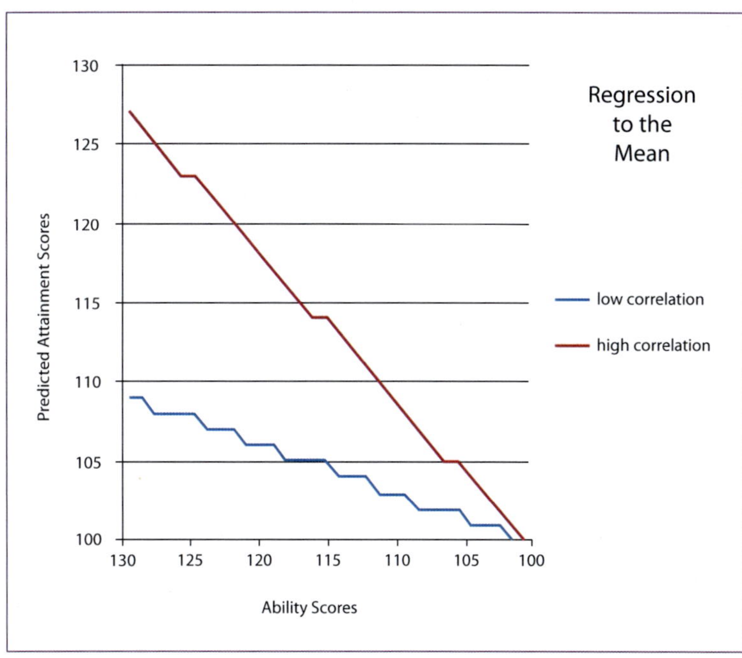

Figure 5.2: Regression of Attainment Scores from Ability

It can therefore be concluded that assessors should be particularly cautious when assessing clients of relatively low or high cognitive ability and where they want to attempt some form of prediction of expectation of attainment from the measured cognitive ability. The general advice is to ensure that all tests used have high standards of reliability coefficients and if co-normed tests of ability and attainment are available, then these should be the preferred choice at all times. In addition, there are major theoretical issues concerning the use of ability-attainment discrepancy analysis. These are discussed in Chapter 18.

In the next chapter, we will continue to see how *Excel* can help us deal with the influences of simple regression on test scores when using a range of tests at our disposal.

Chapter 6
A Simple Regression Table

Introducing the use of *Excel* to obtain a simple regression table for ability-attainment comparison.

In the previous chapter, you learned how to calculate an expected score from one set of ability and attainment scores. The busy assessor needs to be able to work efficiently, not having to perform relatively arduous calculations every time they are involved with their clients. In this case example, we learn how to create a table of regressed scores ranging across the normal distribution of ability for you to save and apply at appropriate times.

Case Example 6

You assess three young children, Anne, Suzie and Poppy, all of similar school age, on the KBIT-2 and obtain measures of their composite IQ standard scores. You then administer a test of reading comprehension to the children. You obtain the correlation coefficient for the KBIT-2 and the test of reading comprehension which is 0.54. The standard scores on all the tests are recorded in Table 6.1.

Table 6.1: KBIT-2 Composite IQ and Reading Comprehension Scores

	Composite IQ	Reading Comprehension Score
Anne	95	105
Suzie	75	80
Poppy	135	100

You want to have available a look-up table of IQ and predicted attainment scores in order to be able to confirm quickly if the scores on the comprehension test are within expectation or not.

Points to Consider

The previous chapter stated that regression to the mean has more impact for very high or very low scores. Therefore, you would expect that by application of the simple regression formula we used in the previous case example that Anne's IQ standard score of 95 would lead to a regressed, predicted attainment score not too dissimilar to a score of 95. In contrast, we would expect Poppy's high IQ standard score of 135 to lead to a significantly regressed attainment score. Likewise, we would expect Suzie's expected attainment score to be regressed significantly to the mean from the opposite direction of the standard normal distribution curve. The latter case example perhaps helps the assessor faced with a 'low IQ/but higher attainment level' case understand that such scenarios are to be expected as a product of the statistical phenomenon of regression to the mean.

Chapter 6 A Simple Regression Table

In fact, the actual regressed scores can be show as in Figure 6.1.

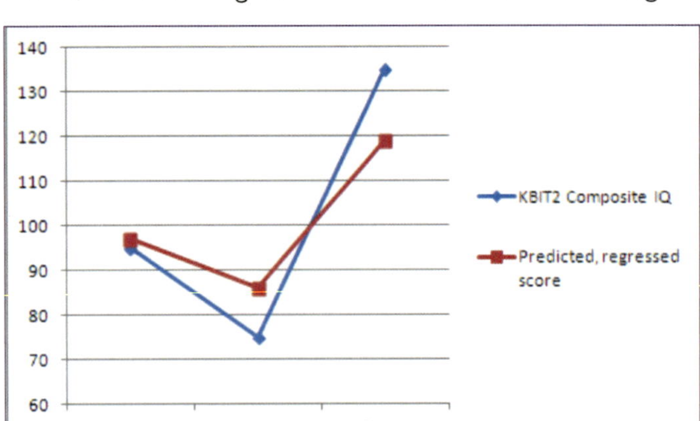

Figure 6.1: Regressed Scores

The Statistics

Excel provides a means of generating a useful look-up table to use when comparing ability and attainment test scores but where it is anticipated that for each pair of selected ability and attainment tests there will be a particular correlation coefficient and where it should be expected that the correlation coefficients for each pair selected will differ again for the age ranges within these tests.

Figure 6.2 shows a sample from a table designed using *Excel*, a version of which is available in Appendix E.

	A	B	C	D	E	F	G	H	I	J	K	L	M	N	O
2	Standard						Ability-Achievement Correlation								Standard
3	Score	0.30	0.35	0.40	0.45	0.50	0.55	0.60	0.65	0.70	0.75	0.80	0.85	0.90	Score
25	139	112	114	116	118	120	121	123	125	127	129	131	133	135	139
26	138	111	113	115	117	119	121	123	125	127	129	130	132	134	138
27	137	111	113	115	117	119	120	122	124	126	128	130	131	133	137
28	136	111	113	114	116	118	120	122	123	125	127	129	131	132	136
29	135	111	112	114	116	118	119	121	123	125	126	128	130	132	135
30	134	110	112	114	115	117	119	120	122	124	126	127	129	131	134
31	133	110	112	113	115	117	118	120	121	123	125	126	128	130	133
32	132	110	111	113	114	116	118	119	121	122	124	126	127	129	132
33	131	109	111	112	114	116	117	119	120	122	123	125	126	128	131
34	130	109	111	112	114	115	117	118	120	121	123	124	126	127	130
35	129	109	110	112	113	115	116	117	119	120	122	123	125	126	129
36	128	108	110	111	113	114	115	117	118	120	121	122	124	125	128
37	127	108	109	111	112	114	115	116	118	119	120	122	123	124	127
38	126	108	109	110	112	113	114	116	117	118	120	121	122	123	126
39	125	108	109	110	111	113	114	115	116	118	119	120	121	123	125
40	124	107	108	110	111	112	113	114	116	117	118	119	120	122	124
41	123	107	108	109	110	112	113	114	115	116	117	118	120	121	123
42	122	107	108	109	110	111	112	113	114	115	117	118	119	120	122
43	121	106	107	108	109	111	112	113	114	115	116	117	118	119	121

Figure 6.2: Predicted Scores for a Range of Correlation Coefficients

Columns A and O give you the IQ scores, starting with an IQ of 139 in row 25 (rows 4-24 have been hidden) and descending to an IQ of 121 in row 43. Row 3 gives a range of correlation coefficients starting with 0.30 in cell B3 and rising in units of 0.5 up to 0.90 in cell N3. Thus by selecting a particular IQ score and confirming the correlation coefficient for the two tests selected, you identify the relevant column from the range B-N. The selected cell for the IQ value will then give you the predicted, regressed attainment score.

Therefore, Poppy's IQ of 135 with a correlation coefficient of 0.54 for the tests of ability and attainment gives you a predicted, regressed score of 119.

Now obtain the respective regressed scores for Anne and Suzie from Appendix E. Anne's IQ of 95 gives a regressed score of 97 and Suzie's IQ of 75 gives a regressed score of 86.

As predicted, and as shown in Figure 6.1, Anne's regressed score does not differ greatly to her IQ score of 95 because it lies near to the mean of 100. Table 6.1 can be extended as shown in Table 6.2 to give the predicted, regressed scores and the differences between these predicted and observed scores.

Table 6.2: Predicted Reading Comprehension Scores from KBIT-2 Composite IQ Scores

	KBIT-2 Composite IQ	Reading Comprehension Score	Predicted Regressed Score	Difference between Predicted and Observed Score (p-o)
Anne	95	105	97	+8
Suzie	75	80	86	-6
Poppy	135	100	119	-19

Let us see how the look-up table was created. We do this by examining the formula bar, and with a sample of the table for Poppy's regressed score of 119 as given below in Figure 6.3.

G29			fx	=$G$3*(A29-100)+100										
	A	B	C	D	E	F	G	H	I	J	K	L	M	N	O
2	Standard						Ability-Achievement Correlation								Standard
3	Score	0.30	0.35	0.40	0.45	0.50	0.55	0.60	0.65	0.70	0.75	0.80	0.85	0.90	Score
25	139	112	114	116	118	120	121	123	125	127	129	131	133	135	139
26	138	111	113	115	117	119	121	123	125	127	129	130	132	134	138
27	137	111	113	115	117	119	120	122	124	126	128	130	131	133	137
28	136	111	113	114	116	118	120	122	123	125	127	129	131	132	136
29	135	111	112	114	116	118	119	121	123	125	126	128	130	132	135

Figure 6.3: An Example of Looking Up a Regressed Score

Cell G29 is highlighted and, in doing, so the regression formula:

$$y' = r_{xy}(X - 100) + 100$$

that we initially used in Chapter 6 for the creation of the value of 119 is revealed in the formula bar:

G29			fx	=$G$3*(A29-100)+100

If we ignore the $ symbols in the formula for the time being, you can see that G3 cell refers to the correlation coefficient selected. This is multiplied (*) by the total of the ability score given in cell A29 minus 100. 100 is then added. The process can be repeated for the range of the other correlation coefficients in row 3.

$ symbols are used in the formula because these are necessary to freeze the value of certain cells used in the formula when using the 'fill handle' facility in *Excel* to fill other cells.

The following chapters will expand more on how you can advance to the next stage of making decisions about the size of the discrepancies that you are observing as given in the three examples above.

When using Appendix E for correlation coefficients that lie between the values given in the columns, always remember to choose the column for the nearest correlation coefficient.

Chapter 7
Standard Error of the Estimate

Introducing:

- **the Standard Error of the Estimate, making judgements about the degree of discrepancy between ability and attainment scores**

- **converting discrepancy scores into z scores**

- **further consideration of one- and two-tailed judgements of difference**

- **estimating correlation coefficients between tests when they are not known.**

Case Example 7

You administer the KABC-II to Ruth, aged 15 years, and obtain a Fluid-Crystallized Index (FCI) standard score of 128. You then administer the WIAT-II^{UK} Pseudoword Decoding subtest and obtain a standard score of 105. You need a means of deciding if the obtained difference of 23 standard score points is statistically significant and, if so, clinically unusual, i.e. rarely found. You have obtained a correlation coefficient of 0.60 for the FCI and the WIAT-II^{UK} Pseudoword Decoding subtest from Table 8:30, page 125 from the KABC-II manual.

Points to Consider

In Chapter 3, Case Example 4, you learned about the standard error of measurement, SE_m, a type of measure of deviation that helps you to derive confidence ranges. Confidence ranges are calculated by application of the formula for the SE_m:

$$SE_m = SD \sqrt{1 - r}$$

You then take the SE_m, and for this example, a 68% confidence level placed one SE_m either side of your observed score to obtain the confidence range in which your true score lies. So, for example, a standard score of 115 with an SE_m of 5, would give a confidence range of 110-120 at the 68% level of confidence. At the 95% level of confidence it would be 105-125 ($2 \times SE_m$) either side of the observed score of 115, or with more precision 105-125 ($1.96 \times SE_m$ and rounded to the nearest whole numbers).

Now, the standard error of the estimate, SE_e, is a term similar to the standard error of measurement, SE_m. It gives us a measure of the likely spread of **predicted** scores and so we can use it to place a type of confidence range around the **predicted** score, not the **observed** score. (This predicted score is the one obtained from our regression table in the previous chapter, Case Example 6.) In other words the SE_e is used whenever we are concerned with using two tests and where we are having to take into account the effect of regression when trying to predict one score from another score.

You have learned that the **higher** the reliability of a test, the **lower** its standard error of measurement will be and this would consequently lead to the confidence ranges being relatively narrow. In other words, the more reliable a test, the narrower the confidence range of possible scores within which the true score will lie. Likewise, when we are using two tests and trying to predict the score of one from the other, it seems safe to assume that if the two tests correlate highly with one another, the standard error of the estimate, SE_e, will be relatively low. If the two tests have a low correlation, then the SE_e will be relatively high. This is because for the latter we will have less power to predict with a high level of certainty where the predicted score will lie – it will lie within a greater range of possible scores because the two tests are not strongly associated with one another. If we were, for example, trying to predict a child's reading skills level from a measure of his general cognitive ability we would probably have more error with our prediction compared to predicting his reading skills level from a measure of his spelling skills level. This is because reading and spelling skills generally correlate relatively *highly* with one another, whilst cognitive ability and literacy skills generally correlate *moderately* with one another. The larger the uncertainty of prediction, the wider will be the range of predicted scores. The SE_e gives us a measure of the degree of this range. Therefore, when you calculate a predicted score, you will be able to know where this score lies in relation to the degree of scatter of all the potential likely scores we need to consider.

Your formula for the SE_e will need to account for the correlation between the two tests that we are using when trying to predict one score from another and where we are concerned with making judgements about the degree of the disparity between our observed and predicted score.

The formula for the standard error of the estimate, SE_e, is:

$$SE_e = SD \times \sqrt{1 - r_{xy}^2}$$

where SD = the standard deviation of the attainment test, and r_{xy} = the correlation coefficient for the ability and attainment tests that you are using.

So, in Ruth's example, if you have a test of cognitive ability and an attainment test of pseudoword decoding that has a correlation coefficient of 0.6, and the attainment test has a standard deviation of 15, then the SE_e for the predicted attainment score would be:

$$= 15 \times \sqrt{1 - 0.6^2}$$

$$= 15 \times \sqrt{1 - 0.36}$$

$$= 15 \times \sqrt{0.64}$$

$$= 15 \times 0.8$$

$$= 12$$

Therefore, this unit of 12 gives us a value of one standard deviation to use when making a judgement about the degree of a difference between an obtained score of attainment and a predicted score of attainment where this prediction is based on the score on a cognitive ability test.

We need to know if Ruth's obtained standard score of 105 can be regarded as significantly below her predicted score of 111. In other words, we need to know how far the difference of 6 is away from the predicted score in standard deviation units. Only by interpreting the value of 6 in standard deviations can we make judgements about its probability of occurrence – how common is this degree of difference.

We now know that the spread of predicted attainment scores has a standard deviation of 12. This enables you to make a judgement about the value of the discrepancy of 6 between the predicted and actual score that Ruth obtained on the WIAT-II^{UK} Pseudoword Decoding subtest. You can conclude that as the discrepancy of 6 is only half a standard deviation away from the predicted score of 111, then this discrepancy would not be considered unusual: in other words a discrepancy of this magnitude would be commonly found.

Of course, this now begs the question: 'What amount of SE_e should be exceeded before a discrepancy score can be regarded as unusual/rare enough for it to be regarded as indicative of a clinical oddity and therefore part-evidence of an underlying learning difficulty?'

The answer is under your control, but publishing companies and researchers use different amounts of SE_es when making such judgements. However, discrepancies of 1 or 1.5 SE_es are commonly used. In other words, and again using our case example, you would take a discrepancy of greater than 12 (1 SE_e or 18 (1.5 SE_es) as being cut-off decision points.

Note that it is possible to convert our discrepancy score of 6 found in Ruth's case to a z score. This is often used in test manuals such as the WJ III and so it is of benefit for you to be reminded how we do this. The SE_e is a measure of standard deviation and z scores enable us to place precisely a score along the 6 (or sometimes 8) z units along the standard normal curve of spread of scores. Therefore, if we take the discrepancy score of 6 and divide this by the SE_e, which in our case is 12, then the discrepancy of 6 is converted to a z score of 0.5.

If you now wanted to apply your size of SE_e and conform to commonly accepted levels of confidence normally found in the special education arena, then these would be the 90th, 95th and 99th levels of confidence. To remind you once again, our z and level of confidence Table 2.11 is a useful reference for the equivalent amount of z value amounts required for these levels of confidence.

Therefore, for example, for Ruth's discrepancy score to be significant at the 95% level of confidence, then the z score would have to be greater than 1.96 for it to be considered as unusual and not occurring by chance, which in being 0.5 it clearly is not.

Now, Table 2.11 may need to be reconsidered if you are not concerned about Ruth's actual attainment score being above her predicted score, only if it is below this score. This is where you have to consider the one- and two-tailed option referred to in Chapter 4. Following the reason for referral, you are likely to be more concerned with the suggestion that Ruth has a learning difficulty and already know that her attainment for reading is impaired. In other words, you have *a priori* knowledge.

Therefore, you may be concerned only with one tail of the normal distribution curve of possible scores, not two. In which case the z values in the table above can be revised but for the same percentage of level of confidence. These values have been given in Table 3.1.

Remember that a two-tailed test is used when you cannot claim, *a priori*, whether a difference between two scores will be positive or negative. A one-tailed test can be used when you want to explore the degree of any difference in a pre-determined direction but only when you have such evidence to ignore validly the chance of the difference score occurring in the other direction. In other words, in Ruth's case where there is a chance that her Pseudoword Decoding subtest score could be higher than her FCI score.

It follows that by multiplying the obtained SE_e in standardised score units by one of the z values above, having decided on the one- or two-tail option and the level of confidence to be taken, that the obtained amount is the amount, in standardised score units, to be exceeded in order to confirm that the discrepancy score is indeed unusual. As an example, if we wanted to adopt a 99% level of confidence and were concerned with only one tail of the distribution of scores with the assumption that the child would not be scoring higher than expectation, then the z amount required would be 2.33. If the SE_e was 12, then we would need our discrepant score to be larger than (2.33 × 12) = 28.

One potential problem with the above calculations is that to use the SE_e one needs the correlation coefficient for the tests of cognitive ability and attainment. It is often the case that test manuals will have this information, usually within the validity sections of their examiner or technical manuals.

However, in cases where the correlation coefficients are unknown, then the advice in the literature is that they can be *estimated* as a product of using data from national standardisations of many major intelligence and attainment tests (Reynolds & Stanton, 1988). The estimation commonly uses the internal consistency reliability coefficients for the tests used and the formula is:

$$r_{xy} = \sqrt{0.5} \times \sqrt{r_{xx} - r_{yy}}$$

Therefore, if we had a test of cognitive ability that has a reliability coefficient of 0.9 and a test of attainment with a reliability coefficient of 0.8, then our formula for the estimated correlation coefficient would be:

$$r_{xy} = \sqrt{0.5} \times \sqrt{0.9 - 0.8}$$

$$= 0.6$$

We would then use this estimated correlation coefficient in our formula for the standard error of the estimate that you know now as:

$$SE_e = SD \times \sqrt{1 - r_{xy}^2}$$

You can then proceed as you have done above.

You will discover, as has already been mentioned, that test manuals generally do not offer a wide source of correlation coefficients with other contemporary tests. However, reliability coefficients given in the test manuals provide a means to compare test scores across tests that you use. For example Raven's Educational provides two reliability coefficients for the MHV in Chapter 6, page 55 for test-retest reliability (0.916) and parallel forms reliability (0.929). It also provides in Chapter 6, page 53 for the SPM+ a split-half reliability coefficient of 0.936 for the SPM+ and a test-retest reliability coefficient of 0.833.

If you select one of each of these reliability coefficients for the two scales, for example the test-retest reliability coefficient of 0.916 for the MHV and the split-half reliability coefficient of 0.936 for the SPM+, you can use these as a starting point to establish another look-up table involving the SE_e formula above.

Let us now do this with a sample of tests, that you might commonly use for students aged 17-18 years.

Firstly, it is wise to start gathering data on core reliability and validity information from your test manuals that will help you to compare obtained test scores across the tests that you use. A simple *Excel* file that will incrementally grow could start to look like Figure 7.1.

	A	B	C	D
1		reliability coefficents		
2	17-18 years	test-	parallel	split half
3		retest	forms	
4	SPM+		0.833	0.936
5	MHV	0.916	0.926	
6	CPM		0.87	0.97
7	CVS	0.88		0.96
8	ART Accuracy	0.88		0.85
9	ART Rate	0.76		0.97
10	ART Comprehension	0.79		0.81
11	KTEA-II Phono Aware (B)			0.83
12	KTEA-II Spelling			0.93
13				
14				
15				

Figure 7.1: Storing Reliability and Validity Data in Excel

The tests referred to here are the *Raven's Educational UK SPM+* and *MHV* (Raven, 2008); the *Raven's Educational UK Coloured Progressive Matrices* and *Crichton Vocabulary Scale* (CPM and CVS; Raven 2008); the ART and three of its subtests; and the Phonological Awareness subtest from the KTEA-II. The example repertoire of tests is in Column A and would expand downwards as new tests are used, as indicated by the arrow.

You then open another worksheet in the same file to establish a worksheet of estimated correlation coefficients using the following formula:

$$r_{xy} = \sqrt{0.5} \times \sqrt{r_{xx} + r_{yy}}$$

Note the two tabs at the bottom of Figure 7.2. The two worksheets we have created have a tab named *r table* for the worksheet that we are establishing as our record of reliability coefficients and the other tab named *Rxy* for our record of estimated correlation coefficients between selected pairs of tests that we are interested in. *Excel* enables you to switch between these two sheets when in a single file in order to obtain the reliability coefficients for each of the tests you are using and then apply them to the above formula in the respective worksheet. As you select with your mouse each relevant cell after changing sheets by clicking on the sheet tab, then the formula in the formula bar will recognise your selection as you proceed to its completion.

As an example, in worksheet Rxy, cell C10 gives an estimated correlation coefficient of 0.61. The formula bar gives the formula for this cell as:

```
fx  =SQRT(0.5)*SQRT('r table'!D10*'r table'!B5)
```

On inspecting this formula, you can see it referring to the worksheet *r table* to obtain the reliability coefficients from the other worksheet to drive the calculation. As mentioned, *Excel* performs the wording/referencing of the formula; all you have to do is put the framework of the formula in the formula bar and select the relevant cells across the worksheets to input the data, as in Figure 7.2.

C10			fx	=SQRT(0.5)*SQRT('r table'!D10*'r table'!B5)		
	A	B	C	D	E	F	G

	A	B	C	D	E	F	G
1							
2		SPM+	MHV	CPM	CVS	ART	ART
3						Accuracy	Rate	Cor
4	SPM+	•				0.62	0.67
5	MHV		•			0.62	0.67
6	CPM			•			
7	CVS				•		
8	ART Accuracy	0.62	0.62	0.64	0.64	•	
9	ART Rate	0.67	0.67	0.69	0.68		•
10	ART Comprehension	0.62	0.61	0.63	0.62		
11	KTEA-II Phono Aware (B)	0.62	0.62	0.63	0.63		
12	KTEA-II Spelling	0.66	0.60	0.67	0.67		
19							
20							
21							
22							
23							
24							
25							
26							
27							
28							
29							
30							

r table | **Rxy** | Sheet3

Figure 7.2: Working Across Worksheets in Excel

Chapter 7 Standard Error of the Estimate

Having now obtained a record of estimated correlation coefficients between particular tests, you can use these in the ability-achievement look-up table of regressed scores in Chapter 6 and continue as before.

Let us look at how you could advance your use of *Excel* when using SE_e for ability-attainment comparison purposes.

Figure 7.3 shows a table created in *Excel*.

H3		f_x =G3/'r & SEe table'!B21						
	A	B	C	D	E	F	G	H	I
1		attainment	actual	ability	ability	predicted	predic.		Discrepancy
2	child	test	score	test	score	att. score	minus actual	G/SE$_E$ (z)	>1.96?
3	Billy	Art Accuracy	85	SPM+	120	112	27	2.28	Yes
4	Jane	ART Rate	90	MHV	125	116	26	2.33	Yes
5	Sam	ART Comp	95	SPM+	115	109	14	1.18	No
6	Anne	KTEA2 Spelling	100	MHV	130	118	18	1.50	No
7	Ken	KTEA2 Phono Aw. (B)	75	SPM+	110	106	31	2.64	Yes
8									
9									
10									
11									
12									
13									
14									
15									
16									
17									
18									

discrepancy table / regressed scores / r & SEe table

Figure 7.3: Excel and using Standard Error of the Estimate for Ability-Attainment Comparison

The important aspect of this table is the 'hidden' reference to the worksheet tables accessed by the tabs at the bottom of the screen, titled *discrepancy table, regressed scores*, and *r & SE$_e$ table*.

The table gives you an example of how you could record your clients' test scores where your aim is to determine whether or not the disparities between their attainment and ability scores are significantly different. Clearly, you will be giving different tests to different clients and so this table reflects this real-life scenario but only with a small set of example tests.

Consider Billy, who has been scored on the ART Reading Accuracy and the SPM+. You want to know if the Reading Accuracy score of 85 is significantly below that of the SPM+ score of 120 with a difference of 15.

Your first task is to obtain the value of the predicted ART Reading Accuracy score that takes into account regression. You already have created a table of regressed scores for a range of ability-attainment tests' correlations as explained in Chapter 6, demonstrated in Figure 6.2 and available in total in Appendix E. For convenience purposes, you then copy and paste this table to the second worksheet of the above *Excel* table and label it '*regressed scores*'. Similarly, you have already created a table of estimated correlation coefficients (Figure 7.2) so again copy and paste this table to the third worksheet and label the tab '*r & SEe*' – short for 'reliabilities and standard errors of estimates'. These extra worksheets will allow you to work towards your goal of calculating the statistics necessary to determine the significance of the differences between the ability and attainment tests without having to leave the *Excel* file you have just created.

Consider now the last worksheet you created, which needs some more work in order for you to have a source of standard error of estimates, SE_e (Figure 7.4).

C20		f_x =15*SQRT(1-C8^2)		
	A	**B**	**C**	**D**	**E**

	A	B	C	D	E
1					
2		SPM+	MHV	CPM	CVS
3					
4	SPM+	*			
5	MHV		*		
6	CPM			*	
7	CVS				*
8	ART Accuracy	0.62	0.62	0.64	0.64
9	ART Rate	0.67	0.67	0.69	0.68
10	ART Comprehension	0.62	0.61	0.63	0.62
11	KTEA-II Phono Aware (B)	0.62	0.62	0.63	0.63
12	KTEA-II Spelling	0.66	0.60	0.67	0.67
18					
19		SE_E	SE_E	SE_E	SE_E
20	ART Accuracy	11.82	11.72	11.50	11.54
21	ART Rate	11.08	11.18	10.92	10.97
22	ART Comprehension	11.82	11.90	11.69	11.73
23	KTEA-II Phono Aware (B)	11.73	11.81	11.59	11.63

discrepancy table / regressed scores / r & SEe table

Figure 7.4: A Source of Standard Errors of the Estimates in Excel

Rows from 20 downwards of this table extend the look-up data to give you a source of SE_e for the total set of permutations of ability and attainment scores. So, for example, the SE_e for cell C20 is 11.72 and the *Excel* formula for the SE_e is given in the formula bar as:

C20		f_x =15*SQRT(1-C8^2)

Note that the C8 cell referred to in the formula is the estimated correlation coefficient between the ART Reading Accuracy and MHV subtests that we calculated before. Also note that in *Excel* to square a number you input the number and select the *Shift and 6 keys* for the symbol, '^' (hat). This symbol may appear in a different place, depending on the keyboard.

We now return to the new worksheet and the row of data for your first client, Billy. In your *Excel* file you now have a source of the estimated reliability coefficient via the third tab, *r & SEe tab*, which for the ART Reading Accuracy and SPM+ subtests is 11.82. So, then switch to the second tab, *regressed scores*, and look up the predicted score for the SPM+ ability score of 120, which is 112. We then insert this value in cell F3 of the *Excel* table for Billy.

We then subtract the predicted attainment score from the actual attainment score for the ART Reading Accuracy and note that it is 27.

If we then divide this difference score by the SE_e, this gives us a z score that expresses the discrepancy in standard deviation z units. Note the formula bar below for the cell H3 that returns in Billy's case a z score of 2.28. If we select the 95% confidence level (two-tailed) the z value is 1.96, and so our last column asks us to compare the obtained z score differences with this cut-off confidence level. In Billy's case, the z score of 2.28 exceeds the cut-off z level of 1.96 and so we can conclude that the difference observed between Billy's actual ART Reading Accuracy score and his SPM+ score is statistically significant. We record a 'YES' in the last column to record this conclusion. In Figure 7.5 this can be done automatically using =IF(H3>1.96,"YES","NO") and then clicking on the cell, dragging the bottom-right corner down to cell H7, allowing *Excel* to check if each of the values in column H is greater than 1.96 or not. Always remember that the confidence level and the choice of tails (one or two) need to be set by you. This should always be done in advance and never retrospectively to resist creating significant discrepancies.

Note how Anne's KTEA-II Spelling subtest score of 100 is deemed not be significantly different to that of her MHV test score of 130. At first sight the difference of 30 standard score points would appear to be an obvious significant difference. However, the regressed, predicted score is only 118 and this reflects the fact that her MHV score of 130 is prone to a significant regression effect as it is an extreme score on the standard normal distribution curve. Also, the reliability of this test is not particularly high and so the SE_e is relatively large. When we use the SE_e as a denominator in our equation for cell H3, then the resulting z difference is reduced accordingly, as can be seen in Figure 7.5.

H3			f_x	=G3/'r & SEe table'!B20				
	A	B	C	D	E	F	G	H	!
1		attainment	actual	ability	ability	predicted	predic.		Discrepancy
2	child	test	score	test	score	att. score	minus actual	G/SE$_E$ (z)	>1.96?
3	Billy	Art Accuracy	85	SPM+	120	112	27	2.28	Yes
4	Jane	ART Rate	90	MHV	125	116	26	2.33	Yes
5	Sam	ART Comp	95	SPM+	115	109	14	1.18	No
6	Anne	KTEA2 Spelling	100	MHV	130	118	18	1.50	No
7	Ken	KTEA2 Phono Aw. (B)	75	SPM+	110	106	31	2.64	Yes

Figure 7.5: An Example – Comparing Billy's ART Accuracy Score with his SPM+ Score

In summary, this chapter enables the assessor to refine her ability to make comparisons between test scores by taking into account the range of correlations between these test scores. The availability of a means of approximating correlation coefficients when they are not available is a useful tool.

Chapter 8
Regression and Confidence Ranges

Further discussion about:

- **confidence ranges**
- **simple regression**
- **standard error of measurement**
- **standard error of the estimate.**

Case Example 8

David, aged 15 months, scored a scaled score of 18 on the Fine Motor subtest of the Bayley-III. You want to calculate a confidence range at the 95% level of confidence but take into account regression to the mean, given that this is an extreme score towards the top end of the normal distribution curve.

Points to Consider

You have already learned how to calculate confidence ranges by finding the standard error of measurement, deciding on your level of confidence and then placing either side of your observed score the necessary amounts of SE_m. So, for example, at the 95% level of confidence, your observed score would be placed within a range of approximately $\pm 2 \times SE_m$ or more precisely $\pm 1.96 \times SE_m$. You have now discovered how to allow for regression to the mean when trying to predict one score from another, usually from a test of cognitive ability to a score on a test of attainment. You learned to apply the formula for the standard error of the estimate, SE_e, which you will remember as:

$$SE_e = SD \times \sqrt{1 - r_{xy}^2}$$

In the formula, the term, r_{xy}^2, refers to the correlation coefficient for the two tests, the degree to which they are related to one another. You also used the formula:

$$y' = r_{xy}(X - 100) + 100$$

where you needed to estimate the regressed score, y', with X being the observed score and r_{xy} being the correlation coefficient, again for the two tests used.

This formula can be revised to take into account the fact that in David's case, the test uses scaled scores, scores with a mean of 10 and a standard deviation of 3. So, the formula is:

$$y' = r_{xy}(X - 10) + 10$$

However, how do you calculate the standard error of the estimate for one test when you want to calculate confidence ranges to take into account regression to the mean for a score that is extreme, one that lies in either of the tails of the normal distribution? Here there is no other test involved, and so r_{xy}^2 is not relevant. This may be particularly important to consider when you are using a test that has a relatively low level of reliability because this will also affect the degree to which the regression affect will occur.

The Statistics

Firstly, you obtain an estimated score from David's observed scaled score of 18 by applying the formula:

$$y' = r \times (X - 10) + 10$$

where y' = the estimated score, and r = the reliability of the FM subtest, which we know from Table 4.8, page 102, of the test manual to be 0.72.

Therefore:

$$y' = 0.72 \times (18 - 10) + 10$$

$$= (0.72 \times 8) + 10$$

$$= 5.76 + 10$$

$$= 15.76 \quad = 16 \text{ (nearest whole number)}$$

In effect, this formula helps you determine the degree to which a score regresses on itself. Now that we have an estimated score that takes into account the regression to the mean of the extreme score of 18, we use the following formula to calculate the standard error of the estimated score:

$$SE_e = SD \times r\sqrt{(1-r)}$$

where SD = the standard deviation of the test, which is 3, and r is again the reliability coefficient of the test, which is 0.71:

$$SE_e = 3 \times 0.71 \sqrt{(1 - 0.71)}$$

$$= 3 \times 0.71 \sqrt{0.29}$$

$$= 3 \times 0.71 \times 0.5385$$

$$= 1.147$$

$$= 1.15 \text{ (rounded up to two decimal places)}$$

You decided to adopt the 95% level of confidence, and so your confidence range would be $\pm 1.96 \times SE_e$, which is:

$$\pm 1.96 \times 1.15$$

$$= \pm 2.25$$

$$= \pm 2 \text{ (nearest whole number)}$$

and place this value either side of the estimated score of 16, which gives us the range 14-18. If we now remember that David's actual score was 18, you can see that 18 does not lie at the mid-point of the range 14-18, which is why, when you observe confidence ranges in some test manuals, they appear to be asymmetrical, particularly for extremely low or high scores and where the test's reliability is not particularly high. Remember, you are trying to take into account the error factor that is inherent within your observed score. To do this with a score that lies towards either tail of the normal distribution you need to remember that the range within which your true score lies is being pulled towards the mean. Therefore, when you calculate the confidence range, you need to allow for this 'pull' of the the the regression.

Figure 8.1 demonstrates how confidence ranges calculated using the standard error of the estimate differ from those calculated using the standard error of measurement.

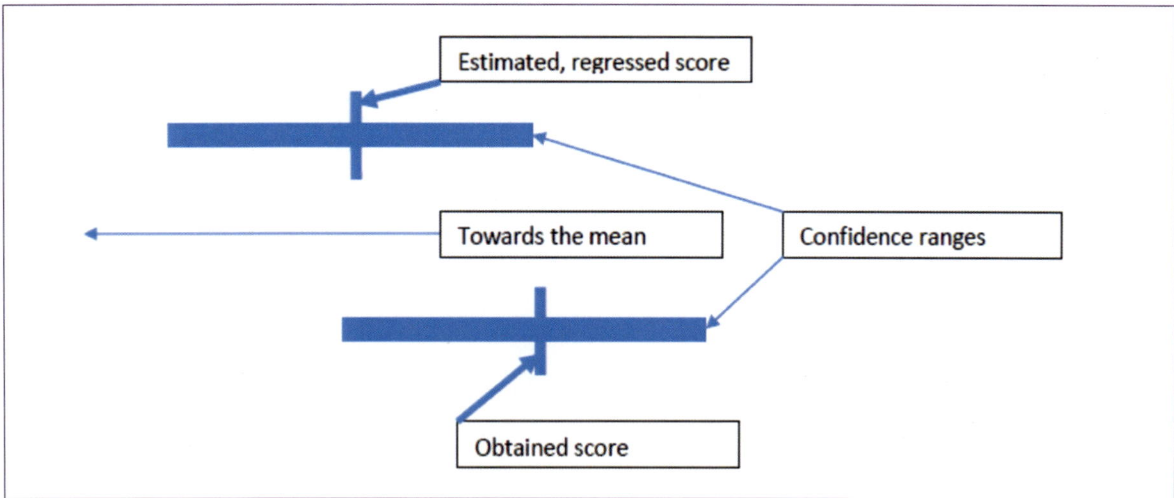

Figure 8.1: Comparing Confidence Ranges Derived from the Standard Error of Measurement and the Standard Error of the Estimate

The obtained score is shown with its confidence range. However, the estimated score that takes into account regression lies to the left of the obtained score because it is pulled towards the mean. When the estimated score's confidence range is calculated it also will be pulled to the mean in comparison to that of the obtained score.

It must be noted that it is often the case that for highly reliable tests, confidence ranges calculated using the standard error measurement and standard error of the estimate do not give very different ranges.

Chapter 9
Test-Retest

Case Example 9

You administer the DASH Copy Best subtest to Jimmy, aged 15 years, who obtains a scaled score of 7. You then repeat this subtest after 30 weeks and he then obtains a scaled score of 11. You want to know if the increase of 4 scaled scores is significant or not.

Points to Consider

A scaled score is a form of standard score with a mean of 10 and a standard deviation of 3. Chapter 3 stated that for scores on two different tests that were significantly different from one another, we used the SE_{mdiff} formula, which for two tests with the same standard deviation is:

$$SE_{mdiff} = SD \times \sqrt{2 - r_a - r_b}$$

If we wish to compare two scores on the same test, then the formula can be amended to:

$$SE_{mdiff} = SD \times \sqrt{2 - (2 \times r_a)}$$

So, for our case example we have the standard deviation as 3 and the test-retest reliability coefficient from Table 6.2, page 80 of the DASH manual for this age as 0.72, making the formula:

$$SE_{mdiff} = 3 \times \sqrt{2 - (2 \times 0.72)} = 2.45$$

If we then multiply 2.45 by 1.96 that is derived from the z score amount of scores that lie outside 95% of the total number of scores within the normal distribution, we obtain the amount 4.8 in units of scaled scores. This is the amount that needs to be exceeded for you to conclude that the second test score is significantly different to the first score at the 95% level of confidence. The value of 4.8 scaled score points is higher than the observed difference of 4 scaled score points, so you cannot conclude that the difference is significant at the selected level of confidence in this case.

Clearly, the choice of z is crucial for your investigation. At the 90% level of confidence, z would be 1.645.

Applying this value to the SE_{mdiff} would give 2.45 x 1.645 = 4.03, which you would accept as being a significant difference for this level of confidence.

Note that the above formula does not consider the influence of practice effects as a result of a client taking the same test again. This is another reason why using parallel test forms is recommended.

The formula for the SE_{mdiff} is:

$$SE_{mdiff} = SD \times \sqrt{2 - r_a - r_b}$$

As explained in Chapter 3, this enables you to determine if the difference between the obtained two scores is reliably different from one another or not. An additional formula is available (Reynolds, 1990) to help you decide if the difference can be regarded to be unusual. This formula can be used when you have no direct source of information as to how many children actually display a range of differences across the two relevant tests. The formula is:

$$\textit{Severe Discrepancy} = SD \times z_a \times \sqrt{2 - 2r_{xy}}$$

where SD = the standard deviation of both tests (recalculated into a common metric, if necessary), z_a = the z score corresponding to the point on the normal curve that you decide designates the frequency of occurrence of a 'severe discrepancy', and r_{xy} = the correlation coefficient between the two tests.

Note that the above formulae, both for the confirmation of a reliable difference between scores and the degree of the difference indicating a severe discrepancy, make no allowance for regression affects.

The major weakness of comparing standardised scores over time periods is the impact of practice/learning effects on the repeated measures where the client profits from knowledge of the test items and procedures, and the related problem of deciding on the time period(s) for repeat measurements. Teachers often prefer to have knowledge about their students' progress over relatively short time periods in order to evaluate efficiently and quickly the impact of their teaching inputs. It is unsafe to repeat the same psychometric test across a short time period. In addition, changes in standardised scores over time are difficult to interpret because they are comparative measures where the comparison group is the test's standardisation sample. Over time, this group of students is also progressing. Thus a student may progress over time in relation to his own baseline score on a test, but in standard score terms may be seen as deteriorating in relation to his peers as they also continue to learn. Chapter 10 highlights why Growth Scale Value (GSV) scores have therefore been created in an attempt to overcome these problems.

Chapter 10
Growth Scale Values and Normal Curve Equivalents

Introducing:

- **Growth Scale Values as a means of monitoring progress over time**
- **Normal Curve Equivalents as a variation of percentile scores.**

Case Example 10

Katie is 7 years and 10 months, and you are reviewing her progress with her parents at the end of her second academic year in your class. She has a specific learning difficulty (SpLD) that causes her to find the learning of literacy skills a slow and laborious process. Nonetheless, you have the view that given the extent of Katie's difficulties she has progressed reasonably well over the years. You have administered the Letter and Word Recognition (L&WR) and Phonological Awareness (Long) (PA) subtests from the KTEA-II on four occasions at six-monthly intervals using Forms A and B at alternate times. The raw and standard scores for the tests are shown in Table 10.1.

Table 10.1: Raw and Standard Scores over Time

Age (years:months)	Scores	L&WR	PA
7:10	Raw score (B)	13	14
7:10	Standard score	66	71
7:04	Raw score (A)	11	12
7:04	Standard score	66	69
6:10	Raw score(B)	7	7
6:10	Standard score	69	73
6:04	Raw score(A)	4	4
6:04	Standard score	70	75

When the above standard scores are plotted on a chart (Figure 10.1), the progress looks disappointing to the parents. In their eyes, they see evidence that Katie has deteriorated over the two years. In fact, as we will demonstrate, Katie has improved. For this reason, you want to give them correct evidence that Katie has progressed from her own baseline.

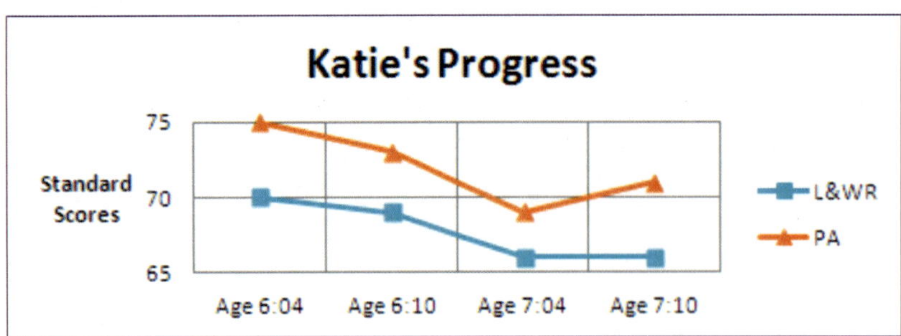

Figure 10.1: Charting Progress over Time Using Standard Scores

Tests such as the KTEA-II and the *Wechsler Individual Achievement Test – Third Edition* (WIAT-III; Wechsler, 2009a) are now introducing Growth Scale Values (GSVs) as a relatively new metric for reporting on client's skill and ability levels. This reflects in part the need to implement legislation such as the US's *Individuals with Disabilities Education Improvement Act* (IDEA 2004) and utilise 'Response to Intervention' (Fuchs & Fuchs, 2005) models of tracking individual students' progress over relatively short periods of time and where the amount of progress may be relatively small. Raw scores on test items within a test do not provide a metric using interval scaling and therefore are limited in their ability to give reliable and valid measures of amounts of progress. An interval scale is one in which a particular difference in scores designates the same size of difference in the underlying skill or ability regardless of where on the scale it occurs. When engaging with parents, teachers are often forced to refer to raw score improvements across repeated administrations of test forms when they observe that although a child appears to have improved over time, his standardised score has either not changed significantly or has even deteriorated after the first test administration.

Unlike percentiles, GSVs are scores on an equal interval scale and are used primarily to track achievement over time. 'Equal interval' refers to the fact that the size of the distance between units of scores is the same. They are created by the use of Item Response Theory (IRT; Embretson and Reise (2000)). The Rasch (1960) model of employing IRT is one of the most commonly used methods in the test industry. An introductory text on IRT is Embretson and Reise (2000). One of its assumptions is that the probability of a particular person with a given level of ability answering correctly a particular item with a particular level of difficulty is determined solely by the ability of the person and the difficulty of the item. In other words, if a person has a high cognitive ability they will probably get an easy item that measures that ability correct. Conversely, if a person has a low cognitive ability and the item is difficult, they will probably get the item wrong. Getting an item correct therefore depends on our ability and how difficult the question is. The probability of getting a right answer to a particular test item with a level of ability can therefore be calculated by applying the appropriate statistical analysis. By employing such techniques, subtests from assessments such as the KTEA-II can be transformed into GSV scales where raw scores on any one test can in effect be equated with a metric that is interval scale based. Traditionally, older tests were developed using Classical Test Theory, where passing/failing items produce data that are of ordinal, rather than interval, metric. Strictly speaking, ordinal level data cannot be used for parametric statistics such as mean, standard deviation and the unrelated T Test (Chapter 12).

GSVs are different from normative scores (i.e. standardised scores obtained by application of the statistical principles of the standard normal distribution curve) such as standard scores and percentiles. As stated in Chapter 2, percentiles do not have equally spaced scores. In addition, standardised scores compare a person's level and progress with a normative population. GSVs reflect absolute performance (within the child) and not relative, comparative standing (within a population). Nonetheless a child's individual GSV score can be compared with the mean GSV scores of his age peers. They are particularly useful for a child who is making slow progress over time where use of standardised scores may not recognise such individual progress as a result of the impact of normative comparison with other children.

In the KTEA-II manual, Table 1.13 on pages 291-2, gives subtest raw scores corresponding to GSVs. Each raw score equates to a different GSV for each different subtest. The GSV numbers do not have any meaning in themselves, therefore they can only be compared within the scale of GSVs for either one subtest or composite set of subtests. They cannot be compared across subtests or composites. Katie's GSV scores are shown in Table 10.2.

Table 10.2: Growth Scale Values Over Time

Form	Age (years:months)	L&WR Test	GSV	PA Test	GSV
(B)	7:10	13	97	14	194
(A)	7:04	11	92	12	189
(B)	6:10	7	80	7	185
(A)	6:04	4	71	4	179

If you now plot Katie's GSV scores for the two subtests, small, but positive, trends can be observed, as shown in Figure 10.2. The trends reflect Katie's progress within herself in that the GSVs are based directly on her raw scores and so their values reflect directly her responses to the test items. The metric of the GSV enables you to compare amounts of progress within each test because the unitary intervals between measurement points have equal value. For example, the GSV difference of 5 between the L&WR administrations at ages 7:04 and 7:10 can be compared to the GSV difference of 9 between the administrations at ages 6:04 and 6:10. In other words, the progress made within the former age range was nearly half that made within the latter age range.

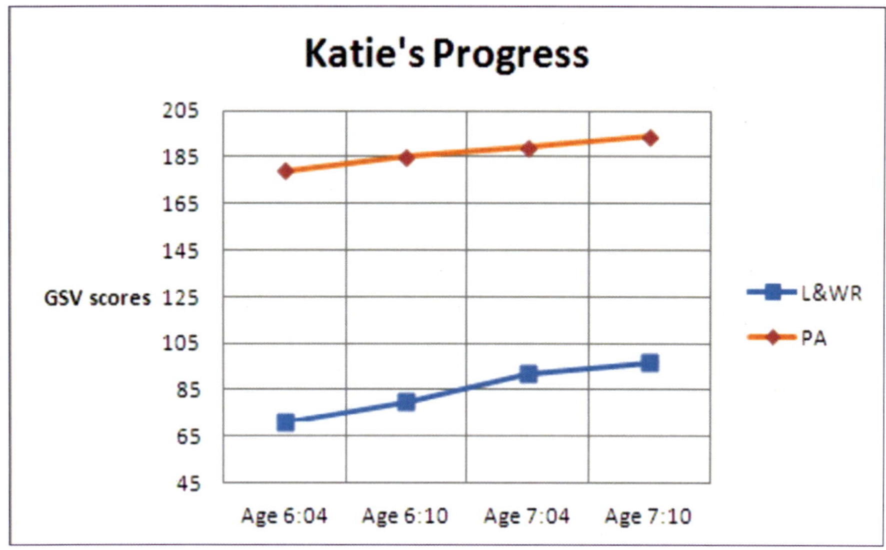

Figure 10.2: Charting Progress over Time Using Growth Scale Values

It is worth reflecting on the differences between standardised scores and GSVs and what their trendlines reflect. A clear understanding of their differences will be helpful when attempting to describe to parents the implications both for progress within the child and in comparison to similar-aged peers. Table 10.3 compares trends of increasing and decreasing standardised and GSV scores.

Table 10.3: Trends of Growth Scale Value and Standardised Scores

GSV Trend	Standardised Score Trend	Scenario
Increase	Increase	Very favourable. Not only has the student improved her skill levels over time, the rate of improvement is faster than her age peers. The gap between her skill levels and the mean standardised score for the population has reduced.
Increase	No change.	Satisfactory. The student has progressed in relation to her own baseline and the gap between her skill levels and her peers has not changed.
Increase	Decrease	Some positive features. The student has progressed in relation to her own baseline but her peers have progressed at a faster rate over the same period of time.
No change	Decrease	Some concern. The student has neither improved nor lost skills over the time period. However, her peers have progressed at a faster rate over the same time period.
Decrease	Decrease	Of concern. The student has lost skills over the time period and the gap between her skill levels and those of her peers has increased over the same time period.

The specialist teacher of children with protracted specific learning difficulties will now be aware of the usefulness of GSVs when reviewing their progress with their parents. GSVs allow for sensitive and yet objective appraisal of the evidence for progress or not, both within the child (intra-comparison) and compared to other children (inter-comparison). Parents in particular will see GSVs as a useful metric that relates to the world of their own child. Teachers will value GSVs as a means of confirming small changes that reflect the impact of their teaching. In this sense, GSVs are useful for those children who could be described as having qualitatively different learning paths and styles compared to the normal distribution of children. GSVs can be seen as a sensitive complement to the assessment methods that are based on Classical Test Theory. They may therefore be a more useful source of data compared to the norms of 'special groups' such as children on the autistic spectrum, children with hearing impairment etc, that some test manuals provide via Classical Test Theory.

TOWRE-2 does not use GSVs but does provide in its manual (pages 32-33) a similar means of comparing raw scores obtained from repeated administrations of the different forms of the same subtest. Each of the two subtests has four alternate/parallel forms, A to D. Because the individual forms of each subtest are closely equated for difficulty as evidenced in Table 6.6, page 85, of the manual (where the raw score totals for each age across the parallel tests are nearly the same, with differences of only one or two raw score points) it is argued that this is sufficient for raw scores to be compared. TOWRE-2 has spaces provided in its Response to Intervention booklet for monitoring improvement across time for both subtests. Raw scores cannot be summated across subtests. The limitation of TOWRE-2's use of raw scores for progress monitoring is that changes cannot be compared at different range points along the raw score continuum.

Normal Curve Equivalents

Occasionally, you will see reference in some assessment manuals to a type of standard score called the Normal Curve Equivalents (NCE) (see Figure 10.3). For example, CELF-4[UK] has Appendix F, Table F, which gives equivalent scores for scaled, standard, percentile ranks and stanines, and the KTEA-II has a similar table, Table N.8, page 305, in its Norms Book.

NCE scores are standard scores with a mean of 50 and a standard deviation of 21.06. The latter value allows a percentile of 1 to be equivalent to a NCE of 1 and a percentile of 99 to be equivalent to an NCE of 99. NCEs were designed to provide an interval metric to a modified percentile range. Percentiles only provide ranked data, and are therefore limited in their ability to give information about change or comparison across percentile score ranges.

A formula to add to our other formulae for changing the metric of z scores to NCE scores is:

$$NCE = 21.06z + 50.$$

The numbers on the NCE line run from 1 to 99, and are therefore very similar to percentile ranks in that they indicate an individual client's rank, or how many nominal clients out of a hundred had a lower score. However, NCE scores have a major advantage over percentiles in that they can be averaged across tests because of the introduction of standard deviation values between each NCE. Percentiles cannot be averaged because they are only rank units, not interval.

NCEs became popular in the US because of the need to obtain summative, average scores across areas of attainments that cannot be done by using percentiles that only have a ranking quality. However, the similarity with percentiles still lead people to have an understanding of a student's relative (ranking) score compared with other students. This therefore maintained their popularity in those academic settings that could be described as competitive where, for example, students were competing for limited places on postgraduate courses or awards.

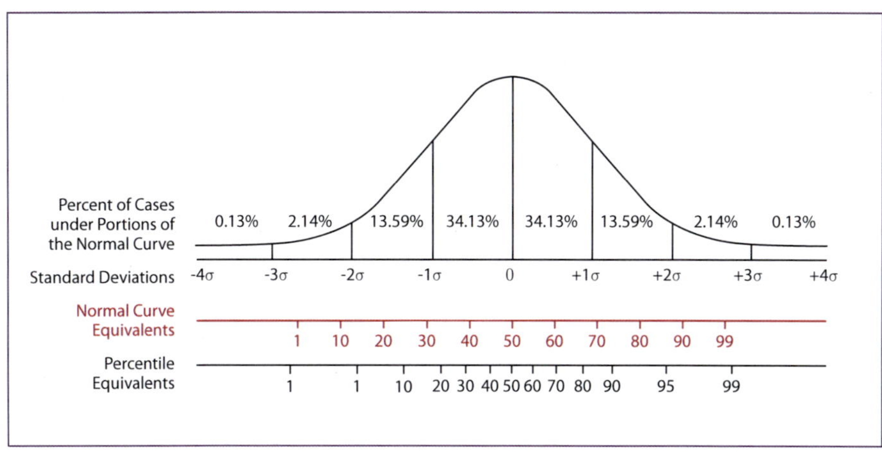

Figure 10.3: Normal Curve Equivalents and Percentiles on a Standard Distribution Curve

Chapter 11
Coefficient of Determination

Introducing basic principles of the concepts of:

- **the coefficient of determination and its relevance to the measurement of 'intelligence'**

- **the General Ability Index and the Matthew Effect.**

A teacher is concerned that one of her pupils has a measured Mental Processing Index of 120 on the KABC-II, but obtained a General Intellectual Ability score on the WJ III of only 110. She is concerned as to which score should be taken as the most valid and reliable score to reflect the pupil's cognitive ability.

Table 8.22, page 116, of the KABC-II manual gives the correlation coefficient between the two tests as 0.77. We have learned in previous chapters how to compare scores on tests by taking into account standard error in order to determine whether two scores are statistically different from each other.

However, one statistic that is useful to highlight the importance of the differences that can exist between IQ test scores, is that of the coefficient of determination. This concept measures the degree to which there is a shared test score variance across the two relevant tests. The formula is simply the square of the correlation coefficient for the two tests. Therefore, in the example above, the square of the correlation coefficient of 0.77 is 0.59. In other words, the two tests only share 59% common variance. The remaining 41% is partly due to random error but is also due to the two tests measuring different abilities as constructed by the validity considerations when the tests were designed. Different tests of cognitive ability are based on the theoretical models of intelligence being applied. These may be quite different. This aspect is defined as 'construct validity'. In other words, a test has construct validity if it is based on a valid model of the concept it is supposed to be measuring. Item selection and, relatedly, subtest construction are concerned with 'content validity' to ensure that the items selected for the test are a valid sample of the total set of abilities within the population as a whole. Therefore, it is understandable that tests of cognitive ability can differ along a number of dimensions. An example is the KABC-II, which offers the user the choice of two theoretical models: Cattell-Horn-Carroll (CHC; Flanagan *et al.,* 2000); and Luria's Neuropsychological Theory of Processing (Luria, 1973) of intelligence before calculating 'IQ'.

IQ score differences are to be expected across different intelligence tests because of such construct validity considerations. Additionally, the presence of high correlations between two IQ tests does not imply that particular pairs of IQ scores for one client will necessarily have the same value.

Table 11.1 shows IQ scores for 10 students on two tests of intelligence, Test A and Test B. The IQ scores for each student on the two tests are different, sometimes very different. However, when a Pearson Product-Moment correlation coefficient is calculated, then the correlation coefficient of (+) 0.98 obtained is extremely high. A high correlation coefficient across tests does not imply close alignment of values of pairs of scores, as can be seen in Table 11.1.

Table 11.1: Comparing IQ Scores on Two Tests

Student	Test A	Test B
1	70	80
2	73	80
3	80	90
4	92	110
5	101	110
6	106	111
7	108	117
8	114	120
9	120	130
10	125	137

For example, student 10 displays a difference of 12 standard score points across the two tests of intelligence that correlate highly with one another.

Note that the risk areas are always towards the two tails of the distribution of test scores along the normal distribution curve. It is in these areas that reliability coefficients of tests are often lower than elsewhere. Therefore, clients of very low or very high intelligence may show more variability across tests of intelligence.

Table 11.2 highlights how the coefficients of determinations (top right-hand sector, red italics) differ across the range of correlation coefficients (bottom left-hand sector) typically found across IQ tests. They are all positively correlated, demonstrating what is called a 'positive manifold', i.e. the phenomenon that performance on any two reliably measured tasks is positively correlated. Understandably, in this example, the positive manifold occurs because general cognitive ability (g, or intelligence), however it is conceptualised and measured, is required for all ability tests.

Table 11.2: Tests' Coefficients of Determination and Reliability Coefficients

	IQ Test 1	IQ Test 2	IQ Test 3	IQ Test 4	IQ Test 5
IQ Test 1		*0.16*	*0.20*	*0.25*	*0.30*
IQ Test 2	0.40		*0.36*	*0.42*	*0.49*
IQ Test 3	0.45	0.60		*0.56*	*0.64*
IQ Test 4	0.50	0.65	0.75		*0.72*
IQ Test 5	0.55	0.70	0.80	0.85	

The Coefficient of Determination will also be referred to in the section on report writing. It is used for the purpose of creating trendlines when interrogating data plotted on charts.

It follows that if a psychologist or specialist teacher needs to select a measure of general cognitive ability in order to make some sort of comparative analysis involving skill levels of attainments, then the outcome will most probably be significantly influenced by their choice of test of cognitive ability. This again supports the position that if possible, co-normed tests of cognitive ability and attainment should be used where possible. Examples here are the co-normed KTEA-II and the KABC-II.

The choice of type of IQ score for comparison with attainment scores is also another factor to consider. Contemporary theoretical models of intelligence now incorporate working memory and speed of information processing and this is reflected in psychometric tests of intelligence such as WAIS-IV[UK] and the WISC- IV[UK]. However, because these particular ability factors are often causally related to specific learning difficulties, children with such specific learning difficulties often score with lower IQ scores on these contemporary tests of intelligence in comparison to earlier versions. Hence some test developers have provided additional measures of types of general ability, such as the General Ability Index that are based only on crystallised and fluid measures of cognitive ability (Raiford et al., 2005). Such measures are recommended when a client's cognitive profile is highly irregular and where there are significant statistical differences between subtest and ability cluster scores. Guidelines are given within the test manuals as to which type of ability measure should be selected.

It has been claimed that when children with specific learning difficulties are administered intelligence tests over their lifespan, the trend is one of them performing less well in comparison to other children (Shaywitz et al., 1995). This phenomenon is called the 'Matthew Effect' from the biblical reference, *'To all those who have, more will be given, and they will have an abundance, but from those who have nothing, even what they have will be taken away.'* (Matthew 13:12). In essence, it is argued that because children with learning difficulties are disadvantaged in acquiring cultural knowledge (crystallised learning) over the years, then their scores on intelligence tests will be likewise detrimentally affected, particularly as their scores are compared normatively with the scores of children without learning difficulties on the same tests.

The diagnostic assessor therefore needs to reflect on her choice of intelligence test. She needs to be aware that the test selected may incorporate ability factors such as speed of information processing and working memory. The relevant subtests may disadvantage the client with learning difficulties but this does not necessarily mean that they should not be used. A client may score poorly on a test of working memory and this is likely to present with important diagnostic information. Whether the working memory score should be subsumed within a measure of the client's general cognitive ability is another matter. Intelligence tests can differ significantly as a consequence of construct and content design decisions and the IQs of certain children may appear to decline in relation to those of their peers as a result of the normative process of test score comparison. Chapter 18 will discuss the implications of these features in more detail.

Chapter 12
Standard Error of the Mean

Introducing:

- **the standard error of the mean**
- **the importance of sampling size.**

Case Example 11

A teacher wants to find out whether her current teaching group of 20 has performed significantly differently to her previous year's group on a test of spelling. She knows that the mean scores for the two groups are different, but she does not know if this is statistically different. She is also interested in the spread of the students' scores and wants to find a measure that assesses this.

So far, this book has been mainly concerned with approaches for the statistical analyses of the scores of the individual. However, teachers in the classroom are not just concerned with the individual student but also with the performance of their students as a group. Lessons are arranged to suit the context of the teaching day that are rarely concerned with how students operate as individuals. Teachers need information on how such groups of students perform over time and to what extent groups are different from one another, both at the same time and across teaching years. It is therefore valid for teachers to want to research the properties of groups of students as well as the profile of the individual student. In addition, such a focus on groups will help teachers obtain a yardstick for the individual, outlying student whose scores on tests appear to be unusual and disparate from the scores of the other students.

Table 12.1 shows sets of standard scores on a test of spelling from the WIAT-II^{UK}-T for two different groups of students. Group A was taught the previous year by a teacher who wants to compare their performance with her current teaching group, Group B. For this exercise, we are assuming that the two groups are of equal numbers.

Table 12.1: Standard Error of the Mean – Spelling Scores for Two Groups of Students

Group A		Group B	
Student 1	89	Student 1	115
Student 2	89	Student 2	112
Student 3	67	Student 3	116
Student 4	79	Student 4	99
Student 5	97	Student 5	117
Student 6	110	Student 6	116
Student 7	89	Student 7	70
Student 8	90	Student 8	112
Student 9	90	Student 9	120
Student 10	93	Student 10	121
Student 11	94	Student 11	110
Student 12	82	Student 12	100
Student 13	82	Student 13	100
Student 14	87	Student 14	95
Student 15	101	Student 15	70
Student 16	102	Student 16	84
Student 17	110	Student 17	102
Student 18	78	Student 18	98
Student 19	70	Student 19	97
Student 20	110	Student 20	135

One feature that the teacher observes is that in Group A, students 6, 17 and 20 have the highest shared score of 110, whilst student 3 has the weakest score of 67. Therefore, one statistical feature that is already evident is that Group A's scores have a range spanning the score range of 67-110, which is 43.

Group B, on the other hand, has students 7 and 15 with weakest scores of 70 for the group, whilst student 20 has the strongest scores of 135. Therefore, the range for this group is 70-135, which is 65.

Unfortunately, describing data in this way is not particularly helpful to obtain a statistical representation of scatter of scores across a group of people. It does not take into account the values of the other scores and it places too much emphasis on the extreme scores selected at either ends of the distribution of scores. As can be seen from the scatter chart in Figure 12.1, one needs a means of acknowledging the impact of each single score when trying to obtain an overview of the scatter of all of the scores. Scatter plots are very useful as a visual means of inspecting range as well as identifying any unusual 'outliers'.

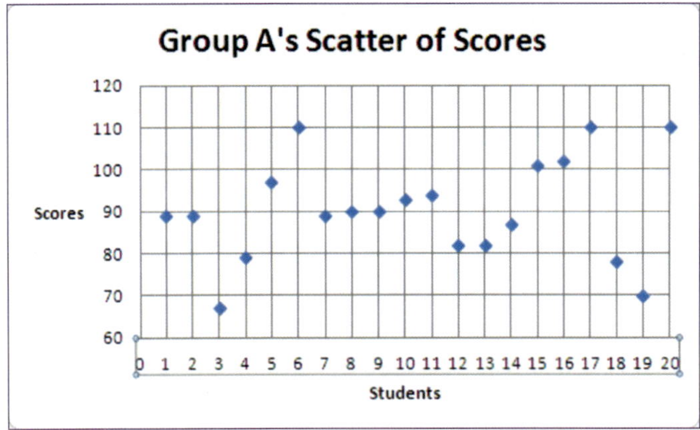

Figure 12.1: Scatter Plot of Scores

In Chapter 1, you learned about standard deviation and variance and how these were the best measures to obtain a measure of spread or range. You also learned that the choice of formula for the standard deviation had variations that were dependent on whether or not you were concerned with an actual population or a sample of an assumed population. If you are concerned with an actual population, then the formula to select is:

$$SD = \sqrt{\frac{\Sigma(X - \bar{X})^2}{N}}$$

When your assumption is that your population is a sample, then the formula is:

$$SD = \sqrt{\frac{\Sigma(X - \bar{X})^2}{N - 1}}$$

Let us return to the two groups of students' scores above. If we wish to compare their properties with regard to each group's variance and whether or not the two groups are different from one another, instantly we are drawn into perceiving each of the two group's scores as being samples of a much wider population of possible scores. Thus, your decision is to use the N – 1 option for the calculation of their standard deviations. From Chapter 1 you learned that, in *Excel*, the formula for the standard deviation (N – 1 option) is:

B21		f_x	=STDEV(B1:B20)

Therefore, placing your cursor on cell B21 (Figure 12.2) and inputting the above formula for cells B1 to B20 by selecting these cells with your mouse, would give you a standard deviation of 12 for Group A. For Group B in D21, the standard deviation is 17. You now can conclude that Group B's standard deviation is approximately 1½ times that of Group A's.

B21			f_x	=STDEV(B1:B20)
	A	B	C	D	E
16	Student 16	102	Student 36	84	
17	Student 17	110	Student 37	102	
18	Student 18	78	Student 38	98	
19	Student 19	70	Student 39	97	
20	Student 20	110	Student 40	135	
21		12		17	SD

Figure 12.2: Standard Deviation Calculations for Groups A and B

Chapter 12 Standard Error of the Mean

This now brings us to the concept and formula for the standard error of the mean, SE_{mean}. The two means for Group A and Group B are 90 and 104. The *Excel* formula for this calculation is:

$$f_x \quad \text{=AVERAGE(B1:B20)}$$

You want to know whether the means of your two sample groups are statistically different to one another. You therefore have to have some way of taking into account the 'standard error' in your calculation of the sample means because you know that if you were to take different samples then the random error effect will lead you to record a different mean every time you perform this act.

The standard error of the mean is represented by a very simple formula:

$$SE_{mean} = \frac{SD}{\sqrt{N}}$$

where SD = the standard deviation of each of your sample, and N = the sample size.

In that we have calculated the standard deviation of Group A as 12 and for Group B as 17, then their respective standard errors of their means are:

$$SE_{mean} \text{ Group A} = \frac{12}{\sqrt{20}} \qquad SE_{mean} \text{ Group B} = \frac{17}{\sqrt{20}}$$

These compute to:

$$SE_{mean} \text{ Group A} = 2.7 = 3 \text{ (nearest whole number)}$$

$$SE_{mean} \text{ Group B} = 3.8 = 4 \text{ (nearest whole number)}$$

You can now apply the concept of confidence ranges to the obtained mean scores. This is similar to the use of the standard error of measurement (Chapter 1) to calculate the confidence ranges to place around obtained scores.

For Group A's mean of 90, and selecting a 68% confidence level, then the confidence range would be 90 ± 3 (87 to 93). For Group B, the range would be 104 ± 4 (100 to 108).

Therefore, at the chosen level of confidence, it can be concluded that the two mean scores obtained are statistically different. Group B students, as whole, have a higher level of scores than Group A students. You can therefore conclude that the two groups are statistically different from one another.

The width of the confidence intervals will depend heavily on the sample size. Smaller sample sizes have wider confidence intervals because the means are estimated less precisely. Larger sample sizes have narrower confidence intervals because there is more statistical power to estimate the means precisely.

Note that a similar approach to examining the differences between two samples is that of using the T Test. This test compares the difference between the observed means of the two samples but uses in its formula the standard error of the difference that you read about in Chapter 3. This test is best applied using *Excel* where it is available in the formula bar because the arithmetical calculations for the formula are quite tedious to perform manually. Some knowledge is also required concerning the understanding and use of the term *degrees of freedom*, that is, the number of values in the final calculation of a statistic that are 'free to vary'. It should also be noted that there are variations of the T Test formula, which relate to the nature of the task to be performed. Carlberg (2011) is useful further reading on this area and for the application of *Excel* with its range of relevant formulae.

Sampling Size

Suppose you did not have a sample of 20 as above for each group. Instead, you decided to have a sample size of 50 for one of these groups. Would your derived mean be more reliable or less reliable as an estimate of the 'true' population mean? Your instincts would probably lead you to say 'more reliable' and you would be correct. The larger your sample size, the more likely it will take on the properties of the 'true' population that you are concerned to make judgements about. This would be with the assumption that your sample was obtained without any extreme bias in the way that you selected your sample. If your sample was 100% then it would be the actual population you are interested in making judgements about. Therefore, you know that N will need to be considered in whatever formula we derive for the error of our sample mean. On reflection, you also know that the wider the standard deviation of our sample, the more error you will have every time you sample and obtain a mean value. If the standard deviation was small, then our range of scores would tend to cluster around the mean and you assume, rightly, that this would lead to less error when making judgements about the true mean of the population.

The best way of having an understanding of the impact of the size of N on the accuracy of sampling to determine a measure of the true value of a population mean, is to draw a chart of the SE_{mean} plotted against different values of N keeping SD as a constant for the purpose of the exercise. If we do this and examine the chart of our findings (Figure 12.3), where we have $SD = 15$, then you can see that after approximately a sample size of 50, the error difference becomes negligible. It is only when the sample sizes are relatively small that the standard error of the obtained means changes dramatically across sample sizes.

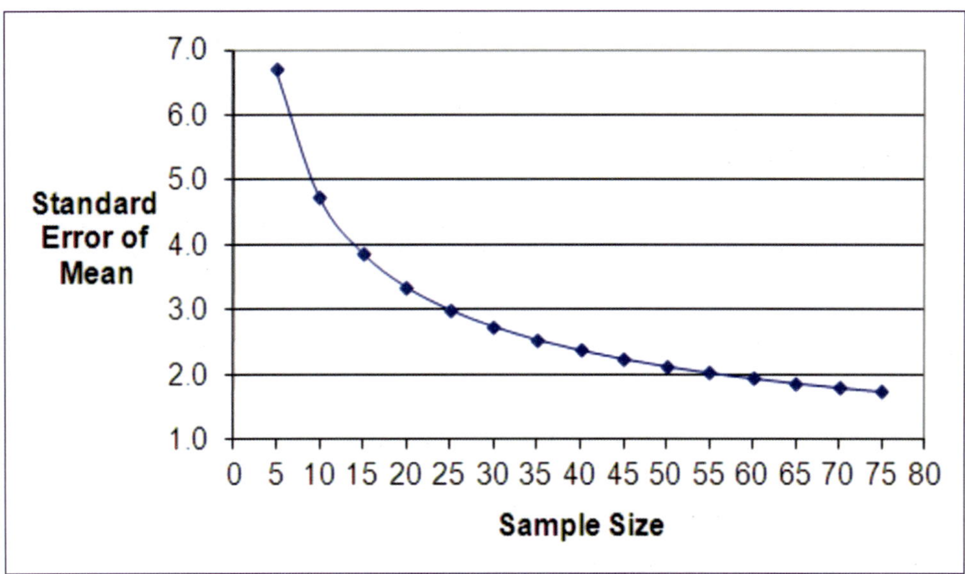

Figure 12.3: Sampling Numbers and the Standard Error of the Mean

This statistical phenomenon is of great help to test developers when constructing their tests. They do not have to undergo extensive and expensive standardisation ventures using extremely large numbers of samples in order to guarantee that their tests will be valid and reliable. After a relatively small sampling for each age group concerned, the law of diminishing returns applies. There is little added value in unnecessarily sampling more units in a population because after a certain number, the sample becomes 'good enough'. Note that test developers tend to go beyond the sampling number of 50 mentioned above in order to maximise reliability considerations.

For the teacher, the statistical phenomenon is also useful. It could allow her to perform small-scale research on evidence obtained from her own (usually group) assessments and even could lead her to mini-standardise and create her own tests, using other features of this book such as converting percentiles into standardised scores explained in Chapter 2. By having access to only a small set of the population, one can still obtain estimates of how this sample population behaves on tests in relation to the true population. The teacher may also be concerned with a particular population of children that is relevant to her own professional area. These children may be a special population, worthy of their own standardisation of academic learning.

Chapter 13
Binomial Distribution Probability and Multiple-Choice Tests

Introducing:

- **the Binomial Distribution Probability**

- **its relevance to multiple-choice test formats and access arrangements for examinations.**

Case Example 12

Jim is a 16-year-old student and you want to ascertain his eligibility for access arrangements in his forthcoming General Certificate of Secondary Education (GCSE) examinations. You believe that his speed of reading comprehension is significantly slow and that this may disadvantage him in timed examinations. You have a test of reading comprehension, the *Vernon-Warden Reading Test (Revised)* (Hedderly, 1996), that uses multiple-choice format, with five response options. You have regularly used this test for a number of years as a group test of reading comprehension. Although this test is not commercially available as a published test, it is accepted by the JCQ as a means of providing part-evidence for access arrangements for examinations. Students select by circling from a choice of five words the word that is appropriate to complete a sentence. Unfortunately, the test does not provide a standardised means of assessing for reading comprehension speed, but it does offer general advice on how to identify students with likely difficulties in this area. It suggests that if, after the standardised time of 10 minutes, any student's raw score 'improves significantly' in the extra time then they can be judged to have slow reading comprehension. This information will be accepted by the examination body as supplementary evidence for allocation of extra time as an access arrangement (www.jcq.org.uk).

You are concerned about the lack of guidance as to how the term 'improves significantly' can be operationally defined because you want to show that you have acted professionally and provided valid evidence that Jim's scores on the test 'improved significantly' after the statutory 10 minutes. Jim's raw score increased by five units across an extra 10 test items. In effect, you need to know whether or not such an increase reflects random chance.

The Statistics

Binomial Probability is concerned with the probability of successive happenings, each of which has only two possible outcomes. In Jim's case this means selection of the correct word or selection of a wrong word for each of the attempted test items. For the purposes of using Binomial Probability it is important to confirm that each test item is independent from the other items within the test. In other words, as Jim processes each item, his actions and each item bear no impact on the outcome of the next test item's word selection.

You know that, in accordance with the test's instructions, Jim has attempted an extra 10 test items after the standard time period for the test. For the purposes of applying the Binomial Formula, this number is referred to as n. Jim's success of five raw score points is referred to as x.

You now need to calculate the odds of selecting by chance a correct word for each item. If you were tossing a coin then you would already be aware that the chances of tossing 'heads' or 'tails' would be the same and the probability, or p, should be 0.5 either way. If you toss the coin again, then the probability of obtaining the same side as before is p^2 (0.5 x 0.5 = 0.25) and for n repetitions, p^n. For the purposes of the formula, p is the probability of success and $(1-p)$ is the probability of failure that we refer to as q.

In Jim's case, we are not dealing with two possible outcomes but five for each test item attempted. Jim can either select the correct word for each test item or one of four incorrect words. His probability of selecting by chance the correct word is therefore one in five, i.e. $p = 0.2$.

We are also dealing with a situation where Jim's extra raw score of five may well have been obtained across the 10 extra test items, i.e. not one after the other, so the p^n probability value cannot be simply applied by calculating 0.2^5.

Be aware that the formula given below is relatively complex and time-consuming to apply manually. However, *Excel* can be used, as can programs such as that provided by *Stat Trek* at **http://stattrek.com/tables/binomial. aspx**. However, the formula is given here and explained to help you to understand the principles involved.

To calculate the probability of obtaining **exactly** x successes within n attempts (test items), the Binomial equation is:

$$\binom{n}{x} p^x (q)^{(n-x)}$$

The statistical term $\binom{n}{x}$ is a statistical term for:

$$\frac{n!}{x!(n-x)!}$$

Note that the use of the exclamation sign in statistics means 'factorial'. Therefore, for example, 6! means 6 x 5 x 4 x 3 x 2 x 1.

In Jim's case, to confirm the probability of him getting exactly five extra test items correctly out of 10:

$$p = 0.2$$

$$q = (1-p) = 0.8$$

$$x = 5$$

$$n = 10$$

The formula therefore becomes:

$$\binom{10}{5} (0.2)^5 (0.8)^{(5)}$$

$$= 0.0246$$

In other words, there is approximately a 2% chance of Jim obtaining this score. You now have a means of judging in a quantifiable way whether the raw score of five can be regarded as a chance event. In Chapter 2 you were made aware of p and z as terms that enabled you to make judgements about scarcity of events when considering the principles of Classical Test Theory. If your general level of confidence was at the .05 level when administering other diagnostic tests to Jim, then the 2% chance calculated above falls well within the level of confidence when making judgements about Jim's raw score increase of five points.

Chapter 13 Binomial Distribution Probability and Multiple-Choice Tests

Figure 13.1 shows a screenshot from *Stat Trek*. Not only does it give you the Binomial Probability for Jim obtaining exactly five extra raw score points, but it also gives the probability for scoring five **or more** – the cumulative probability – given as 0.033 (to three decimal places) on the bottom row. The Cumulative Probability is useful to use as a group benchmark for all students taking the test enabling efficient application of marking and making judgements about eligibility. Other sub-options relating to less than five, five or less, more than five, are also given.

Figure 13.1: Multiple Choice Items – Obtaining Binomial Probability using Stat Trek *(reproduced with permission from* Stat Trek*)*

Excel also provides the means of calculating the Binomial Probability using its BINOM.DIST formula. The formula bar for Jim's case gives the following formula:

```
=BINOMDIST(5,10,0.2,FALSE)
```

The word 'False' is typed in the *Cumulative* section of the Functions Arguments for the probability of scoring exactly five items correctly (Figure 13.2).

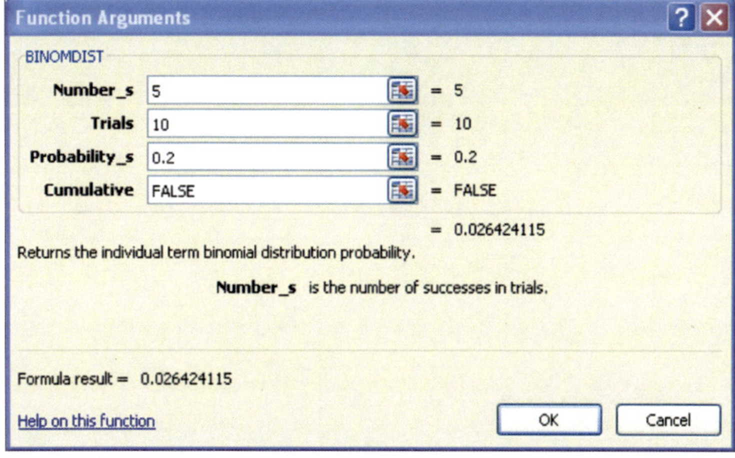

Figure 13.2: Multiple Choice Items – Obtaining Binomial Probability using Excel *(i)*

Note that the probability given in *Excel* when using the word True, as in Figure 13.3, is the probability for scoring **up to and including five**, not five and above, so be careful when interpreting the figures given across different programs on the Internet.

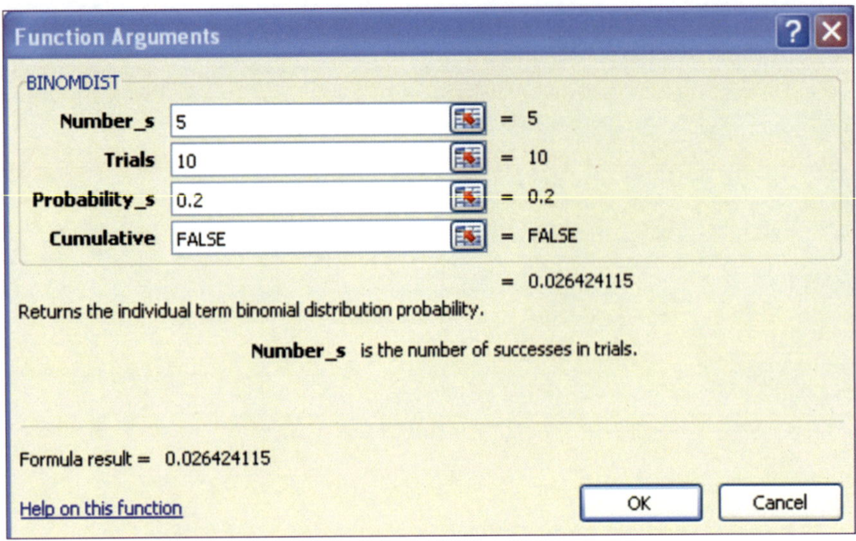

Figure 13.3: Multiple-Choice Items obtaining Binomial Probability using Excel *(ii)*

Therefore, when reporting on Jim's case for consideration of eligibility for access arrangements to allow him extra time for his GCSE exams, you could write the following:

'Jim gave evidence in my assessment that on a test of reading comprehension, the Vernon-Warden Reading Test (Revised), he increased his number of successes on test items by five out of ten when extra time was allowed. Although the test does not provide standardised norms to assess speed of reading comprehension, I calculate that the probability of Jim obtaining this extra score by chance alone is only 2%. I regard this to be within sufficiently safe parameters of confidence to allow him to be eligible to be considered for extra time in his forthcoming examinations.'

The probability of the number of chance successes out of 10 test items can be plotted in *Excel* by selecting *Insert/Scatter* to give the chart shown in Figure 13.4.

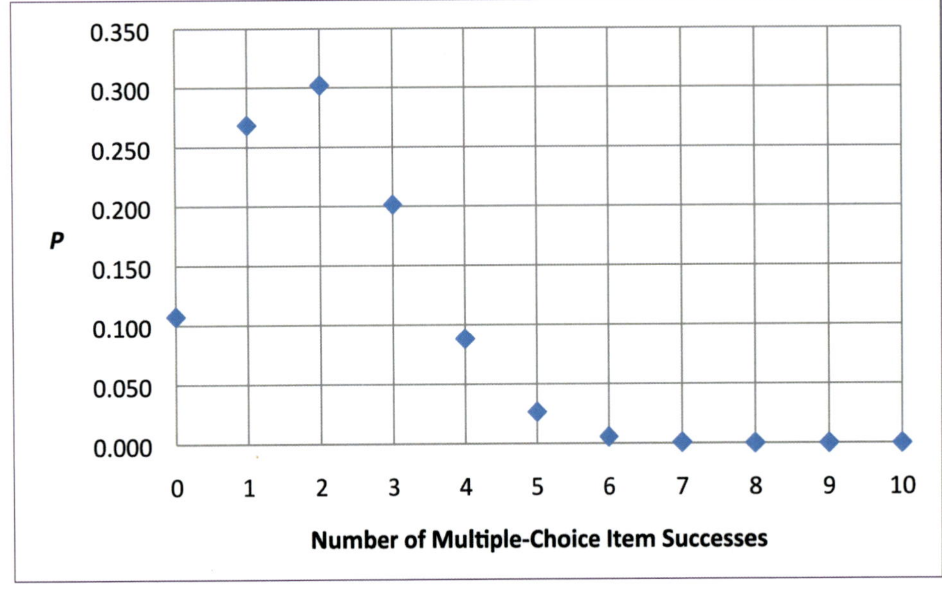

Figure 13.4: Probability (p) of Chance Successes on a Multiple-Choice Test

Chapter 14
Multiple Regression

Introducing multiple regression as a means of predicting an attainment score from more than one variable.

Case Example 13

You want to analyse the combined relationship of a group of children's IQ and their phonological processing ability with their single word reading skills' development. In other words, you want to see how both IQ and phonological awareness scores can be analysed together with regard to how they relate to reading scores. You are particularly keen to use this group information to help you predict the level of Blodwyn's single word reading skills from the knowledge you obtain from the data on these children. You administer to students the WASI-II and the long version of the Phonological Awareness and Letter and Word Recognition subtests from the KTEA-II.

Points to Consider

You have learned that simple regression can help you examine the relationship between sets of scores on two different tests by seeing how one score can be predicted from another using the regression formula given in Chapter 6. In this chapter, we extend the area by considering methods by which two or more sets of scores can be examined with regard to their combined relationship with another set of scores of, for example reading attainment using multiple regression. Multiple regression is best applied by using the formulae already prepared for you in commercial packages such as *Excel*. For the purposes of this book, all you need to understand is the rudiments of what multiple regression is and how it can be applied.

The Data

Figure 14.1 shows a hypothetical set of scores for 10 students. In practice, you will need a larger sample size than this (see below).

	C14			f_x	=TREND(C4:C12,B4:B12,B14)	
	A	B	C	D	E	F
1						
2		WASI IQ	Reading			
3						
4	Alice	125	90			
5	Barbara	120	98			
6	Claire	110	115			
7	Debbie	100	125			
8	Eleanor	90	105			
9	Frances	85	95			
10	Gail	80	90			
11	Heidi	75	85			
12	Imelda	70	100			
13						
14	Blodwyn	110	103			

Figure 14.1: Multiple Regression – Step 1

To predict Blodwyn's Reading Skill score for cell C14, the formula for the formula bar is:

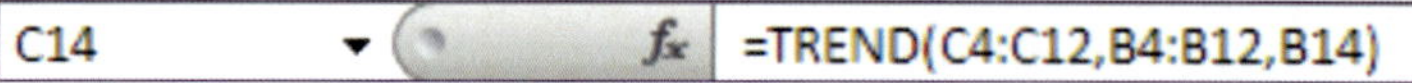

With this data set, the formula returns the value 103 for Blodwyn's predicted score on the Word Recognition subtest. This is based on Blodwyn's WASI II IQ of 110 recorded in cell B14 and using the trend projection calculated from the set of other scores for the other nine students. This is a simple regression formula, aimed at using IQ to predict Blodwyn's reading score where the IQ and reading scores of the other nine students are used as a sample to help us make judgements about Blodwyn's likely reading score, given that her IQ is 110. The formula is primarily concerned with analysing the type and degree of the correlation between the IQ and reading scores for this analysis.

Now consider the set of scores shown in Figure 14.2 that give data on the same set of students, but this time for their scores on phonological awareness and reading.

C14		f_x =TREND(C4:C12,B4:B12,B14)			
	A	B	C	D	E	F
1						
2		Phonological	Reading			
3		Awareness				
4	Alice	80	90			
5	Barbara	95	98			
6	Claire	120	115			
7	Debbie	125	125			
8	Eleanor	100	105			
9	Frances	105	95			
10	Gail	85	90			
11	Heidi	90	85			
12	Imelda	95	100			
13						
14	Blodwyn	90	93			

Figure 14.2: Multiple Regression – Step 2

This time, Blodwyn's predicted score is 93, as highlighted in cell C14, where this prediction is based on the set of scores for the other nine students but where IQ is not the predicting variable.

We therefore have two prediction values for Blodwyn's reading skills, one based on her IQ and the other based on her phonological awareness skills. Clearly, if there were some way in which the two predictors could be combined in a valid way, then we would obtain a more accurate means of predicting Blodwyn's reading score.

Figure 14.3 gives the three sets of the students' scores for IQ, phonological awareness and word recognition.

E6				f_x {=TREND(B6:B14,D6:D14)}						
	A	B	C	D	E	F	G	H	I	J	K
1											
2		WASI IQ	Phonological	Reading	Reading	Reading	Reading				
3			Awareness		predicted by	predicted by	predicted by				
4					IQ	Phonol. Awar.	IQ & Phon.				
5							Awareness				
6	Alice	125	80	90	91	85	89			IQ/Reading r	0.232241
7	Barbara	120	95	98	94	97	99			Phon. Aw./Reading r	0.90747
8	Claire	110	120	115	100	116	118				
9	Debbie	100	125	125	104	120	120				
10	Eleanor	90	100	105	97	101	100				
11	Frances	85	105	95	93	105	104				
12	Gail	80	85	90	91	89	88				
13	Heidi	75	90	85	90	93	91				
14	Imelda	70	95	100	95	97	94				

Figure 14.3: Multiple Regression – Step 3

Figure 14.3 shows in columns E and F the predicted Word Recognition scores for the nine other students based on IQ (column B) and phonological awareness (column C). For prediction from IQ (column B) this calculation is performed by applying the following formula in the formula bar:

E6	▼	f_x	{=TREND(B6:B14,D6:D14)}

The procedure here is to highlight cells E6-E14, type in the formula as shown, and then 'array-enter' it with a Ctrl+Shift+Enter key combination. The highlighted cells are then automatically filled with the predicted values. The procedure is repeated for column F predicted from column C (phonological awareness) with the relevant cells being typed into the formula bar.

Now examine the highlighted cells G6-G14 in Figure 14.4. These cells are the predicted values based on the combined relationship of **both** the IQ and Word Recognition subtest scores. Note that in the formula, cells B6-C14 are highlighted to cover both the IQ and Phonological Awareness columns.

Pearson r correlation coefficients are give in columns K for IQ/Word Recognition (0.232241) and Phonological Awareness/Word Recognition (0.90747). The much higher correlation for Phonological Awareness/Word Recognition compared with that for IQ/Word Recognition is reflected in row 16 when we examine the totality of Blodwyn's scores. Note how the predicted score based on the score for phonological awareness is much nearer the combined predicted score than that for the predicted score based on IQ. However, as the IQ scores have a small but positive correlation with the Word Recognition scores, the combined multiple regression analysis refines the prediction to give a predicted score of 89.

G6	▼	f_x	{=TREND(D6:D14,B6:C14)}

	A	B	C	D	E	F	G	H	I	J	K
1											
2		WASI IQ	Phonological	Reading	Reading	Reading	Reading				
3			Awareness		predicted by	predicted by	predicted by				
4					IQ	Phonol. Awar.	IQ & Phon.				
5							Awareness				
6	Alice	125	80	90	91	85	89			IQ/Reading r	0.232241
7	Barbara	120	95	98	94	97	99			Phon. Aw./Reading r	0.90747
8	Claire	110	120	115	100	116	118				
9	Debbie	100	125	125	104	120	120				
10	Eleanor	90	100	105	97	101	100				
11	Frances	85	105	95	93	105	104				
12	Gail	80	85	90	91	89	88				
13	Heidi	75	90	85	90	93	91				
14	Imelda	70	95	100	95	97	94				
15											
16	Blodwyn	110	90		103	93	89				

Figure 14.4: Multiple Regression – Step 4

This example is based on the scores of only nine students. In real life, it is advisable to have a sample size much larger than this. For multiple regression, you need (at least) the larger of: (1) N >=50 + 8m students to test the multiple correlation, and (2) N>=104 + m students to test individual predictors (Tabachnik & Fidell, 2007). In the formulae, m refers to the number of predictor variables (independent variables). Therefore, if you have two predictor variables then you need a sample size of 104 + 2 = 106. The sample size requirements depend on the size of the relationship between the predictors and the dependent variable (larger effect sizes need fewer students). Such an analysis would not only help you form a view about whether or not Blodwyn's actual score for Reading Recognition was satisfactory, taking into consideration her IQ and phonological processing scores and the scores from the other nine students, but also help you make judgements about the usefulness of certain tests for future use for the same purpose. If the scores were real, then you would conclude that phonological awareness is a stronger predictor than IQ of reading skills. Similarly, you may consider dispensing with the IQ test in favour of another test that may have more added value for your needs. Tests with high predictive value of students' future attainment skills are extremely valuable.

Additional means by which *Excel* can be used for multiple regression analysis can be accessed by using the Data Analysis/Regression option in *Excel*. This can be accessed by confirming that the Analysis Toolpak add-in is installed in your computer. Check that this is installed by clicking on the File menu and choosing *Options*. Then select Add-ins and make sure that Analysis ToolPak and Analysis ToolPak-VBA are selected in the available menu. Once confirmed, you can use the data analysis functions in *Excel*. Select *Data Menu/Data Analysis* that then gives you a dialogue box for Data Analysis. Select *Regression* and then proceed with your analysis. You will need to be aware of a range of statistical concepts and procedures to proceed. Useful references for further reading on these areas are Carlberg (2011), Field (2009) and Tabachnik and Fidell (2007).

Section 2:
Report Writing

Chapter 15
Range Descriptors

Introducing the term 'range descriptor' (also known as descriptive categories or qualitative descriptors) and their relevance to report writing.

Case Example 14

You have assessed Glynn, aged 16 years 3 months, and obtained four sets of scores from the CELF-4[UK] Word Definitions subtest, KTEA-II Decoding Fluency (Form A), the Logical Memory subtest of the *Wechsler Memory Scales – Fourth Edition* (WMS-IV; Wechsler, 2009b) and the WIAT-II[UK]-T Spelling subtest. You observe that the range descriptors given within the test manuals for these test scores are not the same, yet want to write a report that describes Glynn's performance across the four tests in a way that is consistent and understandable to the lay reader. You also experience some confusion about how range descriptors relate to confidence ranges.

Points to Consider

Some people confuse range descriptors (also known as descriptive categories or qualitative descriptors) with confidence ranges. A range descriptor is a term that describes a test score with a qualitative phrase, for example, *low average*, and where the score can be placed within the score range for that particular range descriptor. So, for example, for the WIAT-II[UK]-T, the score range from 80-89 has the range descriptor 'low average'. So, any obtained score within this range can be described as being a 'low average' score. All range descriptors for this particular test can be observed on its record form.

Table 15.1 shows the obtained scores for the four subtests.

Table 15.1: Standard and Scaled Scores for Subtests

	CELF-4[UK] Word Definitions	KTEA-II Decoding Fluency (A)	WMS-IV Logical Memory	Spelling WIAT-II[UK]-T
Standard Score		65		82
Scaled Score	6		16	

You are now aware that scaled scores have a mean of 10 but that standard scores have a mean of 100. As mentioned previously, in order to help the lay reader your first task is to convert the scores into a common metric, and we will select standard scores for this purpose. This task will also clarify any confusion between confidence ranges and range descriptors. Look-up tables can be used such as Table 5.1, page 151, in the WMS-IV Technical and Interpretative Manual, and the manual calculation uses the formula:

$$z = \left(\frac{X - M}{SD}\right)$$

where you can convert the scaled scores into *z scores*. So for the scaled score of 6, the formula becomes:

$$z = \left(\frac{6-10}{3}\right)$$

where $M = 10$ and SD is 3 for scaled scores.

Therefore $z = -1.33$ (to 2 decimal places).

Now that you know the *z score*, this can be converted to a standard score using the formula:

$$\text{Score on new scale} = (z \times SD_{new\ scale}) + \overline{X}_{new\ scale}$$

$$= (-1.33 \times 15) + 100$$

$$= 79.75 = 80 \text{ (to nearest whole number)}$$

where $SD_{new\ scale} = 15$ and $\overline{X}_{new\ scale} = 100$.

Likewise, applying the same conversion procedure, the scaled score of 16 for the WMS-IV Logical Memory subtest is converted to a standard score of 120.

The scores for the CELF-4[UK] Word Definitions and WMS-IV Logical Memory subtests enable the conversion to revise Table 15.1 to Table 15.2.

Table 15.2: Standard Scores for Subtests

	CELF-4[UK] Word Definitions	KTEA-II Decoding Fluency (A)	WMS-IV Logical Memory	WIAT-II[UK]-T Spelling
Standard Score	80	65	120	82

You now need to source or calculate the confidence ranges for the four scores, and you have decided to set the confidence level at the 95% level.

The CELF-4[UK] source table is in Table 7.9, page 226. This gives the SE_m for a 16-year-old child on the Word Definitions subtest as 1.16, but you realise that this figure is given in scaled score units. Table 7.3, page 219, gives the coefficient alpha reliability coefficient as .85 and so the SE_m can be calculated from the formula:

$$SE_m = SD\sqrt{1-r}$$

$$= 15\sqrt{1-.85}$$

$$= 15\sqrt{.15}$$

$$= 5.8$$

Having obtained the SE_m, you can then obtain the confidence range for the 95% confidence level by application of the formula:

$$\pm 1.96 \times SE_m = \pm 11.4 = 11 \text{ (to nearest whole number)}$$

Therefore, your standard score of 80 now can lie within the confidence range of 69-91.

Progressing to the standard score of 65 for the KTEA-II Decoding Fluency (A) subtest, referring to Table N.7, page 302 of the KTEA-II Norms Booklet, you observe that the confidence range for this score is ±11 at the 95% confidence level that gives a range of 54-76.

The WMS-IV Logical Memory subtest has an SE_m of 1.34 as confirmed from Table 3.3, page 49, from the Technical and Interpretative Manual. But again, you are aware that the metric is scaled scores and so you need a source of value of reliability coefficient to calculate the SE_m. Table 3.1, page 46, gives the split-half reliability coefficient as .80. Thus, the SE_m is calculated as 6.7, giving a confidence range at the 95% level of ± 7 (to nearest whole number).

The WIAT-II(UK)-T Spelling confidence range information is available in Table D1, page 154. This is given as a 'confidence interval magnitude' for this subtest, which relates to 2 SE_ms, totalling 9 standard score points at the 95% confidence level, and so we can complete the second row of our table (Table 15.3).

The range descriptors are given in the third row for the four scores. Note how the two CELF-4(UK) Word Definitions and WIAT-II(UK)-T Spelling subtest scores of 80 and 82 are described as marginal (or borderline or mild) and low average, respectively, even though they are very close together.

Table 15.3: Range Descriptors for Subtest Scores

	CELF-4(UK) Word Definitions	KTEA-II Decoding Fluency (A)	WMS-IV Logical Memory	WIAT-II(UK)-T Spelling
Standard Score	80	65	120	82
Confidence range (95%)	69-91	54-76	113-127	73-91
Range Descriptor for score	Marginal	Lower extreme	Superior	Low average

The problem is highlighted by sampling some other tests' range descriptors, as shown in Table 15.4, where the range descriptors are given for the full range of scores (first column) for the CELF-4(UK), KBIT-2, KTEA-II, and the Beery VMI. Note that the CELF-4(UK) gives you a choice of range descriptors for the ranges below the standard score of 85.

Table 15.4: Reference Table for Tests' Range Descriptors

CELF-4[UK]	115 and above	Above Average
	86-114	Average
	78-85	Marginal/Borderline/Mild
	71-77	Low Range/Moderate
	70 and below	Very Low Range/Severe
KTEA-II	131 and above	Upper Extreme
	116-130	Above Average
	85-115	Average
	70-84	Below Average
	69 or less	Lower Extreme
Beery VMI	Above 129	Very High
	120-129	High
	110-119	Above Average
	90-109	Average
	80-89	Below Average
	70-79	Low
	Less than 70	Very Low

It is clear that there is no agreed set of range descriptors for the qualitative categorisation of standardised scores and some test manuals do not provide them at all. Authors select range descriptors based on their preferences which can have a range of influences such as professional background, geographical location, maintaining consistency with previous versions of the test or with similar tests, professional guidelines, theoretical model, etc. Any attempt to re-word the content of test manuals may be deemed to be an infringement of copyright whether this is held by the author or publisher.

The issue becomes sensitive when assessors have to conform to external regulations which define score ranges for their own purposes. For example, in the UK each year, the Joint Council for Qualifications (JCQ) publishes regulations for access arrangement at www.jcq.org.uk for GCSE and GCE examinations and gives its own definition of 'below average' as being any standard score below 85.

There is no legal obligation to apply the range descriptors given in test manuals. Clearly, when assessing for the purposes of interpretation according to external regulations that define score ranges in certain ways, it would be wise and may be essential to follow them. However, you do need to write a report that appears to be consistent to the lay reader, in order to minimise queries and complaints as a result of readers erroneously thinking that you are making mistakes or are inconsistent with your application of range descriptors. If you work within an organisation or are a member of a professional body then it may be advisable to check available guidelines or use those provided by your professional body. If none exist, consider collaborating with others to create a harmonised set of standards which you will all use consistently.

Consider devising a table such as Table 15.4 that will give you a means of speedily looking up range descriptors for all the tests that you use. It is useful to have the other type of standardised score such as T, percentiles, etc, as well in this table.

An additional feature to take into account when writing your report is when the confidence ranges for an observed score overlap the range descriptors. So, in our example for the CELF-4[UK] score of 80 that lies in the marginal/borderline/mild range, we note that the confidence range spans another two range descriptors: low range/moderate and average. When writing the report, the writer may find that their choice of words appears to be somewhat tortuous, such as, *'Glynn's CELF-4[UK] Word Definitions score of 80 lies within a 95% confidence range of 69-91 that can be taken as lying across the marginal, moderate and average ranges.'*

You will also most probably hesitate to use some of the test manuals' range descriptors because of their emotional loading. Descriptors such as *poor, borderline, very poor, very low,* etc, are likely to be received badly by the reader who may be the parent or the young person you have assessed. These descriptors reflect the history of test construction at the time when tests were often primarily used for selection purposes such as immigration control, identification for categories of mental handicap, or placement in special schools (Zenderland, 1998). In addition, it was unusual for assessment reports to be made available to the primary client (the person being assessed) and so less attention was given to the impact on the client of using such terms.

In effect, you have six options. You can:

1) conform to the regulations laid down by an external body (such as JCQ) if your assessment report is for use in that body's arena

2) continue to use each test's range descriptors when referring to the test scores but have some sort of footnote reference within the main body of the report that highlights the issue

3) ignore the test manuals' descriptors; define your own and display them in a table somewhere in the report as a reference for the reader and apply these to your observed test scores

4) do not use range descriptors and explain the scores in different ways for example, by referring to percentiles and explaining what percentile scores mean

5) employ option (3) for the main body of your report but refer to range descriptors within the appendix of the report that provides the reference of all your test scores for the reader to appraise

6) conform to any guidance given to you by the organisation you work for and/or seek guidance from your professional body.

Above all, you need to be consistent with your chosen option within each report.

Note also that in the US and in research settings there is a trend to refer to the normal range as lying between the standard score range of 85-115, i.e. within one standard deviation ($z = \pm 1$) either side of the mean of 100 within the standard normal distribution curve. This is because of the growing preference to distinguish between relative and normative weaknesses for the purposes of definition of specific learning difficulties and certain theoretical challenges to the ability-attainment discrepancy model. It is likely that this range descriptor format will grow in importance and frequency of usage over future years and this area is discussed in Chapter 18.

Chapter 15 Range Descriptors

Whichever option you select, you still need to evolve a style of report writing that enables the reader to understand your report and how your concepts relate to the obtained test scores. Here, it is important to design the overall framework of the report in such a way as to promote communication with the reader. Essentially, it is wise to place scores and references to statistical interpretation in the report's appendix, use the main body of the report to convey your views and arguments, and have a summary that can 'stand alone' and that gives the essence of your diagnostic assessment's findings and final conclusions. In addition, you need to be wary about using vernacular terms such as 'good', 'bright', etc, when report writing whenever describing children. Your description of a child presenting as a 'bright child' where you meant for the adjective bright to refer to, say, his alertness may be interpreted by the parent as confirming that her child has a high level of cognitive ability. Some terms such as 'gifted', tend to have a specific meaning (e.g. 98th percentile or higher) and should only be used when criteria are available to apply when making this diagnosis.

Chapter 16
Data Merging and *Auto Text*

The process of report writing can be time-consuming, repetitive, and prone to error. At the end of a typical diagnostic assessment, the assessor will be faced with a mass of completed record forms, scribbled notes, and thoughts, all of which need to be condensed and communicated into a clear, consistent message to the reader. Time is of the essence in order to trap the dynamic essence of one's views and perceptions about the client before crucial information is forgotten or reconstrued, but care will always be needed to avoid making simple mistakes that could be costly and embarrassing. Commonly observed mistakes are referring to a client with the wrong gender (*'Julie gave good attention, his speech was clear...'*), incorrect dating and age calculation, incorrect transposing of scores from forms to reports, inconsistent referencing of scores within the report (such as referring to a score of, for example 90 on a spelling test in one section of the report and then referring to the score as 100 in another section), getting the client's name wrong within the report, etc.

Therefore, the assessor is strongly advised to learn about useful word processing resources to save valuable time and reduce the chances of making errors.

Most experienced assessors design templates for their report writing but stop at this point without giving further thought to refining the process to give additional help. One danger of such templates is that they tempt the assessor to adopt standard ways of reporting and thus the individuality of the report may sometimes be threatened. Each diagnostic report should be unique, in that each client's circumstances being assessed are unique. Therefore, when using templates, the assessor needs to see them as a framework within which this individuality is protected.

It is advisable to have a goal of regularly refining one's templates and creating core templates that are relevant to certain areas of diagnostic work. An example of such core templates is given in Figure 16.1.

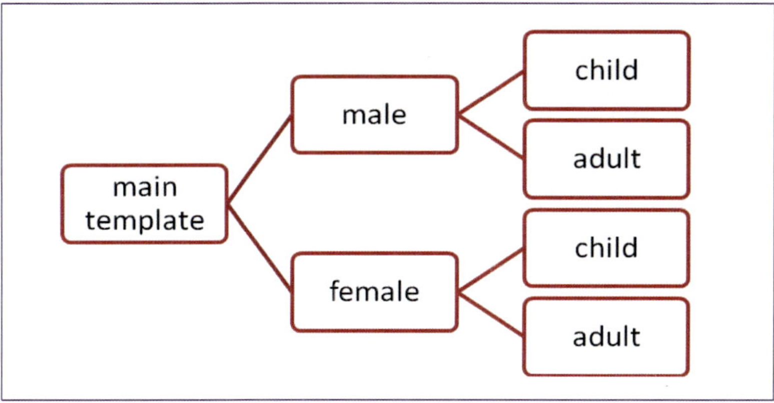

Figure 16.1: Example 1 of Core Templates

Further subdivisions could be considered. Some assessors may decide to base their decisions on a range of frequently used tests, and an example variation here could be as in Figure 16.2.

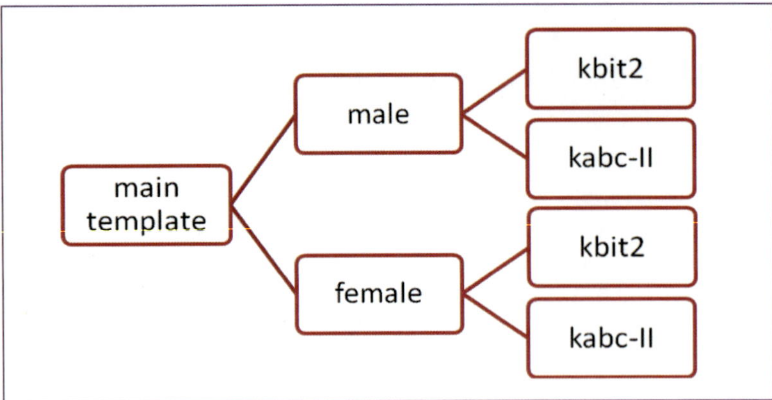

Figure 16.2: Example 2 of Core Templates

Having established a report template, one may obtain something like Figure 16.3. See the sentences as being extracts of the report for our purposes of learning how data can be merged into this template from a data file. (The apostrophe s ('s) inserts are there to enable the first name of the client to be dropped into the preceding space.)

DIAGNOSTIC ASSESSMENT REPORT

NAME:	
Date of Assessment:	Date of Birth:
School:	Age:

's score on the KBIT-2 Verbal scale was which lies within the range. His score on the KBIT-2 Nonverbal scale was which lies within the range...

's score on the KTEA-II Reading subtest was which lies within the range...

Figure 16.3: Preparing a Template for Data Merging

Consider now the extract from an *Excel* file in Figure 16.4. We have created a file that lists clients' personal details such as their name, school, etc, and the scores on a sample of tests that have been administered to them. In our example, all three children attend the same school. This file is presented as a sample of a possible file of data fields (the individual categories of information). The assessor would want to decide on their own fields to fit personal circumstances and the data file is designed in conjunction with the template report shown, in part, above in Figure 16.3. Data merging allows for selection of information to be merged, so reports do not have to give reference to the same tests across clients.

Note first that the *Excel* file shows you how to calculate the age of each child by use of the formula given in the formula bar:

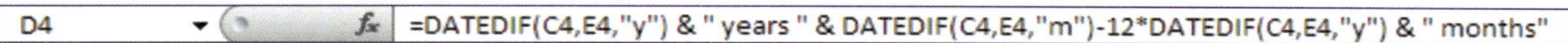

The formula interrogates the columns C (dob) and E (date assessment) and returns the age of the client in years and months by performing the necessary subtraction.

Case Example 15

The example given is for Billy Jones whose age is given as 10 years 3 months in cell D4. Not only does this give you your first check on whether or not you have calculated the correct age of the client, but the format of the information also enables you to 'drop' it directly into your template. 'Pulling down' on the cell D4 will fill the D column for the other children's ages as shown in Figure 16.4.

	A	B	C	D	E	F	G	H	I	J	K	L
1	first name	last name	dob	age	date	school	KBIT2		KBIT2		KTEAII	
2					assessment		Verbal	range v	Nonverbal	range nv	Reading	range re
3												
4	Billy	Jones	21/08/2001	10 years 3 months	25/11/2011	St. Lukes	120	above average	115	average	100	average
5	Paul	Devlin	23/01/2001	10 years 10 months	25/11/2011	St. Lukes	85	average	90	average	75	below average
6	Peter	Brown	16/03/2001	10 years 8 months	25/11/2011	St. Lukes	110	average	93	average	80	below average

Figure 16.4: Data File for Merging

Note how the range descriptors are given for the tests. For the example highlighted, cell D4, the formula for the range descriptor shown below uses the 'IF' function and gives a particular range descriptor for any score lying within any of the ranges which are given in the KBIT-2 manual in Table B.4, page 4, and the KTEA-II manual in Table 3.2, page 25:

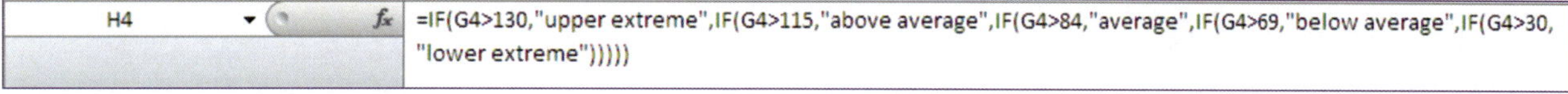

Note that the formula is so long that it continues to a second line. It is wise to check that the number of 'start' brackets equals the number of 'end' brackets in such long formulae, otherwise an error message will be given.

The task now is to drop each client's data into the template to help create his personal report. To do this, we use *Mail Merge in Microsoft Word*.

If you open the *Word* document above, and select *Mailings/ Mail Merge/Step by Step Mail Merge Wizard* you see the information shown in Figure 16.5.

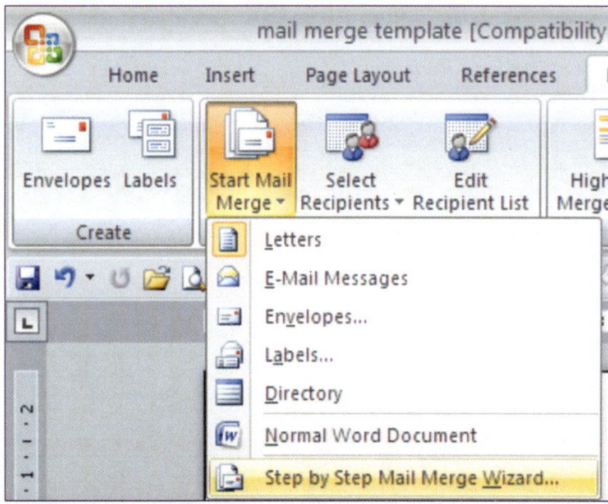

Figure 16.5: Selecting the Mail Merge Wizard in Excel

You then enter a six-step wizard, the first step of which is shown in Figure 16.6.

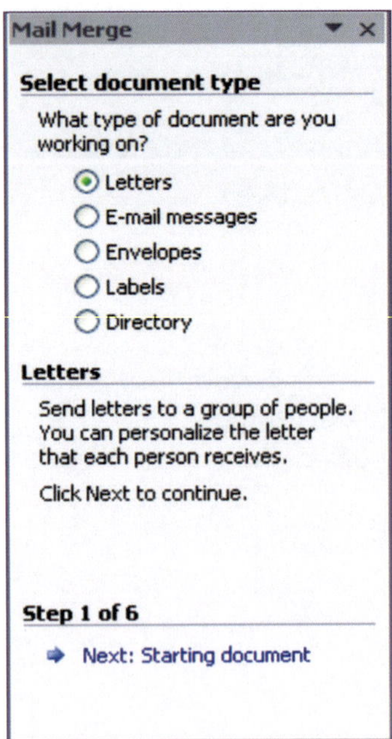

Figure 16.6: Mail Merge Wizard – Step 1

Although you are not using *Mail Merge* for the purposes of writing a letter, you are using it to extract data (personal details and test scores) from one *(Excel)* file and drop it into your report template. The finished product is the 'letter', your diagnostic report. Therefore, in the menu above, you select *Letters* and click *Next* for Step 2 (Figure 16.7).

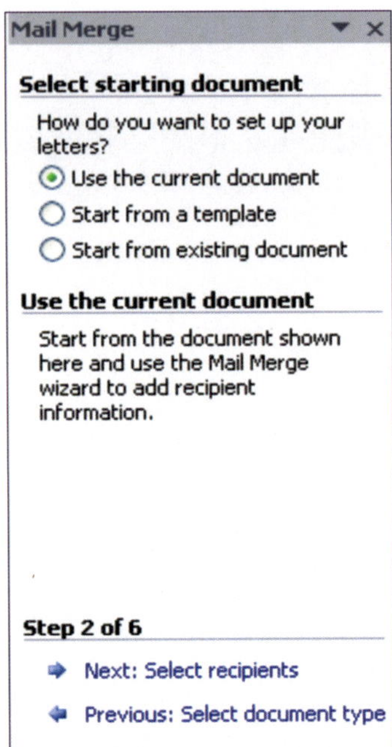

Figure 16.7: Mail Merge Wizard – Step 2

Step 2 is concerned with whether you selected the correct template. If it is already open and ready to use, then select *Use the current document*. Alternatively, select other options to find the template in your computer's directory. Then proceed to the next step, *Next: Select recipients*. This repeats the process of finding the correct file to work on, in this case for the purposes of selecting client details.

This step leads you to opening your *Excel* file and selecting the client, in our case, Billy Jones. Do not be concerned at this stage with the date being in US format (Figure 16.8).

Data Source	✓	last name ▼	first name ▼	dob ▼	age ▼	date
data merge exampl...						assessme
data merge exampl...						
data merge exampl...	✓	Jones	Billy	8/21/2001	10 years 3 months	25/11/20
data merge exampl...		Devlin	Paul	1/23/2001	10 years 10 months	25/11/20
data merge exampl...		Brown	Peter	3/16/2001	10 years 8 months	25/11/20

Figure 16.8: Mail Merge Wizard – Selecting the Client

You are now ready to 'write' your report by going to the next step of clicking, one by one, locations in your template report for each of the field data that will be merged. Select *Next: write your letter* (Figure 16.9).

Figure 16.9: Mail Merge Wizard – Step 3

Your screen will then show your template and the data fields to be selected. At this point, put your cursor on the required place in your document, and click on *Insert* from the *Insert Merge Filed* blue box. Repeat this for all of your required data fields, as in Figure 16.10.

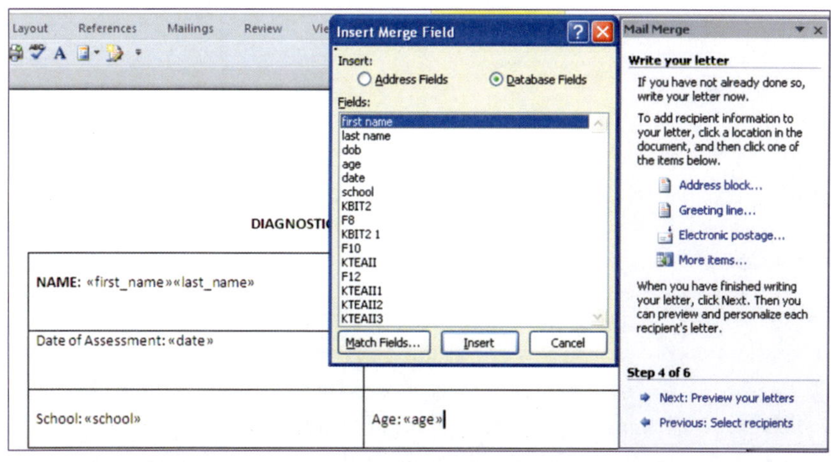

Figure 16.10: Mail Merge Wizard – Inserting Data Fields

You then see your template being prepared to accept the selected data fields by the presence of brackets (Figure 16.11).

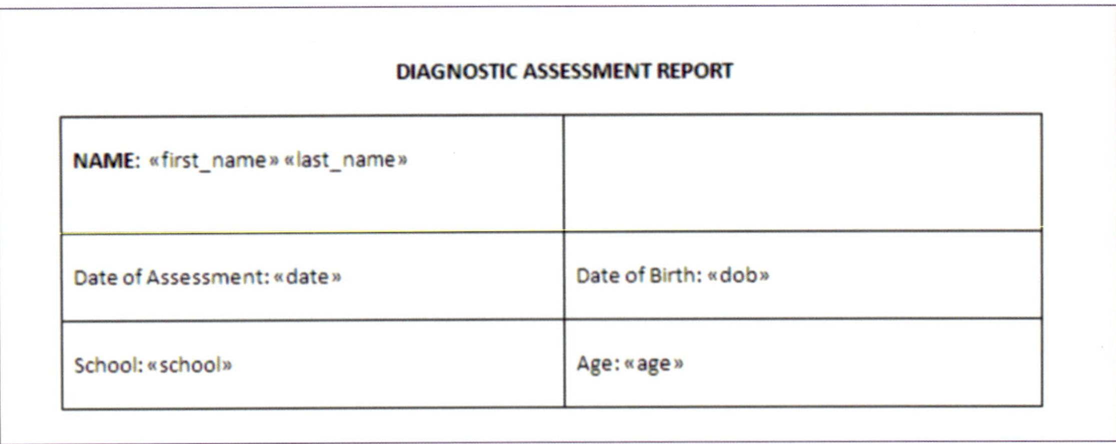

Figure 16.11: Mail Merge Wizard – Template with Data Fields

When you have finished you can check your placements by previewing your report by progressing through Step 4 (Figure 16.12).

Figure 16.12: Mail Merge Wizard – Step 4

This shows you the results of the merge (Figure 16.13). A common mistake noted at this stage is the lack of spaces between insertion points, but do not worry because at every step of the Wizard, you can return to previous steps and make the necessary revisions.

Note that is wise to check that you have set your *Microsoft* and *Excel* Language Options to UK settings. If you find that the date of birth of your client in the merged document as above is given in the US format of months:days rather than days;months, then when previewing your report, Press Alt+F9 together and the date text will be replaced by {MERGEFIELD "DATE"}. Click inside this grey text and add the text { MERGEFIELD "date" \@"DD/MM/YYYY"*Mergeformat}. Repeat this for other dates and age in the document. Good advice on this feature is given at http://www.computeractive.co.uk/ca/pc-help/1913624/change-mail-merge-date-format-excel.

Press Alt and F9 again to return to the preview of the merged field.

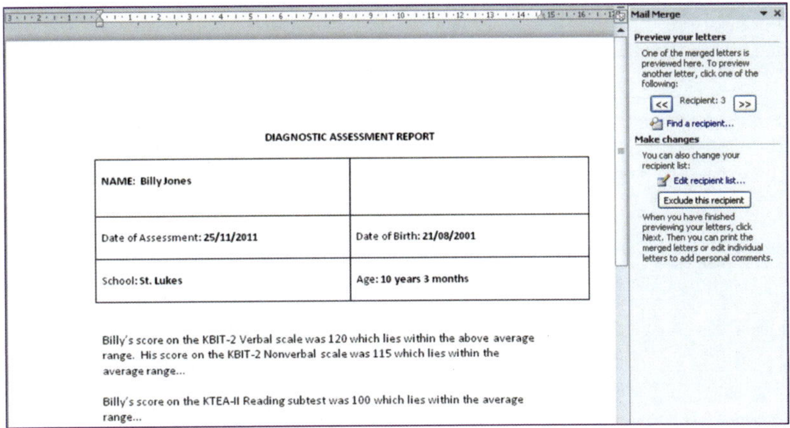

Figure 16.13: Mail Merge Wizard – Step 5

You can then either print the finished report at Step 6 (Figure 16.14) or select it to edit for further revisions, as you would do normally with any *Word* file.

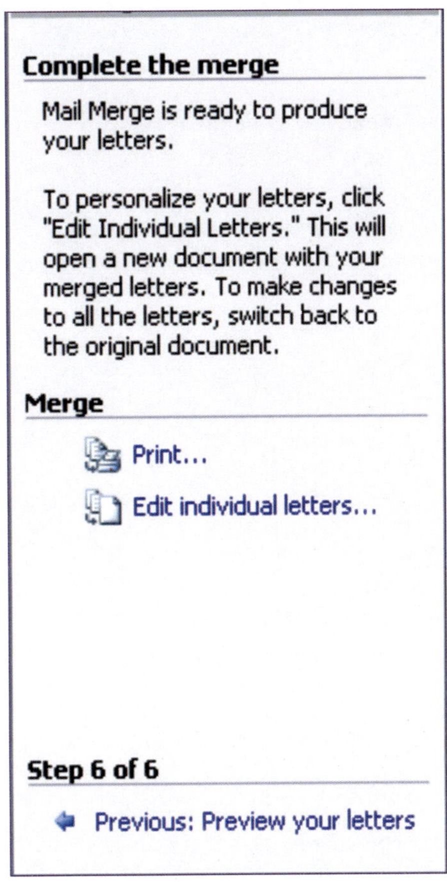

Figure 16.14: Mail Merge Wizard – Step 6

<table>
<tr><td colspan="2" align="center">DIAGNOSTIC ASSESSMENT REPORT</td></tr>
<tr><td>NAME: Billy Jones</td><td></td></tr>
<tr><td>Date of Assessment: 25/11/2011</td><td>Date of Birth: 21/08/2001</td></tr>
<tr><td>School: St. Lukes</td><td>Age: 10 years 3 months</td></tr>
</table>

Billy's score on the KBIT-2 Verbal scale was 120 which lies within the above average range. His score on the KBIT-2 Nonverbal scale was 115 which lies within the average range...

Billy's score on the KTEA-II Reading subtest was 100 which lies within the average range...

Billy's score on the KTEA-II Decoding subtest was 86 which lies within the average range...

Billy's score on the KTEA-II Reading Fluency subtest was 86 which lies within the average range...

Figure 16.15: Final Mail Merged Report

The finished report (Figure 16.15) is guaranteed to reflect the same data selected from the *Excel* file and thus the risk of making transposing errors is significantly reduced. However, errors can still be made during the initial input of your data into *Excel* and it is therefore wise to double-check after this stage. It is advisable to proofread reports from a printed copy.

An added advantage in storing assessment data in this way is that it offers a means by which you can interrogate data across clients to provide overview data for a range of purposes. These could be: to offer a report on your total client involvement in a school or college over the year; obtain revised local norms for the client base selected; research the data using the statistical functions in *Excel* or export the file to a statistical package such as IBM SPSS Statistics; draw graphs for group data; analyse the data across assessors by querying the same data fields for the purposes of moderation; and so on.

Use of *Auto Text*

Building blocks are reusable sections of *Word* documents such as titles or conclusions that are stored in galleries. *Auto Text* is a type of building block.

Auto Text is a useful command option that enables you to reduce the need to type frequently used words, sentences and paragraphs when preparing diagnostic reports. It differs from the use of templates because templates provide you with the same word framework for all reports. *AutoText* is used when you frequently use the same wording across reports, but not always. *Auto Text* is therefore more flexible than templates for the purposes of saving time and promoting individuality across reports.

An example might be the paragraph:

> <<name>> *was very polite during the assessment and he engaged in conversation with me with good social skills and clear speech. He separated well from his parents at the start of the assessment and gave good concentration over the assessment time period.* <<name>> *appeared motivated to try his best with all assessment tasks. He appeared to be well on the day of the assessment.*

You can predict using such a paragraph for the majority of your clients, but not all of them. You wish to store the paragraph for future use but you would rather not place it in your template because of the risk of making an error when reporting about clients for whom the description is inappropriate.

The operation of *Auto Text* differs significantly from *Word 2003* to later versions. The first stage is to add the Auto Text icon to the Quick Access Toolbar. This toolbar is available below the main *Word* tab options, as seen in Figure 16.16. In this example, the Quick Access Toolbar is shown with a range of icons and with the pull-down menu for customising the options also displayed.

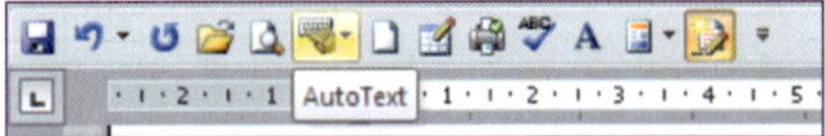

Figure 16.16: Microsoft's Quick Access Toolbar

To insert the *Auto Text* command, click on the Microsoft Office button in the top of the screen, and select *Word Options*. Then click *Customise* and your screen will show in the information in Figure 16.17.

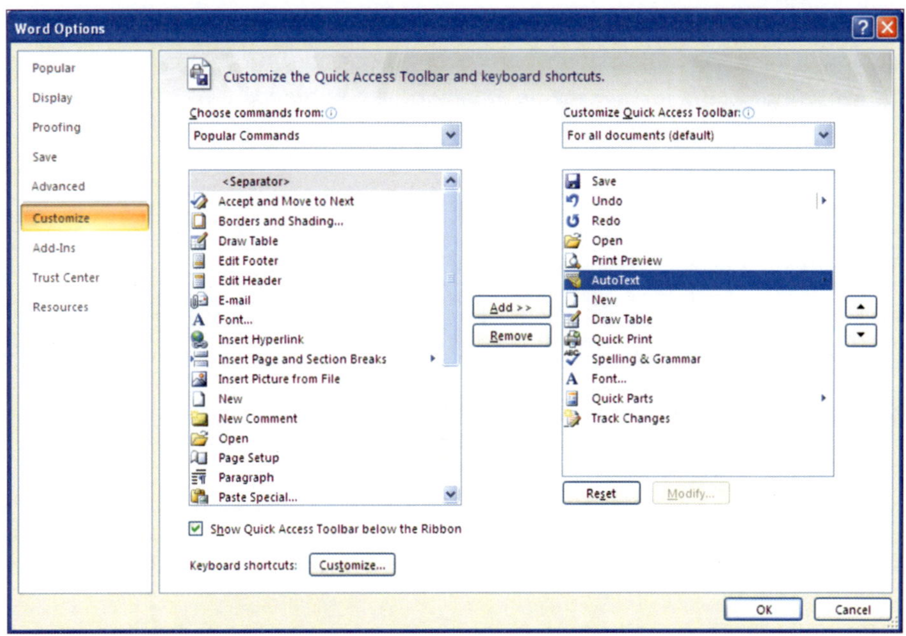

Figure 16.17: Customising the Quick Access Toolbar for *Auto Text*

There are a range of command options in the left hand option box to be selected for the Quick Access Toolbar in the right hand box. Here you can see that *Auto Text* has been selected by clicking *Add* and is highlighted in the right hand box, together with other selected commands. Clicking *OK* will add the *Auto Text* icon to the Quick Access Toolbar.

To create a new *Auto Text*, select and copy the text that you want to use from your *Word* document then click on the *Auto Text* icon. Click *Save Selection to Auto Text Gallery*, and you will see a screen as in Figure 16.18.

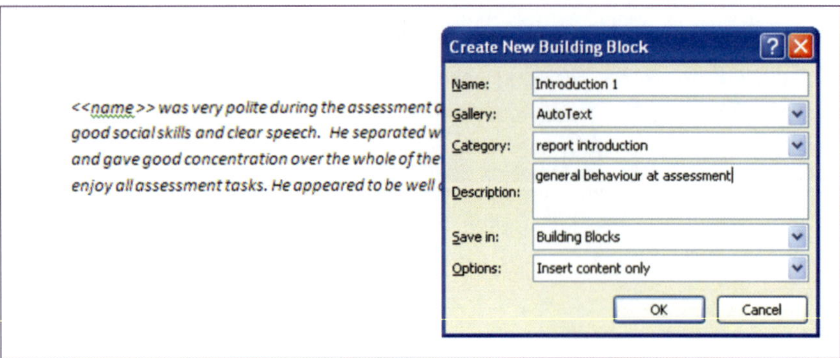

Figure 16.18: Creating a New Auto Text

You then complete the dialogue box as follows.

- Give your building block a unique *Name*. At this point you may wish to consider how you should categorise the names. If you were, for example, building up a bank of recommendations rather than focusing on the introduction section of your report, you could consider *recommendation1*, or *memory1*, etc.

- *Gallery* refers to the type of building block you are concerned with, for example, if you were building up a store of headers, you would select *Headers* from the gallery selection.

- *Categories* refers to the sets of building blocks. For example, you may wish to create collections of *Auto Text* inserts for the categories of *Recommendations, Reasons for Referral, Conclusion, Appendices*, etc.

- *Description* gives you a means of remembering what the *Auto Text* item is, and *Save in* gives you the choice of not saving to a category or choosing a category.

- *Options* enables you to decide if you want the insert to be standard text for merging into continuous text, or to stand alone as a paragraph or as a separate page. An example of a separate page option might be the first introductory page of your report, the title of a section of the report, etc.

To insert an *Auto Text*, click in the document where you want the block to be placed and on the *Insert* tab, in the Text group, click *Quick Parts and then Building Blocks Organizer*. Select your chosen *Auto Text* as highlighted in blue in Figure 16.19 and click *Insert* to place it in your document. Then close the Building Blocks Organizer.

Another useful function is being able to add blocks of text or individual words and phrases to your document as you type. To do this, format your word processor to insert text when you type a code that is associated with the stored text.

Suppose you wanted to be able to insert automatically the following test title, the WIAT-II^{UK}-T.
When you have typed this text, select it with your mouse and click the Microsoft Office button, then click *Word Options* (Figure 16.20).

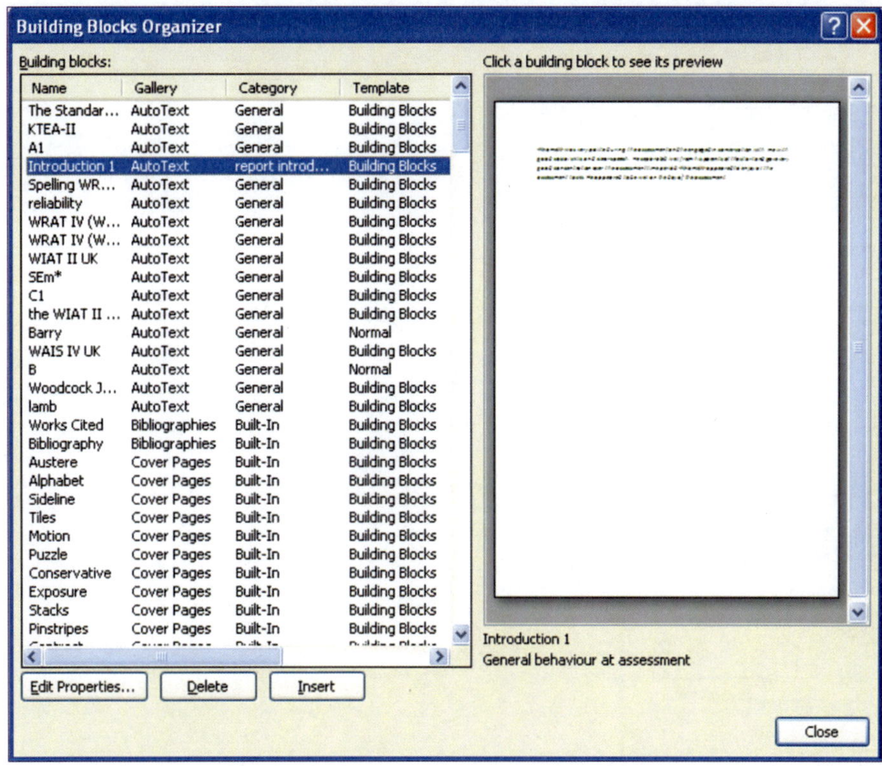

Figure 16.19: Inserting an Auto Text

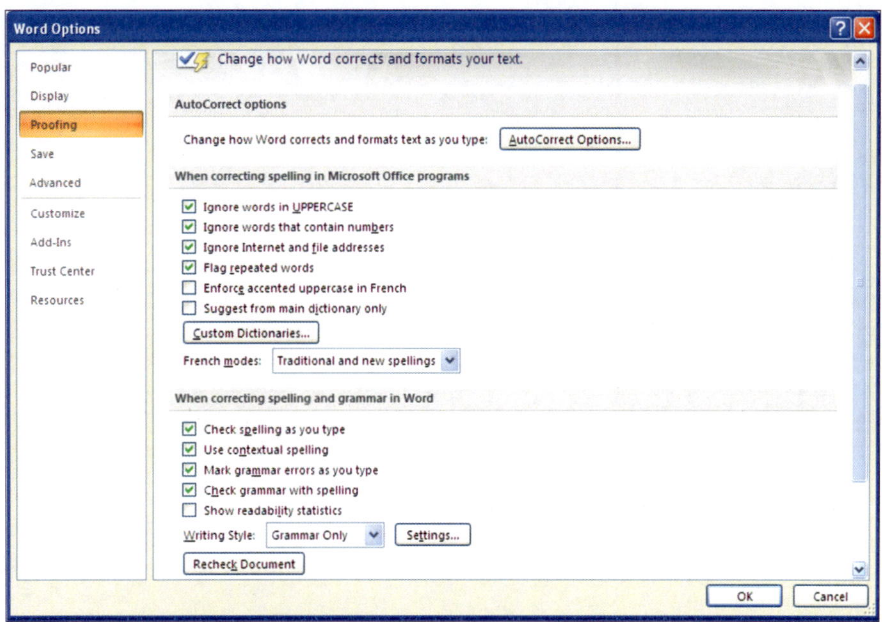

Figure 16.20: Inserting Auto Text *as You Type – Step 1*

Click on *Proofing* (highlighted above), and you see the information in Figure 16.21.

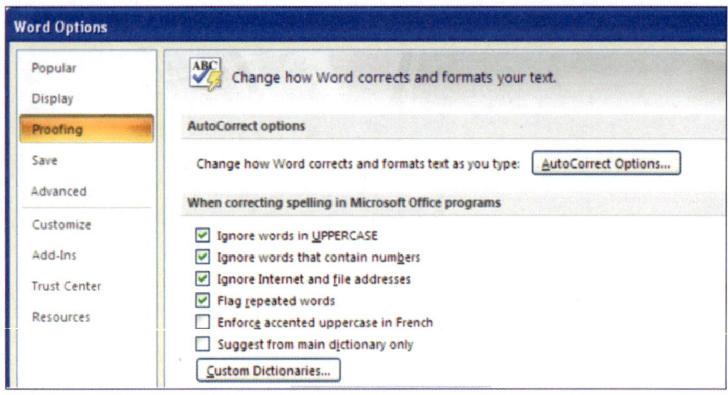

Figure 16.21: Inserting Auto Text *as You Type – Step 2*

Click *AutoCorrect Options* and then the *AutoCorrect* tab to get the Autocorrect dialogue box (Figure 16.22).

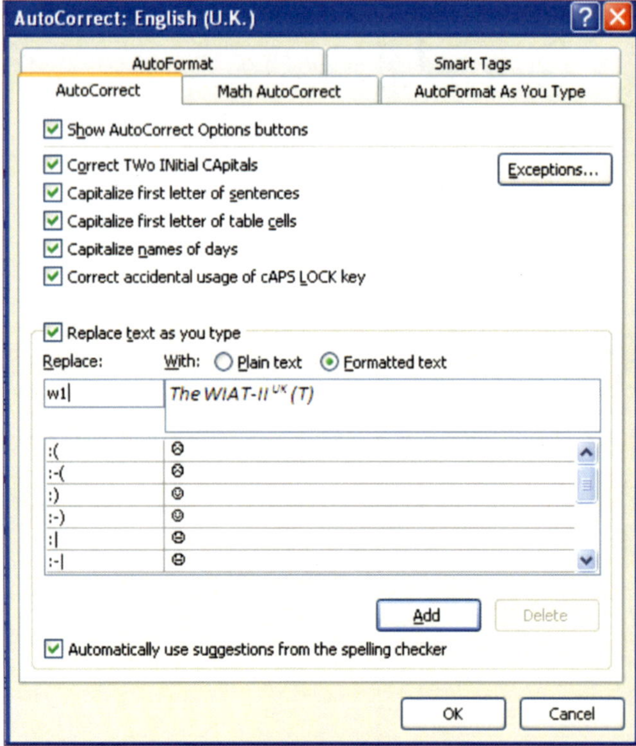

Figure 16.22: Inserting Auto Text *as You Type – Step 3*

It is important to make sure that you now tick the *Replace text as you type* box, if it is empty. You will see your selected text already positioned in the *With window*. Then, under *Replace*, type the characters that you want to use for the automatic text. In the screen shot above, we have selected 'w1'. Then click *Add*.

The next time you type 'w1' and hit the Return or Space key, the text 'WIAT-II^{UK}-T' will appear.

You will need to create a reference log to remember the codes for your inserts. You can create a new file and switch between this file and your report file to retrieve a code. Spilt-screen facility, *View/Split*, can be used to view two pages at the same time. This facility is particularly useful when typing words with sub/superscript fonts and for test titles and their respective subtest titles. If you write many reports, you will save time in the long run by automating repetitive tasks.

When using templates for report writing, it is essential that these templates are content-free of individual client's information. You should **never** use or part-use a previous report as a basis for a new report; a mistake could eventually be made. In addition, it should be remembered that use of a previously written report in electronic format as a palimpsest (a 'canvas' to be painted over again) means that it is likely that personal details of the original client may be able to be recovered via electronic means. Files created by *Word, Excel,* and *PowerPoint* often contain hidden or personal information, such as revisions or comments, that others can access. Depending on the nature of the information, this could place the assessor in an embarrassing or legal position, and even put the assessor's employer at risk.

The assessor needs to know how to respond to requests for reports to be sent electronically via e-mail. If you are employed, then you should adopt the policies of your employer at all times, paying particular attention to any issues that may relate to working at home or across working contexts and use of portable storage devices such as memory sticks. The signing of electronic documents can be a complex area to manage and current legal practice is such that inked signatures of paper documents (i.e. assessment reports) are required. Electronic files can be made more secure using encryption. Encryption is the use of a mathematical system (algorithm) to make information secret from anyone not authorised to use it. It uses a secret key to scramble information applied to files so that only those with the correct key can view them. Modern word-processing systems enable files to be saved in PDF (Portable Document Format). PDF was invented by Adobe Systems and is now the global standard for capturing and reviewing information from almost any application on any computer system and sharing it. PDF files have the advantage of displaying information such as charts and figures in high-quality resolution. They are also more resistant to attempts to modify them by other people. Summary advice for the assessor in this complex area is to:

- have a working knowledge of the Data Protection Act 1988

- confirm if you need to register as a Data Controller

- learn about encryption of report files for sending by e-mail

- evolve a policy on the use of electronic signatures for reports

- avoid distributing unencrypted electronic copies of your scanned signature

- always sign paper copies of reports in blue or black ink

- understand that electronic files often have hidden information within them, even though it cannot be seen

- design templates that are content-free of clients' personal information

- consider saving reports in PDF

- regularly 'clean' the files stored in your computer using commercially available software

- evolve a storage, circulation, and destruction policy for data that is in line with Data Protection requirements. Summarise this policy in your reports. If an employee, adopt your employer's policies.

Chapter 17
Using Charts in Reports

Introducing:

- **charts and inserting them into reports**
- **making use of z scores**
- **using Stock Charts and Error Bars as a means of presenting confidence ranges within a report**
- **creating trendlines within Precision Teaching charts.**

As a diagnostic assessor, you are likely to use terms that lay readers (such as most parents) cannot easily understand. You therefore need to style your reports to communicate their essential features with minimum effort required by the reader. The advantages of providing charts are that they can summate test scores, provide information in a visual medium, and highlight main areas of weakness and strengths. Charts are therefore a useful tool for the assessor. However, the process of designing and inserting charts can be time-consuming and therefore it is important to consider design options in the early stages of report-template creation.

Charts and Z Scores

Z scores are a very useful type of metric of standard scoring. They reflect the deviation from the mean in precise units of standard deviation. As they are the only commonly used score that can be reported with minus and positive values, this feature can be taken advantage of when placing charts within reports. This is because one can centralise easily the mean with minus scores on the left and positive scores on the right of any profile distribution.

For example, Table 17.1 shows scaled scores for subtests from the WMS-IV. Scaled scores have a mean of 10 as discussed earlier.

Table 17.1: WMS-IV Subtest Scaled Scores

Subtest	Scaled Scores
Logical Memory 1	14
Logical Memory 2	11
Verbal Paired Associates 1	8
Verbal Paired Associates 2	7
CVLT-II Trials 1-5	15
CVLT-II Long-Delay	6
Designs 1	10
Designs II	12
Visual Reproduction 1	18
Visual Reproduction 2	8
Spatial Addition	14
Symbol Span	9

If you now create an *Excel* file, and convert the standard scores into *z* scores by using the formula:

$$z = \frac{a - \overline{X}}{SD}$$

where *a* = standard score, and for standard scores $\overline{X}$ = mean(10), *SD* = standard deviation (3).

The *z* scores are as shown in Figure 17.1.

	Sub-test	Scaled Scores	Z Scores
1	Sub-test	Scaled Scores	Z Scores
2	Logical Memory 1	14	1.33
3	Logical Memory 2	11	0.33
4	Verbal Paired Associates 1	8	-0.67
5	Verbal Paired Associates 2	7	-1.00
6	CVLT-II Trials 1-5	15	1.67
7	CVLT-II Long-Delay	6	-1.33
8	Designs 1	10	0.00
9	Designs II	12	0.67
10	Visual Reproduction 1	18	2.67
11	Visual Reproduction 2	8	-0.67
12	Spatial Addition	14	1.33
13	Symbol Span	9	-0.33

Figure 17.1: Creating a Table of Subtest Z Scores in Excel

You can see that the highlighted cell C2 has the above formula in the formula bar. Pulling down the cell reveals the *z* scores for the other subtests.

Now select *Insert, Chart, Bar,* and select the highlighted choice as shown in Figure 17.2.

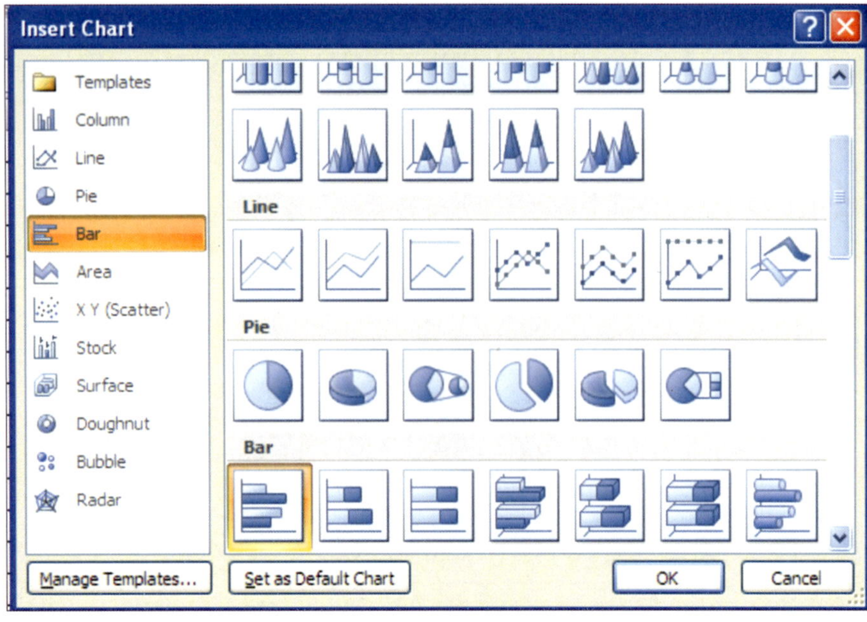

Figure 17.2: Creating a Chart – Step 1

Select *OK*, and you see the chart as shown in Figure 17.3.

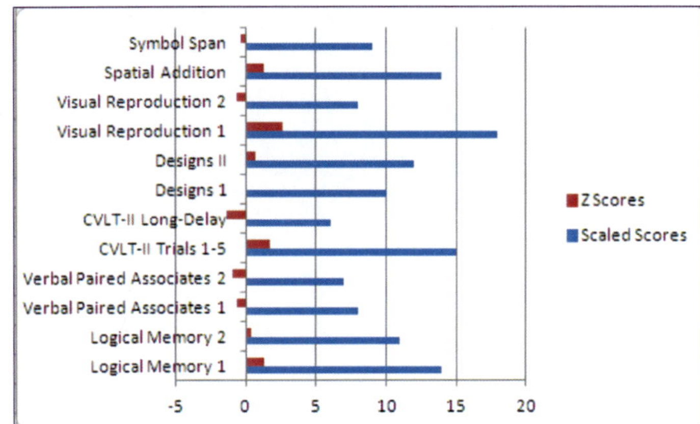

Figure 17.3: Creating a Chart – Step 2

The blue rows represent the standard scores from the table and the red rows are the *z* scores. As you do not want the standard scores in the chart, simply place your cursor on one of the blue rows, right click, and select *Delete*, as seen in Figure 17.4.

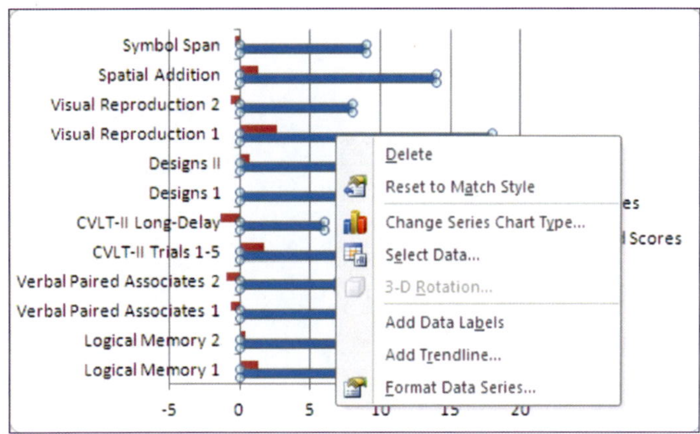

Figure 17.4: Creating a Chart – Step 3

You then see the chart that is shown in Figure 17.5.

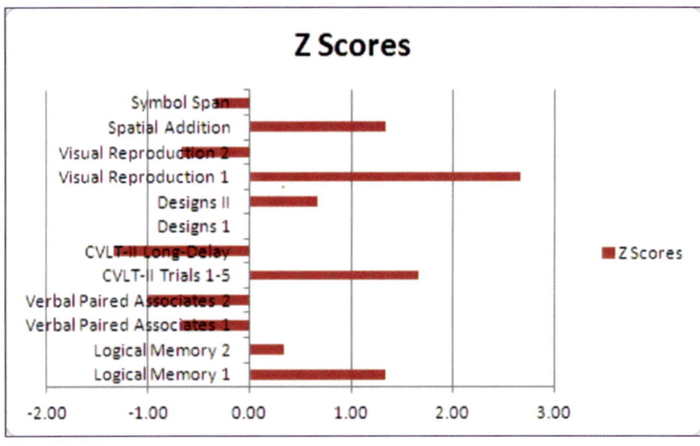

Figure 17.5: Creating a Chart – Step 4

You will see from the horizontal axis at the top of Figure 17.5 that the left-hand side starts with the z value -2 whilst the right hand side ends with +3. To revise the chart to start from -3 on the left and therefore to be balanced and in accordance with the z score range for the standard normal distribution curve, click on the number 2 of this range, see Figure 17.6.

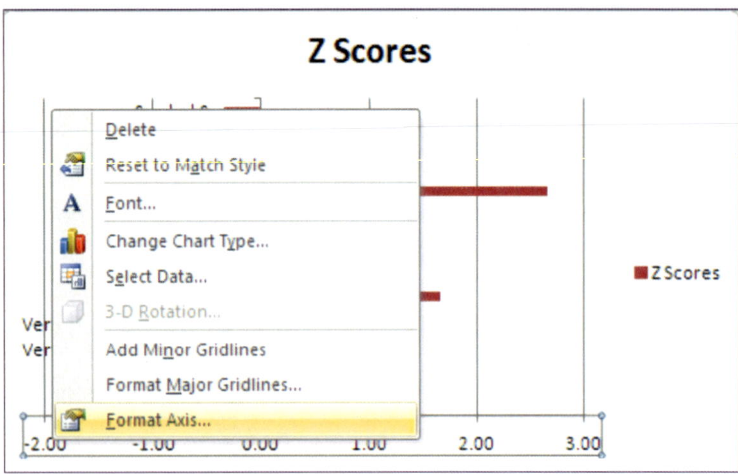

Figure 17.6: Creating a Chart – Step 5

Now select the highlighted *Format Axis* at the bottom of the option column, to see the screen as in Figure 17.7.

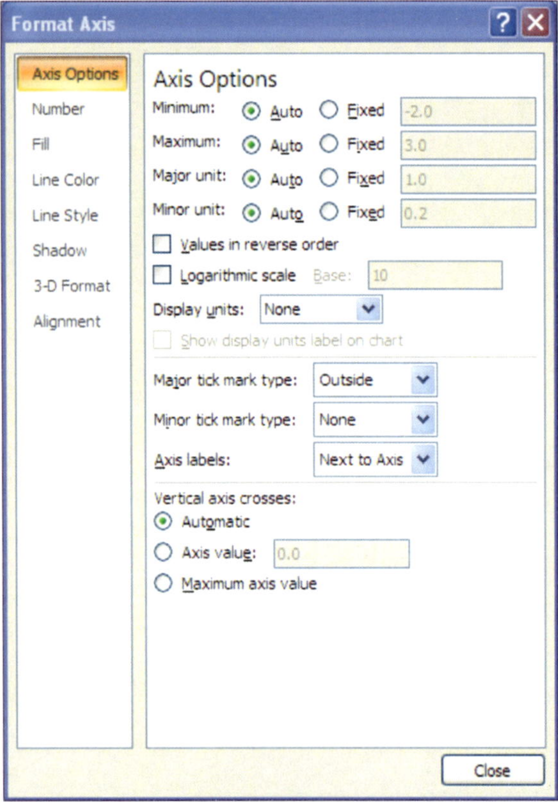

Figure 17.7: Creating a Chart – Step 6

Now click the *Axis Option* button at the top for 'Fixed' and the grey cell to the right of this button becomes active. Type '-3' and go to the bottom right and select *Close*.

The chart extends to cover the z range from -3, as shown in Figure 17.8.

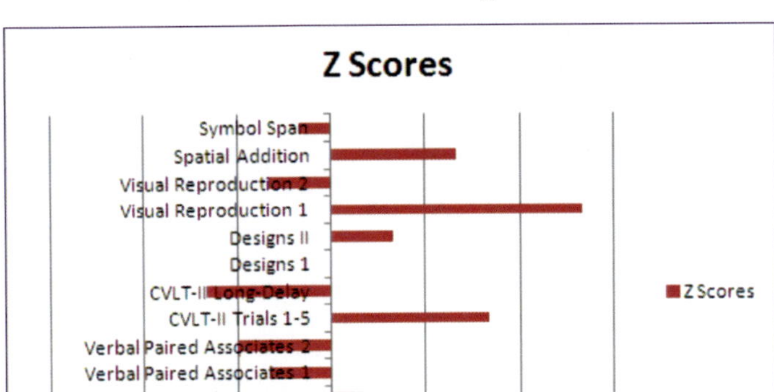

Figure 17.8: Creating a Chart – Step 7

The chart appears confusing to the reader because of the overlapping of words by the red colour, so we now edit the presentation by right-clicking/deleting the legend and title that were automatically created by the *Excel* chart wizard (or substituting your own wording). Then, you need to shift the row titles by right clicking on one of the titles and selecting *Format Axis*. Pull down the *Axis Labels*, and select *Low*, to see, as in Figure 17.9.

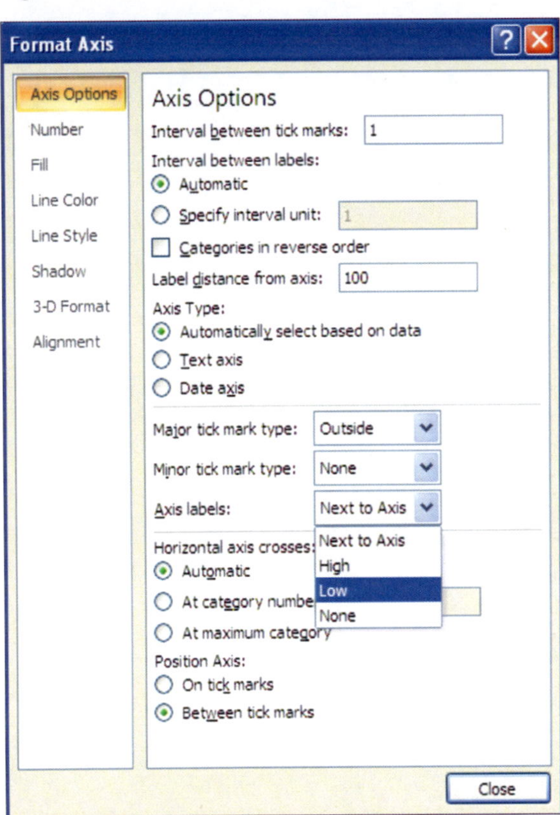

Figure 17.9: Creating a Chart – Step 8

You then see the chart as in Figure 17.10.

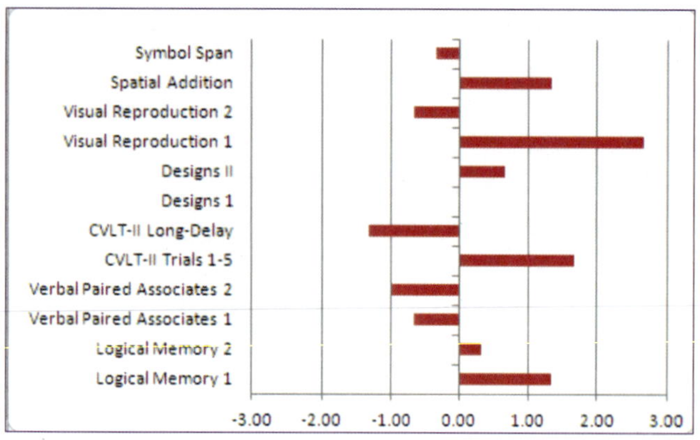

Figure 17.10: Creating a Chart – Step 9

However, note the row for *Designs 1*. Here there is no coloured row and there appears to be a score missing. This is because the score was an average score, which in *z* values = 0. One way to avoid this is to place your cursor on any one of the red rows, right click, and select *Add Data Labels*, as in Figure 17.11.

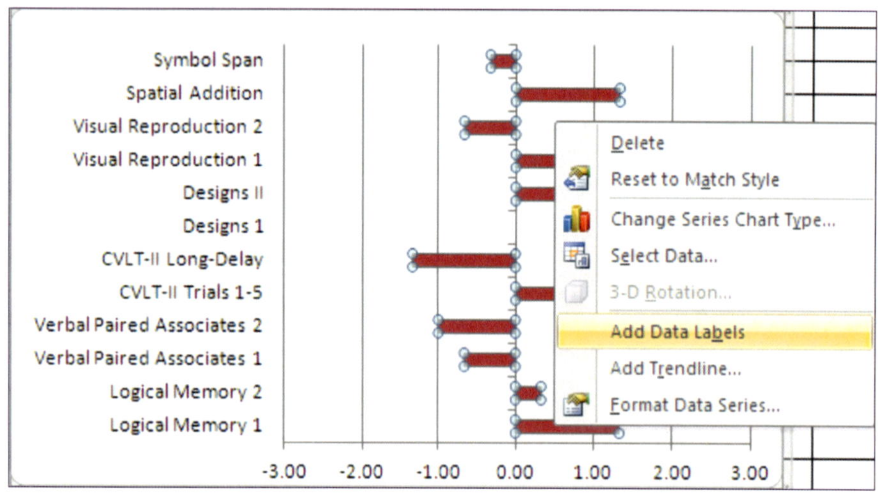

Figure 17.11: Creating a Chart – Step 10

You can see that the *Design 1* row has been given a value of 0, as in Figure 17.12.

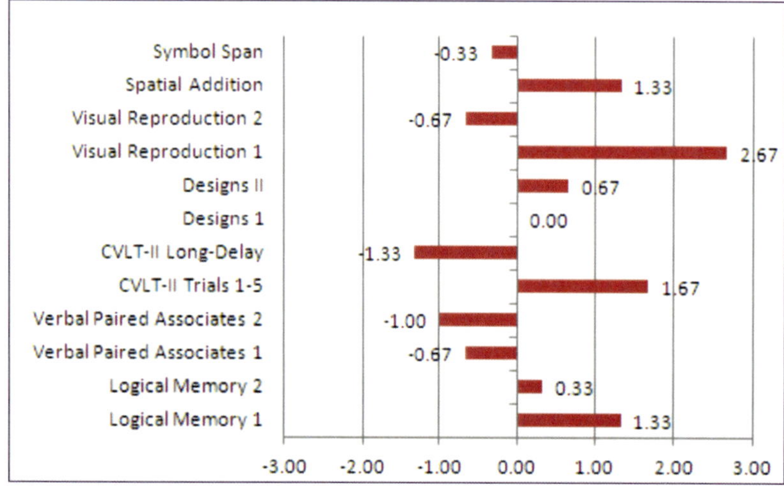

Figure 17.12: Creating a Chart – Step 11

The chart can be edited further to suit personal choice and circumstances. For example, you may decide to exchange the names of the subtests for labels that best describe the abilities being measured. It is also possible to present the scores in a required order such as highest to lowest. You may wish to add minor grid lines, place text or colour to emphasise and contrast weak and strong scores, etc. Right clicking and copying the chart in *Excel* will allow you to work across files and paste the image into your report at the most suitable point, either in the appendices or in the section where you wish to comment on the profile of your client's strengths and weaknesses. In our experience the lay reader focuses more on the visual profile of the chart's representation of the client's strengths and weaknesses, rather than the values of scores represented. This aids conversation between the assessor and the client but, of course, the report retains the scores as permanent record and for additional inspection.

Such a bar chart does not need you to employ z scores. Scaled scores can also be used but you would need to edit the horizontal axis to have the mean of 10 as the intersection value for meeting the vertical axis. Right-clicking on the horizontal axis and then selecting *Format Axis*, gives you the means of altering the range of your scores. Figure 17.13 adopts the range as 4 (minimum) to 19 (maximum). We have also selected the unit of 10 for our *Vertical Axis Crosses*. It is this choice that separates the relatively weak scores from the relatively high scores around the scaled score mean of 10.

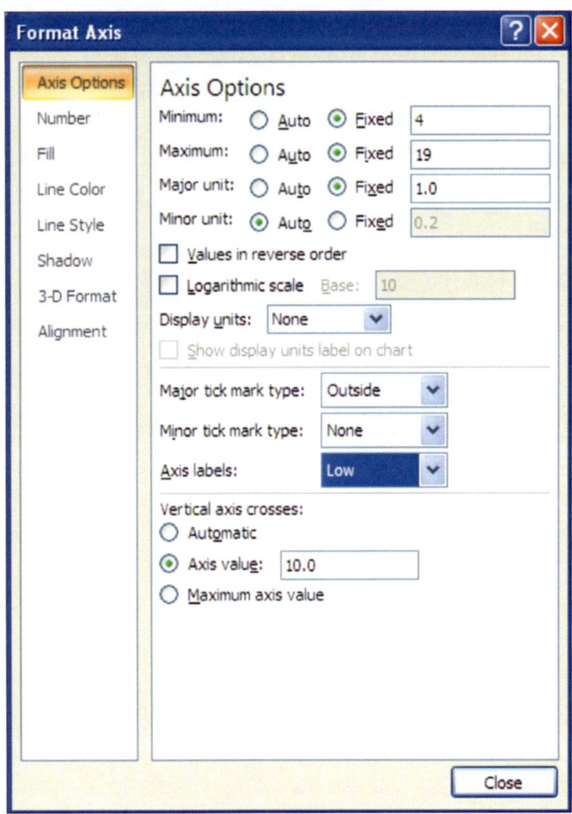

Figure 17.13: Setting the Range of Scores in Excel

After closing, you then get your chart, as in Figure 17.14, which you can edit further according to your styling preference.

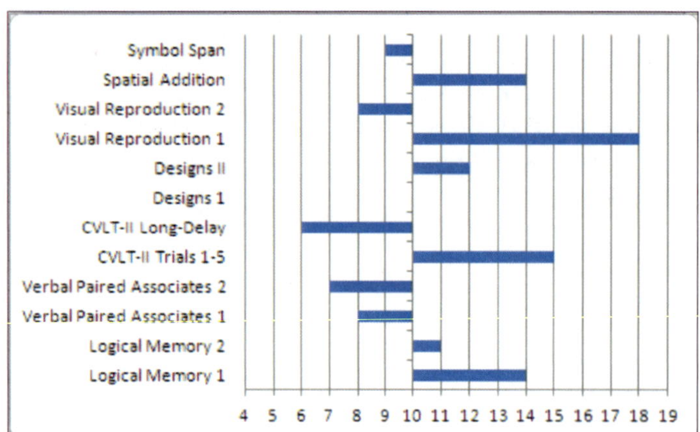

Figure 17.14: Example Chart of Scaled Scores

Creating a Stock Chart

As the name implies, a stock chart was originally designed to illustrate the fluctuation of stock prices. As the concept of confidence ranges are extremely difficult to put across to the lay reader, the use of stock charts is extremely useful. The diagnostic assessor can not only show the client his spread of scores within a clear visual profile but also show the impact of confidence ranges on the diagnostic interpretation of the meaning of the presented profile.

It is always worth considering which data fields you should record in *Excel* as you prepare and organise your report-writing strategies and methods of statistical analyses. Time spent here will save you more time when assessing and preparing your reports. You will not be able to predict your needs and preferences in later months and years, so review your systems at regular intervals and make changes as you go, rather than have to start again from scratch. Rather than reinvent the wheel, note how your colleagues approach their work and learn from them. Considering the data fields required for confidence ranges is a very good example of deciding early on what to record. The following examples give you options to consider.

Case Example 16

Table 17.2 shows scaled scores for CELF-4[UK] subtests for Phoebe, aged 15 years and 11 months.

Table 17.2: CELF-4[UK] Subtest Scaled Scores

Subtest	Abbreviation	Scaled Score
Recalling Sentences	RS	12
Formulating Sentences	FS	14
World Classes (Receptive)	WCR	6
World Classes (Expressive)	WCE	11
Word Definitions	WD	13
Understanding Spoken Paragraphs	USP	5
Sentence Assembly	SA	7
Semantic Relationships	SR	3
Number Repetition Forwards	NRF	15
Number Repetitions Backwards	NRB	8
Familiar Sequences	FSq	10

In Table C, page 308, of the CELF-4[UK] manual you are given a source of confidence ranges and, for the purposes of this example, we will choose the 95% level of confidence. If we create an *Excel* file as shown in Figure 17.15, you will note that we have repeated the subtest scores in the columns, C and D. These repeated scores have the lower limit of their confidence range in column B (CR-), and the higher limit in column E (CF+). Select your data and titles (data labels) and drag from cell A1 to E12.

A	B	C	D	E
CELF4[UK]	CR-	score	score	CR+
RS	10	12	12	14
FS	11	14	14	17
WCR	4	6	6	8
WCE	9	11	11	13
WD	11	13	13	15
USP	2	5	5	8
SA	5	7	7	9
SR	1	3	3	5
NRF	12	15	15	18
NRB	5	8	8	11
FSq	7	10	10	13

Figure 17.15: Creating a Stock Chart – Step 1

From the Insert menu, select *Other Charts/Stock* and from the Stock options available select *Open-High-Low-Close*, as shown in Figure 17.16.

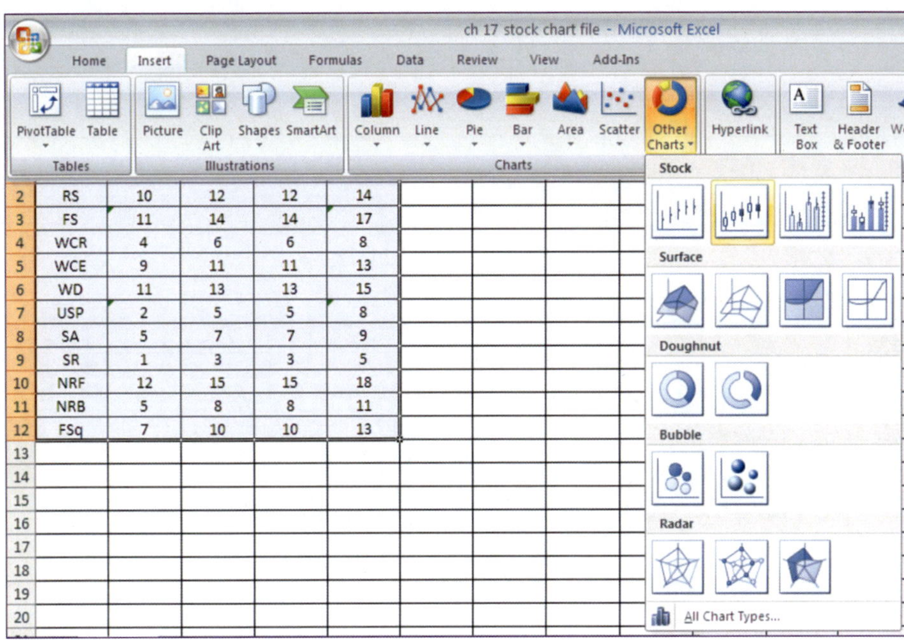

Figure 17.16: Creating a Stock Chart – Step 2

Selecting by clicking will give you the initial chart on your screen as in Figure 17.17.

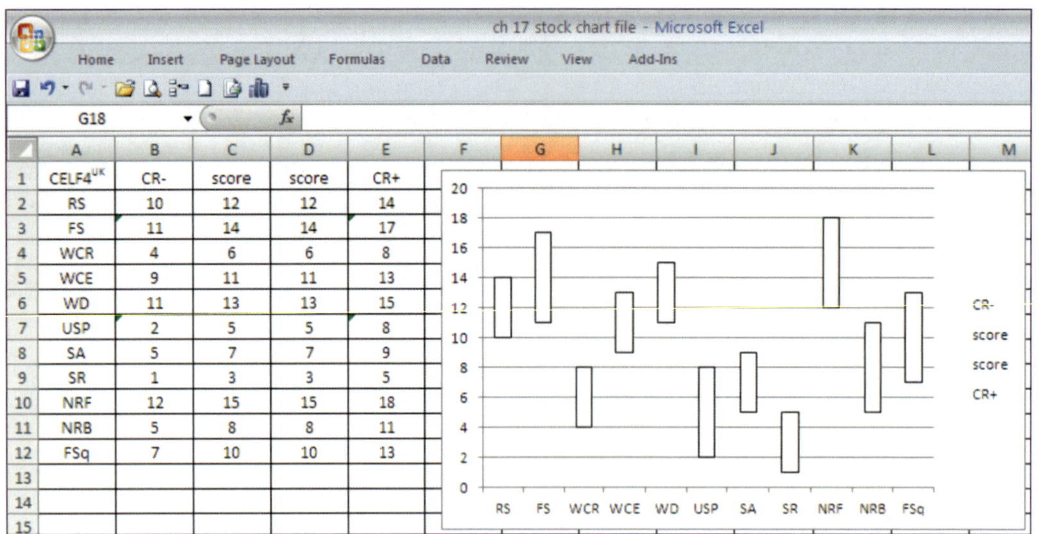

Figure 17.17: Creating a Stock Chart – Step 3

Now, you are ready to redesign the layout of this chart by selecting *Layout* in the Chart menu after you've clicked on the chart. You will find that the *Labels* options shown in Figure 17.18 enable you to restyle your title, change the data range if needed, place more gridlines into the display, and format your stock boxes. The example in Figure 17.19 shows that we have titled the chart *Phoebe's Profile*, inserted minor horizontal gridlines, and coloured the stock boxes.

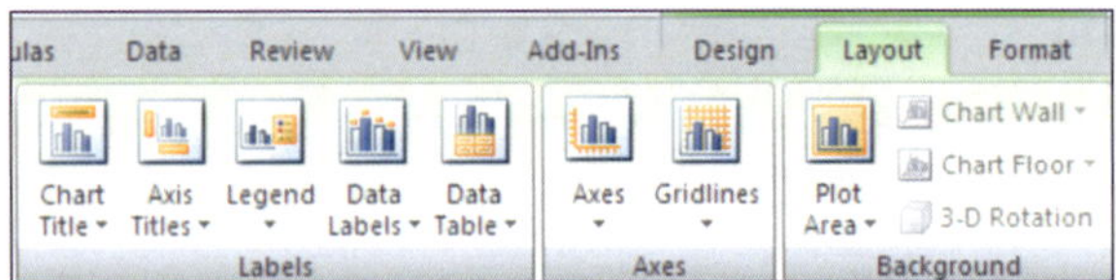

Figure 17.18: Creating a Stock Chart – Step 4

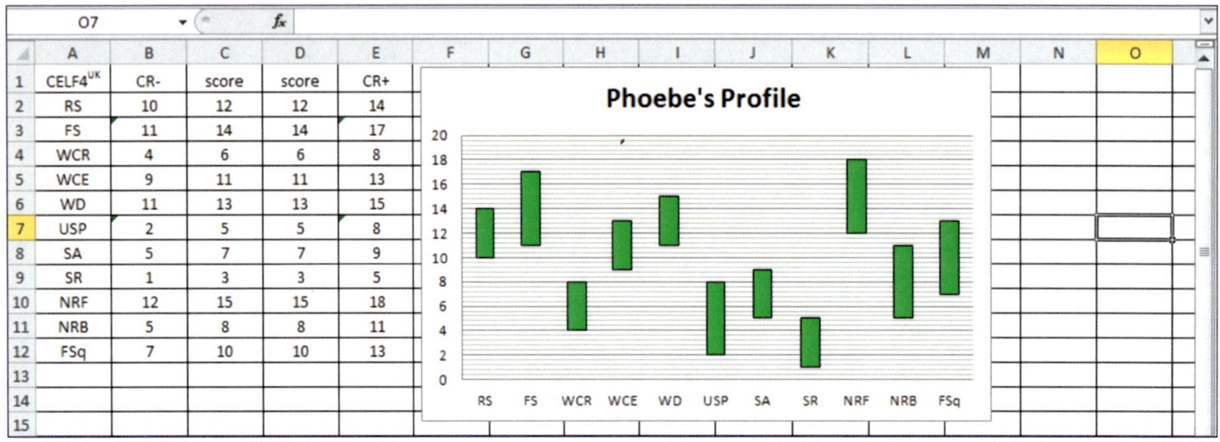

Figure 17.19: Creating a Stock Chart – Step 5

As with the previous examples, if actual score values are to be placed within the chart, then right-clicking on a stock box will give you a menu for preferences.

Another way of acknowledging confidence ranges is perhaps quicker and prevents you having to amend your data file to include what could be described as an artificial column of repeated scores in order to drive the Stock Chart procedures above. Consider again Phoebe's scores on the CELF-4[UK]. You can see in Figure 17.20 that this time we have only one column that gives you the scaled points for creating the confidence intervals. The scaled scores in column C are for each half of the confidence range.

A	B	C
CELF4[UK]	score	1/2 C.R.
RS	12	2
FS	14	3
WCR	6	2
WCE	11	2
WD	13	2
USP	5	3
SA	7	2
SR	3	2
NRF	15	3
NRB	8	3
FSq	10	3

Figure 17.20: An Alternative Way of Creating a Chart – Step 1

In *Excel*, select only the data in columns A and B by dragging from cell A1 to B12; leave column C alone for the moment. Select *Insert*, and *Line* from the Chart Options to get the screen shown in Figure 17.21.

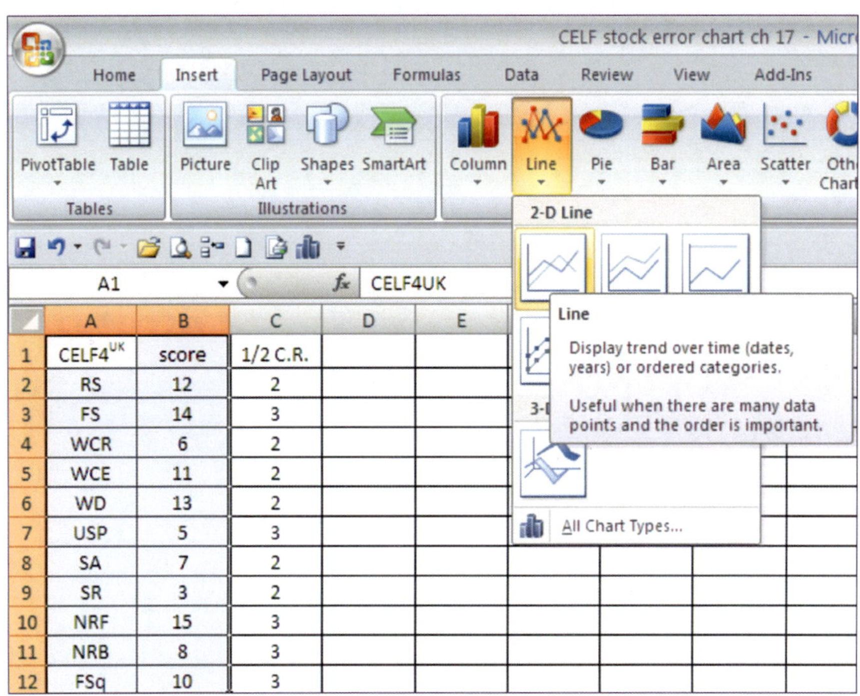

Figure 17.21: An Alternative Way of Creating a Chart – Step 2

Select the first *Line* option highlighted to produce the chart below. Then select *Layout* and *Error Bars* from the *Analysis* options on the right of your screen to get the screen shown in Figure 17.22.

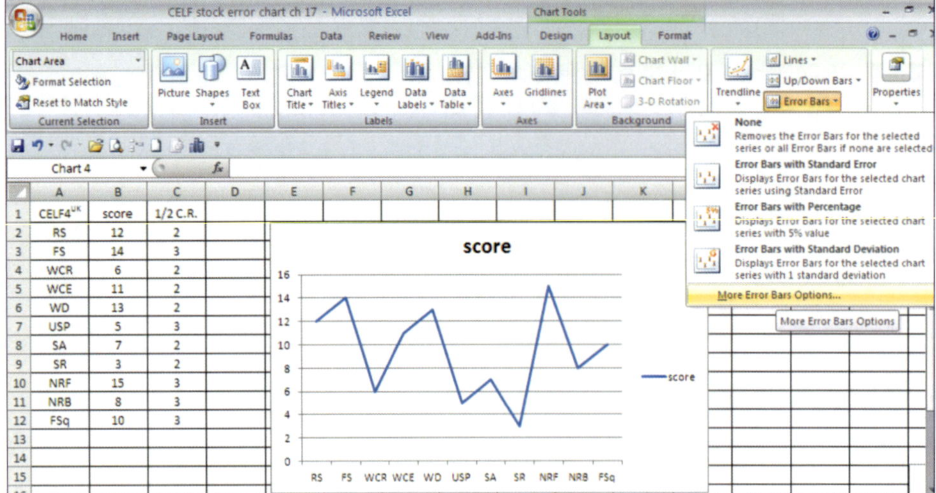

Figure 17.22: An Alternative Way of Creating a Chart – Step 3

Then select *More Error Bars* Options as highlighted in Figure 17.22. This gives you the Format Errors Bars option as in Figure 17.23. Select *Custom* at the bottom as highlighted, and click on *Specify Value*.

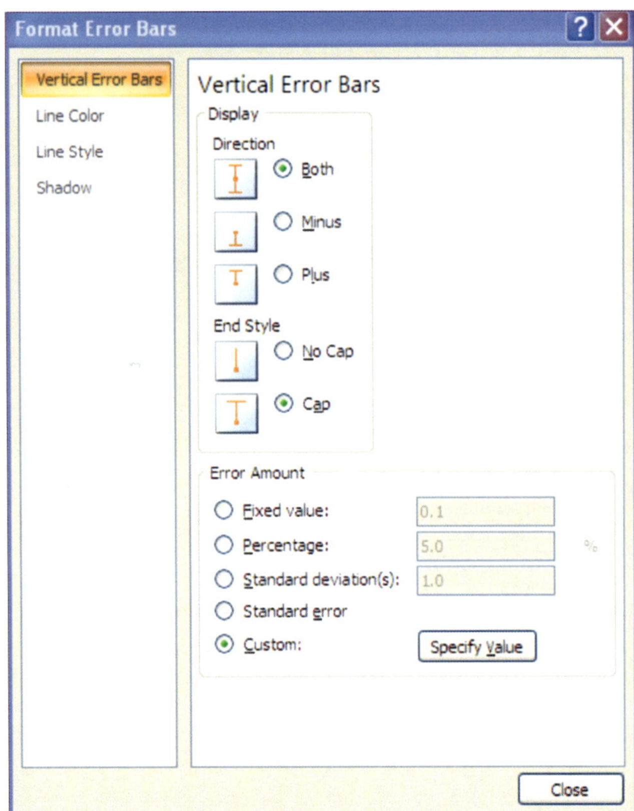

Figure 17.23: An Alternative Way of Creating a Chart – Step 4

You are then requested to insert a data range for the *Positive Error value* (Figure 17.24). Interpret this request to insert the lower half of the confidence ranges values for all of the scores, i.e. the data in column C.

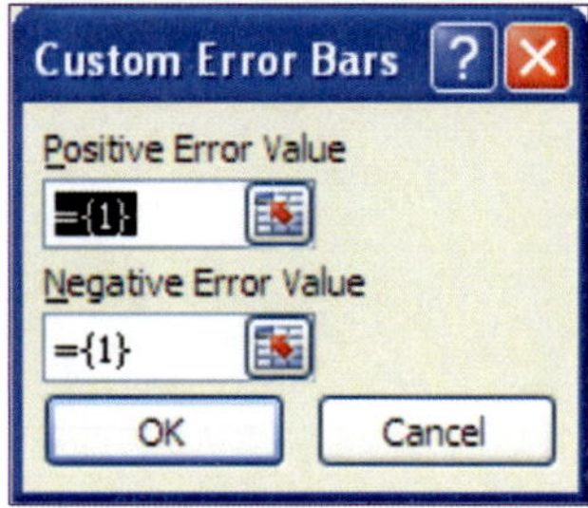

Figure 17.24: An Alternative Way of Creating a Chart – Step 5

Click on the *Collapse* Dialogue button with the small red arrow inside it to get Figure 17.25.

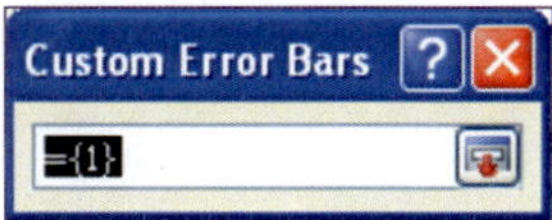

Figure 17.25: An Alternative Way of Creating a Chart – Step 6

Place your cursor on cell C2 and select the data in column C. As you do this, you will see the Positive Window box fill up with the Sheet reference for your selection. Click on the *Collapse Dialogue* button to return to the Custom Error Bars as shown in Figure 17.26.

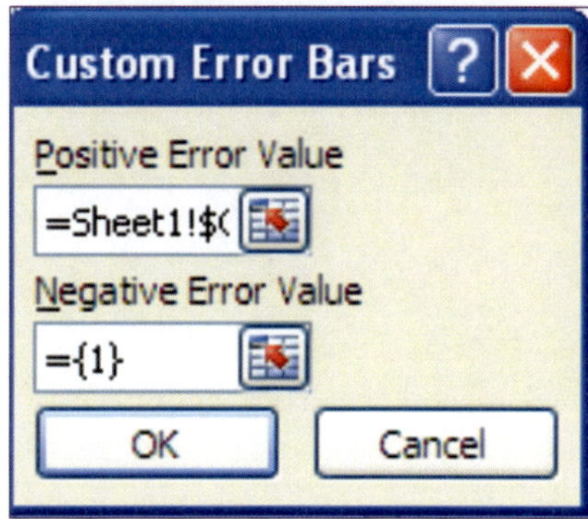

Figure 17.26: An Alternative Way of Creating a Chart – Step 7

Repeat this process for the Negative Error Value by again selecting your data range from column C. Be careful here, however. You will remember from Chapter 7 that we considered the use of confidence ranges where the range was not symmetrical about the standard score. It was noted that it is safer to place confidence ranges around their *estimated* true score as a result of regression to the mean. If you wished to recognise this, then your data table would need another column to obtain the estimated scores before going any further.

Click *OK*, and you are given your basic chart with confidence ranges, as shown in Figure 17.27.

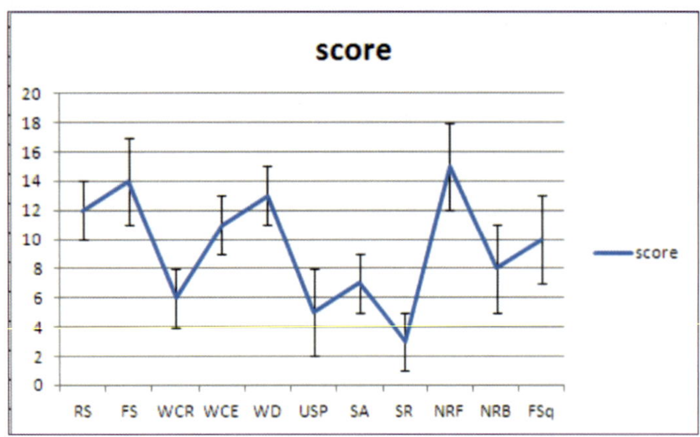

Figure 17.27: An Alternative Way of Creating a Chart – Step 8

Right-clicking on one of the confidence bars enables you to format the bars for width, colour, arrows, data labels, etc, and, as shown in Figure 17.28, you can edit the rest of the chart according to your needs and style preferences.

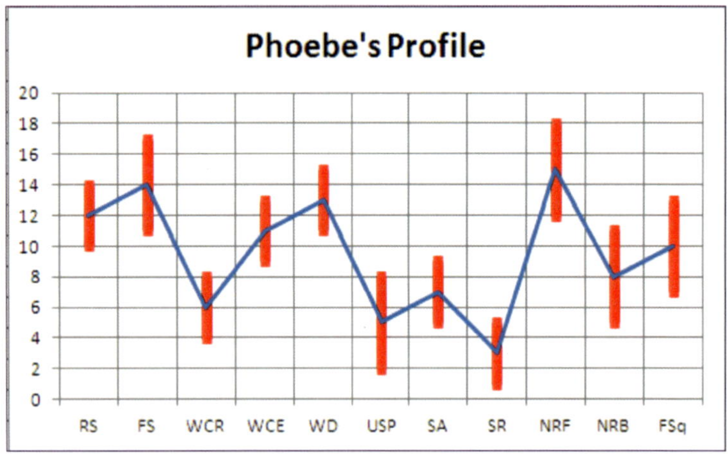

Figure 17.28: An Alternative Way of Creating a Chart – Step 9

Precision Teaching and Using Charts

Precision teaching is a medium that can be used in most types of teaching approaches and application of teaching materials. Its history is based in Direct Instruction techniques and behavioural learning theory (Lindsley, 1991). Precision teaching involves the frequent teaching of small units of information on cards (probes) with monitoring of progress using charts, often with logarithmic scales. A logarithmic scale is a **scale of measurement** using the **logarithm** of a **physical quantity** instead of the quantity itself.

Precision Teaching does not rely on the principles of Classical Test Theory and therefore does not require the application of standardised tests. However, with the increasing trend of psychometric tests being designed with the use of IRT, there is a similarity between probes and short parallel tests provided by the newer tests. For example, the *Wide Range Achievement Test 4 Progress Monitoring Version* (WRAT-4-PMV; Roid & Ledbetter, 2006) provides four very short (only 15 test items each) parallel test forms that can be repeated over relatively short periods of time, allowing for progress to be monitored very closely and in a way similar to the use of probes. Precision Teaching has therefore evolved over the years and been embraced by the Response to Treatment Intervention (Fuchs & Fuchs, 2005) movement but with the application of sophisticated statistical tools. The following section focuses on basic Precision Teaching principles, primarily for the purpose of encouraging the assessor to employ available materials for chart design and report writing purposes.

A simple example is a chart with a vertical axis of equally spaced increments labelled 100, 200, and so on, instead of 1, 2, 3, 4. Each unit increase on the logarithmic scale thus represents an **exponential** increase in the underlying quantity for the given base (10, in this case). Figure 17.29 gives a visual representation of this example.

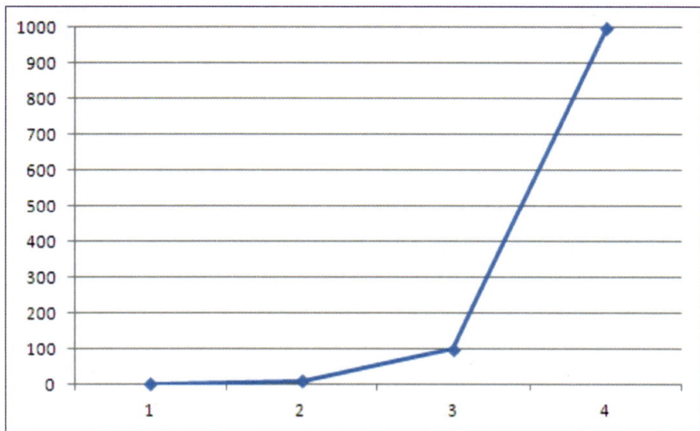

Figure 17.29: Logarithmic Scale for a Chart

Logarithmic paper is often used because initial learning is recorded on a wider scale metric than for later learning. For young children the advantage is that early progress can be visibly seen in apparently large units. Later emphasis on speed/efficiency of learning is enhanced by the narrower width of the logarithmic scales for higher scores.

The emphasis is on fluency of learning and therefore a stopwatch is often used by the teacher to record speed of completion as well as number of information units learned, for example number of c-v-c words recognised correctly on the probe sheet. Precision Teaching is often used when it is thought that the child concerned needs to be more involved with his learning and where self-motivation needs to be encouraged. It can also be used to monitor children's rate of forgetting over for example, a holiday period or weekend, and employed as a research instrument to track outcomes of experimental changes. Children can monitor their own progress by inputting their scores into a computer and obtain instant visual feedback on their trend of progress.

Case Example 17

Table 17.3 shows raw scores obtained by Ruth, an 11-year-old child, attempting to identify correctly a number of single words on a probe sheet within two minutes. You administer the same probe sheet once a week, and for holiday weeks 16 to 18, no score is available. At the start of week 8, you introduce a new phonics-based reading scheme together with involving the child's parents using the scheme at home. You are keen to obtain a measure of whether or not the child will respond positively to the new scheme and if the holiday period will have any detrimental impact on previous skill levels reached.

Table 17.3: Raw Scores on Probe Sheet

Week	Raw Score on Probe
1	20
2	20
3	23
4	23
5	21
6	23
7	24
8	34
9	34
10	39
11	45
12	56
13	67
14	67
15	68
16	
17	
18	
19	45
20	34
21	46
22	50
23	67
24	68

To create a chart in *Excel*, you place Ruth's raw scores numbers in separate, adjoining columns for the baseline period (column B, weeks 1-7), the first experimental period when the new reading scheme is introduced (column C, weeks 8-15), and the post-holiday period (column D, weeks 19-24), as in Table 17.4.

A	B	C	D
Week	Raw Score on Probe		
1	20		
2	20		
3	23		
4	23		
5	21		
6	23		
7	24		
8	➡	34	
9		34	
10		39	
11		45	
12		56	
13		67	
14		67	
15		68	
16			
17			
18			
19		➡	45
20			34
21			46
22			50
23			67
24			68

Table 17.4: Raw Scores on Probe Sheet – Preparation for Excel *Chart*

In Figure 17.30, you can see how the numbers are placed in the rows and columns up to the 13th week.

	A	B	C	D
1	week	raw score	raw score	raw score
2		on probe	on probe	on probe
3	1	20		
4	2	20		
5	3	23		
6	4	23		
7	5	21		
8	6	23		
9	7	24		
10	8		34	
11	9		34	
12	10		39	
13	11		45	
14	12		56	
15	13		67	

Figure 17.30: Charting Probe Scores – Step 1

You then highlight all of the cells from B3 to D26, go to *Insert*, select *Line* and choose the chart *3D line* as highlighted in Figure 17.31.

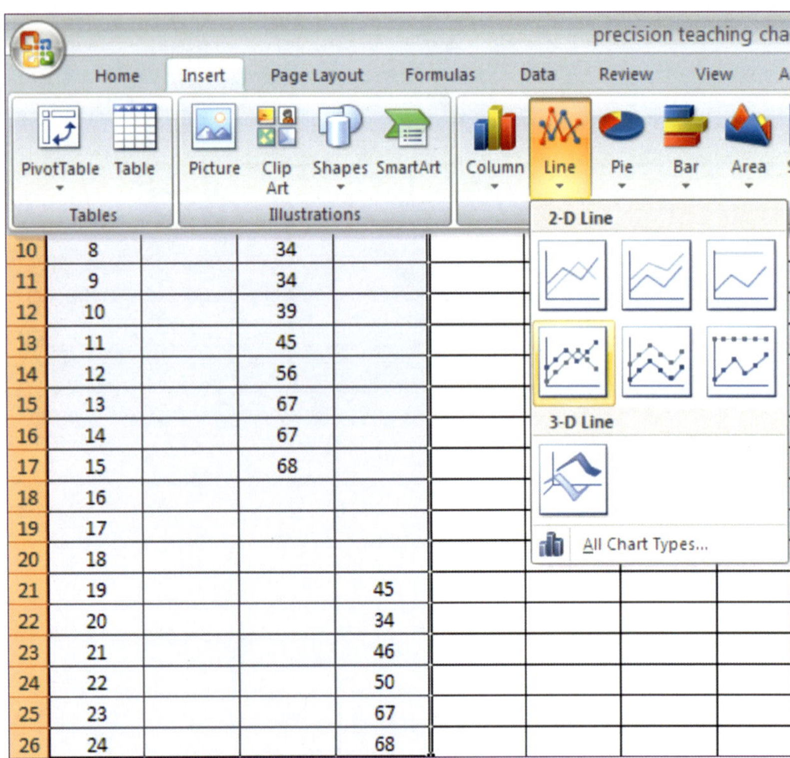

10	8		34	
11	9		34	
12	10		39	
13	11		45	
14	12		56	
15	13		67	
16	14		67	
17	15		68	
18	16			
19	17			
20	18			
21	19			45
22	20			34
23	21			46
24	22			50
25	23			67
26	24			68

Figure 17.31: Charting Probe Scores – Step 2

You then get the chart shown in Figure 17.32, with weekly plots separated for the three sections of your data that you placed in your *Excel* columns.

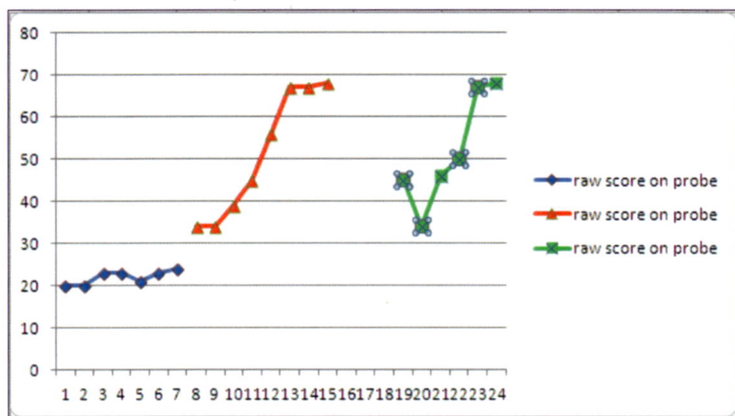

Figure 17.32: Charting Probe Scores – Step 3

At this point you can start to edit the chart, and in the example given in Figure 17.33, Layout 7 (highlighted) has been selected from the Chart Layouts options.

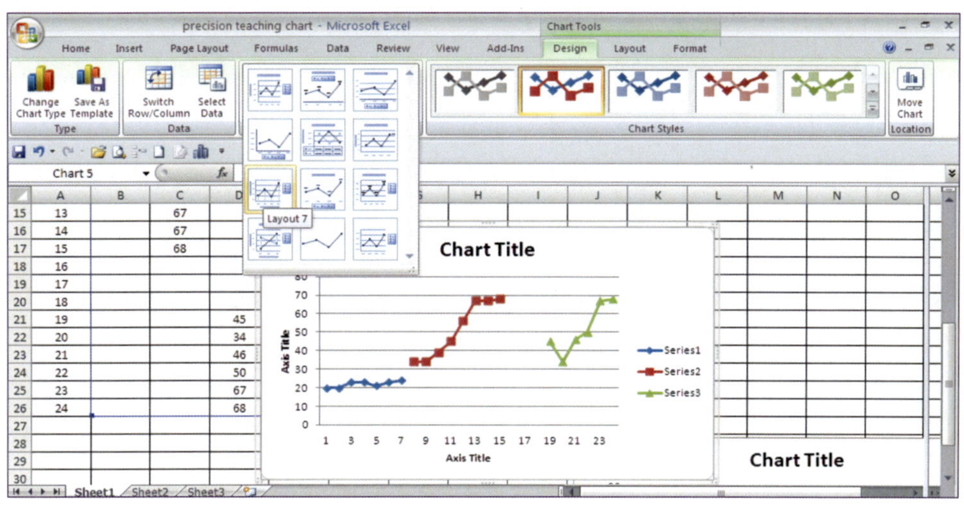

Figure 17.33: Charting Probe Scores – Step 4

Editing the chart by inserting lines to denote changes (start of new reading scheme, holiday period), formatting the data range for weeks (horizontal axis), inserting titles for name and labelling the two axes gives a chart such as that shown in Figure 17.34.

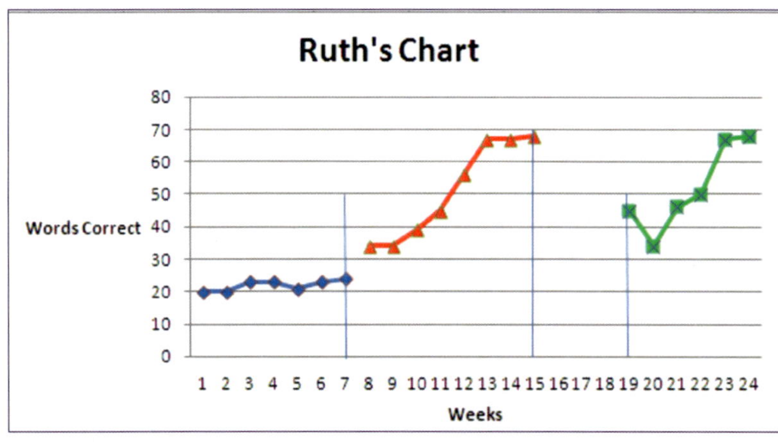

Figure 17.34: Charting Probe Scores – Step 5

Chapter 17 Using Charts in Reports

The visual overview of the trend of progress can now be clearly seen. Such a chart enables the teacher to have a simple means of sharing data with Ruth and her parents and for judgements to be made about the impact of the reading scheme and the holiday period on Ruth's learning status.

Case Example 18

Trendlines can be inserted into such charts in order to obtain a perspective on the progress made as well as set goals for progress. Figure 17.35 shows the chart for Sven, a 6–year-old boy who is learning to recognise numbers at speed. He has been given a daily probe chart and his scores are plotted.

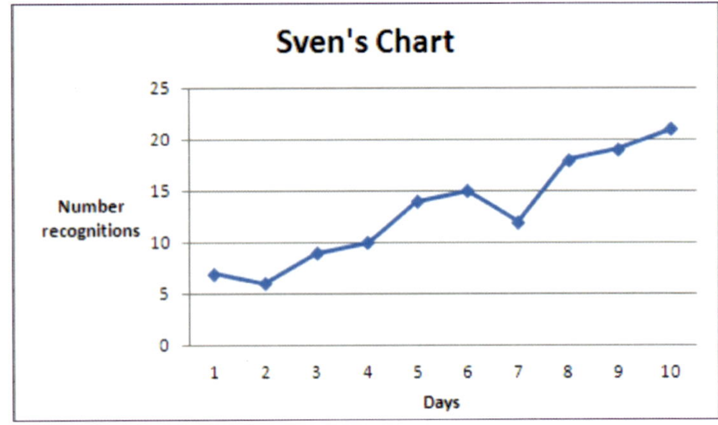

Figure 17.35: Inserting a Trendline into a Chart – Step 1

Right-clicking on the chart line between any data points will offer the functions shown in Figure 17.36.

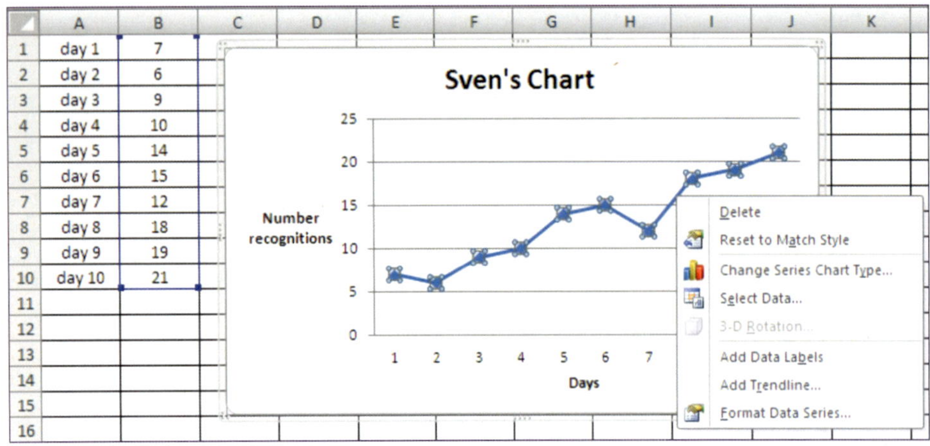

Figure 17.36: Inserting a Trendline into a Chart – Step 2

Select *Add Trendline*, and in the *Trendline Options* shown in Figure 17.37, select *Linear*, and close.

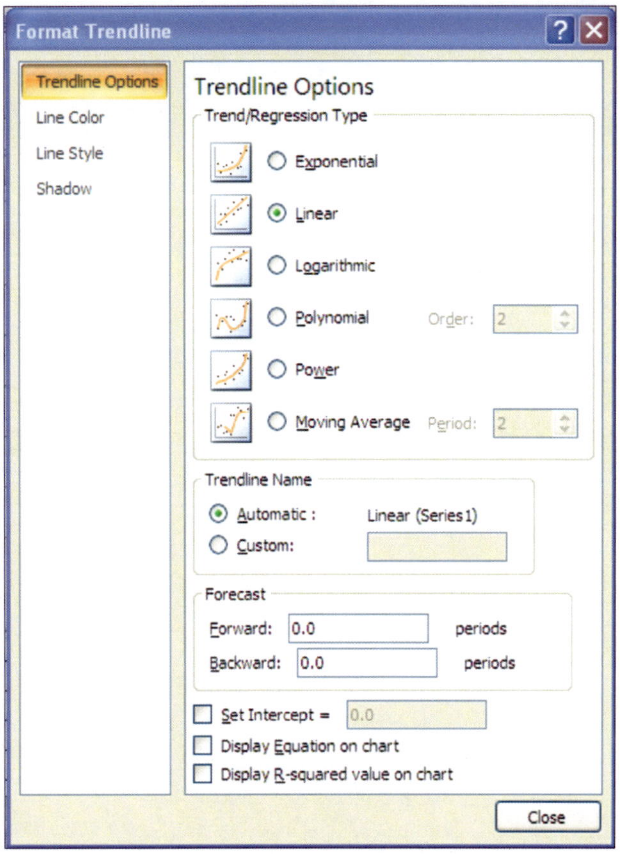

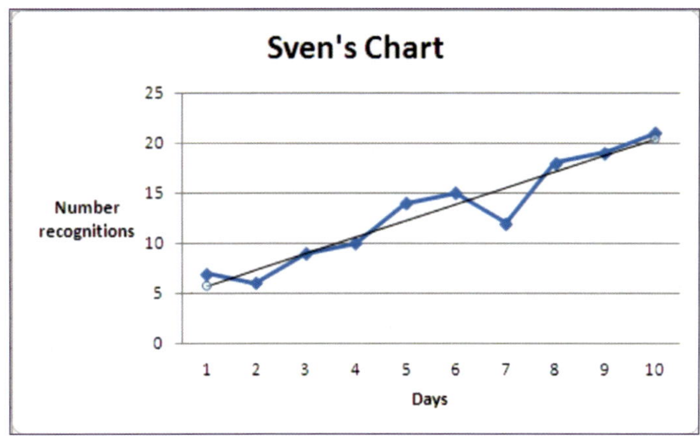

Figure 17.37: Inserting a Trendline into a Chart – Step 3

The chart is then given a trendline, as shown in Figure 17.38.

Figure 17.38: Inserting a Trendline into a Chart – Step 4

You need to be confident that you have chosen the best trendline of those offered by *Excel*. A trendline is most accurate when its R-squared value is at, or near, 1. The term R-squared value is also known as the Coefficient of Determination (introduced in Chapter 11). This value shows how closely the estimated values of a trendline correspond to the actual data plots on your chart. When you fit a trendline to your data, *Excel* automatically calculates the R-squared value. This value can be displayed on your chart. Right-click on your trendline and choose the option *Display R-Squared Value* on Chart at the bottom of the *Trendline Option* box, as in Figure 17.39.

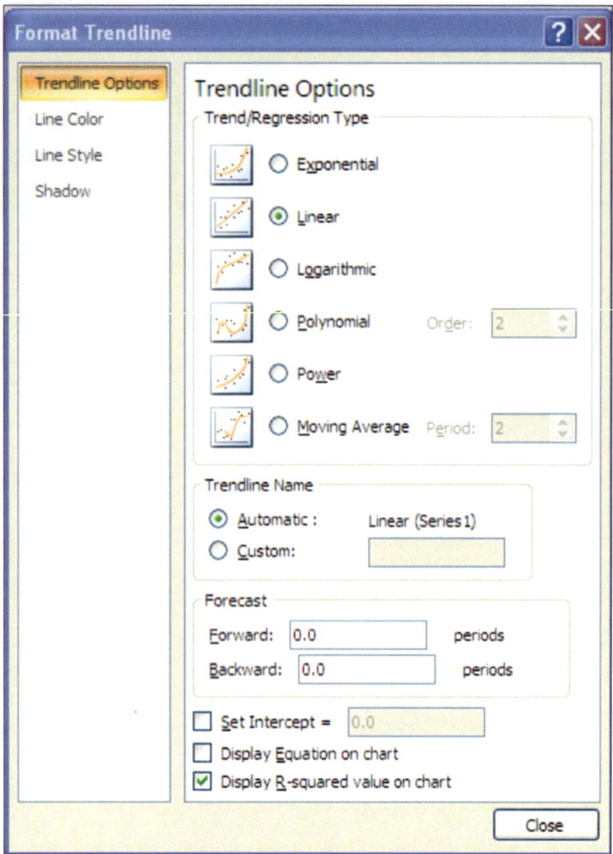

Figure 17.39: Inserting a Trendline into a Chart – Step 5

You can then experiment by switching across the *Trend Regression Types* and seeing which one gives you the highest R-squared value. You will often find that two or three choices will give you very little difference of the R-squared value, but always select the one with the highest R-squared value. The R-squared value ranges from 0 (the trendline does not account for variation over time) and 1 (the trendline fully accounts for variation over time). R-squared is sometimes expressed as a percentage (range 0 to 100%).

If you wish to give the child a monitoring goal using the trendline as a source of daily targets, right-clicking on the trendline (not the chart data line) will give you the screen shown in Figure 17.40.

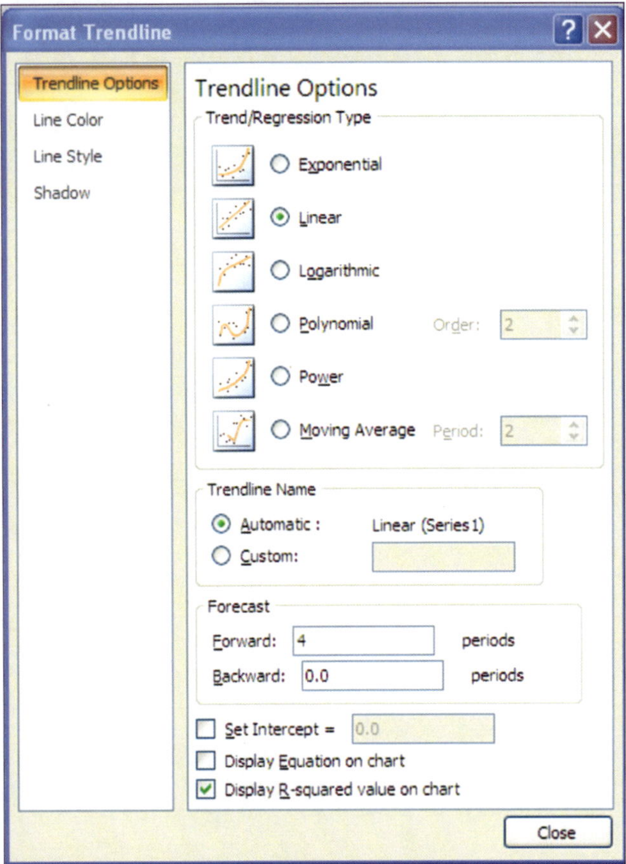

Figure 17.40: Inserting a Trendline into a Chart – Step 6

Here you can see that we have chosen four days in the *Forecast* option *Forward periods* box. In doing so, when closing the *Option* box, the chart is altered (Figure 17.41) to give it the extra four days and the projected trendline for Sven to use as a self-monitoring and/or targeting tool.

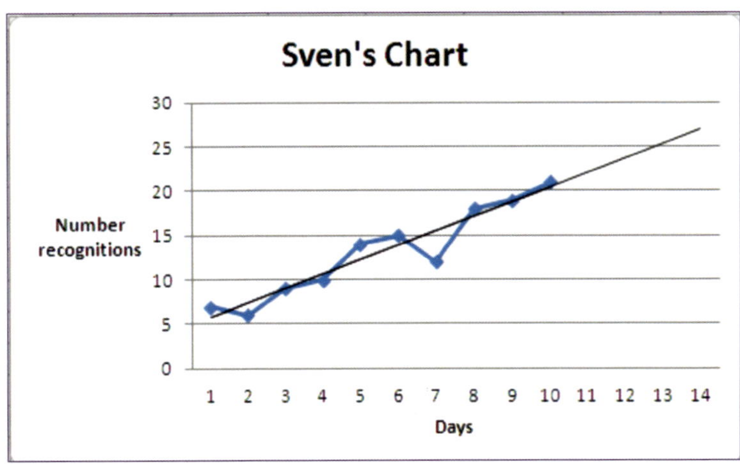

Figure 17.41: Inserting a Trendline into a Chart – Step 7

It must be emphasised that the use of such charts is to aid interpretation by the lay reader, give the client a means of self-monitoring and motivation for learning, and give the assessor a tool for evaluating effectiveness of instruction over a time period.

Section 3:
The Future

Chapter 18
The Future: Trends and Issues

Refinement of the ability-attainment model[1]

The use of ability-attainment discrepancy analysis (comparing cognitive ability and academic attainment levels) continues to be prevalent within the fieldwork practices of psychologists and specialist teachers who assess clients for specific learning difficulties. There are many reasons for this but it is important to note that in the UK there are contemporary professional guidance directives that either require or encourage psychologists and specialist teachers to provide such analysis as evidence of specific learning difficulties. For example, the Revised SEN Code of Practice states: '... *academic attainment is not in itself sufficient for LEAs to conclude that a statutory assessment is or is not necessary. An individual child's attainment must always be understood in the context of ... expectations of the child's performance.*' (DfES, 2001). Note however that at the time of writing this book there are plans in the UK to review the general area of special educational needs' identification and resourcing as outlined in the *Draft legislation, Reform of provision for children and young people with Special Educational Needs* presented to Parliament in September 2012. Further information is available at http://www.official-documents.gov.uk/document/cm84/8438/8438.pdf.

Also, the SpLD Working Group 2005/Guidelines (DFES, 2005) state that '... *although a discrepancy between ability and attainment in literacy skills is not a diagnostic criterion... where such discrepancies do exist, they provide further supporting evidence... the effect of Specific Learning Difficulty... on a student's learning can be evaluated more effectively when underlying ability is taken into account.*' Indeed, psychologists and specialist teachers who do not consider the issue of ability-attainment discrepancy in their assessment formats run the risk of their reports for Disabled Students' Allowance (DSA) being rejected. This is because Student Finance England (SFE) in its current advice to key delivery partners states that assessment of specific learning difficulties should contain, in part, '... *evidence of a significant discrepancy between the abilities in reading, writing, spelling and numeracy and the level of those abilities expected of the student in terms of their general intellectual ability* [2].' (*Assessing Eligibility Guidance 2011-2012 Student Finance England*).

It is therefore understandable that UK fieldwork practitioners seem not to have taken into account the significant amount of (mainly US) research and related opinion that is critical of ability-attainment discrepancy analysis and that has led to alternative paradigms being offered as more valid means of assessing and thereby treating specific learning difficulties (see Flanagan, *et al.*, 2006, for an introduction). Examples of the latter are the various *Response to Treatment Intervention* (Fuchs & Fuchs, 2010) programmes that most US states have now employed. Notwithstanding this criticism, the use of ability-attainment discrepancy models are still permissible via US legislation (IDEA, 2004) and the academic debate about the validity of these models and their possible integration and compatibility continues (Flanagan *et al.*, 2006; Kavale, 2005; Hale, 2006).

The debate around the claimed failings of ability-attainment discrepancy analysis has stimulated developments to create better assessment models. Over the last decade, there has been increasing interest in, and refinement of, aptitude-achievement consistency analysis (A-ACA) as an alternative to ability-attainment discrepancy analysis (Flanagan *et al.*, 2006). This is sometimes referred to as the 'Modern Operational Definition of SLD' (Lichtenberger & Breaux, 2010).

---

[1] Some of the points raised in this section have been referred to in the article, Johnson, B. E. E. (2011). Aptitude-achievement consistency analysis: an alternative to the ability-attainment discrepancy model. Dyslexia Review, 22, 14-16, with permission of the journal editor.

[2] For more information about DSA regulations, see www.assist-tech.co.uk/DSA1112.html and also www.patoss-dyslexia.org/SupportAdvice/DisabledStudentAllowances

Chapter 18 The Future: Trends and Issues

Rather than attempt to compare broad measures of intelligence with attainment levels, A-ACA has its focus on *aptitudes* ('narrow' clusters of abilities), which are proposed as conceptual bridges between broad cognitive abilities and academic skills. The process is to determine the degree to which a weakness in an area of academic achievement is consistent/positively correlates with known related cognitive abilities/aptitudes. In doing so, implications for teaching are better identified. This has led to publishing companies investing heavily in the design of attainment and cognitive ability tests that are co-normed and that reflect the contemporary Cattell-Horn-Carroll (CHC) model of intelligence (Flanagan *et al.*, 2000). The CHC model of intelligence supports the view that, rather than perceive cognitive abilities and academic attainments as qualitatively different and thus distinct from one another, it is better to perceive them as part of a *hierarchy ranging from general to specific* abilities. A-ACA also requires confirmation of average or above-average levels in ability and attainment areas that are not associated with the identified specific learning difficulties in order to discount general slow learning. It also logically demands that there should be sufficient analysis performed to exclude the impact of any contextual factors that may explain why the client appears to have low attainment levels. Lastly, and importantly, A-ACA requires that for an SLD to be confirmed, the competencies within the attainment and related aptitude areas need to be operating below the average range that is operationally defined as less than one standard deviation below the mean (Flanagan *et al.*, 2006). This latter feature reflects the adoption of the concept of a *normative* weakness as a *necessary* component of the process of confirming the presence of an SLD. It is probable that this latter necessary criterion reflects resourcing and selection issues and contrasts significantly with ipsative models of SLD where intra-comparisons of a person's individual relative strengths and weaknesses are performed. It is likely that such pragmatic forces will shape specialist assessment models in the future.

Another model that has been proposed is the Concordance-Discordance model of SLD (Hale & Fiorello, 2004; Hale, 2006), sometimes referred to as the Pattern of Strengths and Weaknesses (PSW) model (Lichtenberger & Breaux, 2010). In order to meet the criteria of this model to confirm the presence of an SLD, two cognitive ability test scores need to be statistically discrepant from one another. The cognitive ability strength needs to be dissociated from the attainment area of weakness and this is done by reference to established research findings, which include normative evidence from co-normed tests of abilities and attainments. Likewise, the cognitive ability weakness needs to be associated with the attainment area of weakness, again as evidenced by reference to research findings. Therefore, it is likely that such cognitive weaknesses will be, for example, working memory and information processing speed. The statistical means by which the evidence for significant differences across scores is arrived at is the standard error of the difference, referred to in Chapter 3. Note that the most important difference between the A-ACA and PSW models is the normative weakness necessary criterion for the A-ACA model.

It is likely that the ability-attainment model will be refined and not rejected, given the trends evident in the US. There will be a greater demand for co-normed tests of cognitive abilities and attainments that reflect contemporary models of cognitive ability and its development and these should therefore include tests of working memory and speed of information processing. Such refinement will continue to require that specialist teachers and psychologists understand the theoretical platforms of the range of operational models available and be able to apply suitable statistical analyses to their test scores.

The Rise of Growth Scale Value Scores

The current trend of focusing on impact and effectiveness, rationalising and efficacy of resourcing, involvement of parents and carers (Peacey, *et al.*, 2010) will continue to drive assessment models to focus on individual educational plans (Audit Commission, 2002) and intra-client profiles of strengths and weaknesses. Although future UK legislation may dilute the legal status of individual education plans, the DfE is still determined for schools to achieve impact data and demonstrate effectiveness of teaching of children with special educational needs (DfE, 2010). The advantages of obtaining 'granularity' in attainment levels and encouraging formative, small-scale assessment models for students with special educational needs has been demonstrated and recommended (Audit Commission, 2010). These features could further stimulate the trend towards the use of Growth Scale Value (GSV) scores (introduced in Chapter 10) and the equivalent W and Relative Proficiency Index scores from the Woodcock-Johnson repertoire of tests (Jaffe, 2009). These have the advantage of being able to demonstrate learning growth within the individual, rather than emphasise comparison with a population of people that may, as a group, be deemed to be qualitatively different to the individual with specific learning difficulties. GSV scores have the very significant advantage of having the status of a relative metric and are therefore more amenable to quantitative research analyses where researchers wish to apply research methodologies to fieldwork data. Lastly, from the parents' and carers' perspectives, although they would all wish for their children to catch up with their age-equivalent peers, their fundamental perspective is to see their children progressing within themselves, i.e. to use themselves as the benchmark for progress (Collins & Goodnow, 1990). It is highly likely that GSV scores will replace the need for Special Group normative data tables that are often present in test manual's validity chapters or appendices as a source of normative reference.

The Lifespan Perspective[3]

Education is not just about children and young people: it is a life-long process, even more so for those people with specific learning difficulties. Specialist assessors will invariably be drawn into the educational needs arena of adults, particularly within the workplace where competing demands of work output and economic efficiency are paramount but where contemporary employment legislation is now also recognising the rights of the person with learning difficulties (The Equality Act, 2010). Therefore, specialist assessors whose training and experience lies within the developmental arena of intellectual growth and maturation within children and young people will need training and information about lifespan cognitive trends and needs that will include, for example, mild/early cognitive decline in mid-life and associated health risk-factors (Knopman *et al.*, 2001). Consequently, traditional assessment paradigms that employ ability-attainment comparison techniques will need revision and refinement. The focus on statistical analysis of ability-attainment discrepancy is often placed on a platform of children's developing abilities, aptitudes and skills and this may not be particularly appropriate for the adult who is entering a phase of some form of cognitive decline.

It is sometimes forgotten that psychometric standard scores only provide relative information on the status of a person's cognitive profile, in that they are concerned with normative comparisons with the functioning of people within certain narrow age ranges. A 40-year-old person's standard score of 100 on a test does not mean that she performed at the same competency as a 12-year-old child with the same standard score on the same test. These two people's scores simply reflect the fact that they scored at an average level for their chronological age in comparison to samples of their similar aged peers.

---

[3] Some of the points raised in this section have been mentioned with permission of the editor in the article, Johnson, B. E. & Hagger-Johnson, G.E. (accepted for publication in 2012). Older adults with dyslexia in the workplace, or the beginnings of cognitive decline? Emerging implications for assessment. *Dyslexia Review*.

Chapter 18 The Future: Trends and Issues

In *absolute* terms, general cognitive ability grows as children grow older but eventually declines over the adult age range. This normal decline of intellectual functioning is often underestimated, both in the amount of the decline and its start-point. These features can be graphically shown by plotting the z scores that equate with average *raw* scores and their ranges across the age-range bands for this psychometric test. Figure 18.1 is derived from the normative data within the *Wechsler Adult Intelligence Scale – Third UK Edition* (WAIS-III[UK]; Wechsler, 1997) and gives data plots across the life span for five of the subtests.

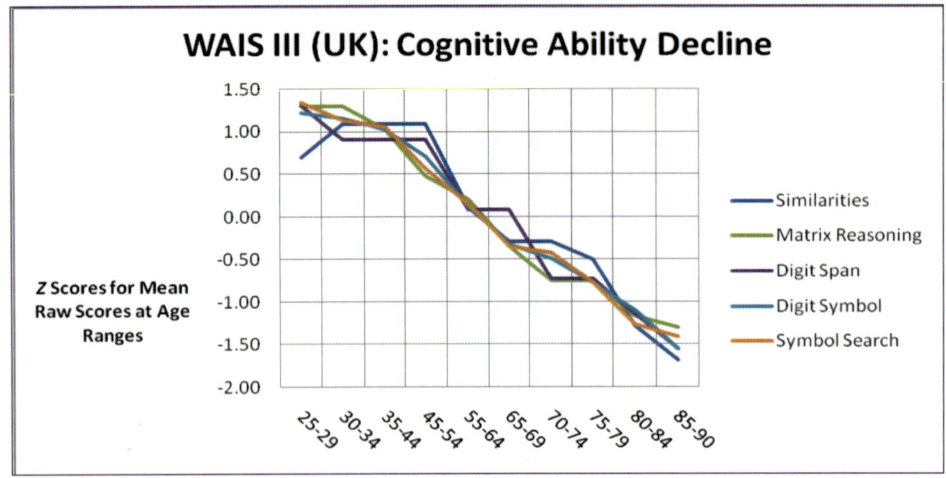

Figure 18.1: WAIS-III[UK]: Mean Raw Scores for Age Ranges

The five subtests referred to consist of one test of fluid reasoning (Matrix Reasoning), one test of crystallised intelligence (Similarities), one test of working memory (Digit Span), and two tests of Speed of Information Processing (Digit Symbol and Symbol Search).

It is well known that types of cognitive abilities differ with regard to their rate of decline over the lifespan. Information processing speed and working memory are particularly susceptible (Deary *et al.*, 2009). Note the age of the start of the decline of the scores for the WAIS-III[UK]. Some start within the 25-29 age range and others appear to start to have significant decline with the 45-54 age range. Decline in reasoning, memory and fluency have also been observed from as young as age 45 in longitudinal cohort studies (Singh-Manoux *et al.*, 2012).

No wonder then, that it is uncommon to see many older people in occupations that require rapid application of cognitive problem-solving and decision-making (fluid reasoning) such as financial trading, air-traffic control, fighter pilot, etc. Relatedly, one factor that may shorten the professional sportsperson's career is the start of the decline of those abilities that are associated with speed of perceptual reasoning and processing. Research also shows that children of lower-than-average ability are more susceptible to decline in cognitive ability as they get older (Deary *et al.*, 1996; Richards, *et al.*, 2004) and that cognitive ability decline can be associated with health problems such as cardiovascular disease (Knopman *et al.*, 2001) and neuroendocrinogical factors (Braverman, 2009). Indeed, measures of cognitive ability are increasingly being interpreted as criteria of what can best be described as a neurological 'cognitive reserve' that is associated with a range of measures of physical well-being (Richards & Deary, 2005). Specialist assessors need to be aware therefore that some susceptible adults may be showing evidence of significant decline on measures of cognitive ability and at relatively early ages.

The frequency of reported learning difficulties may increase in times of economic recession and with the removal of the statutory pensionable age in the UK where the older employee feels unable to retire because of financial or other life-choice considerations. The apparent learning difficulties of adults in the workplace may not be causally related to dyslexia or other types of specific learning difficulties per se but rather to the lifespan process and, in certain cases, susceptibility to cognitive deterioration and related health issues

(Knopman *et al.*, 2001). Relatively high levels of literacy appear to buffer the effects of aging on cognitive decline (Manly, *et al.*, 2003) although there is some evidence that literacy skills also generally decline over the lifespan from age 30 (Willms & Murray, 2007). Concern about apparently deteriorating literacy levels or cognitive fatigue in a middle-aged adult within professional occupations needs careful attention and reflection. This is particularly so if there are co-existing physical illnesses. Deriving baseline and trend data in these situations is problematic. For this reason, access to co-normed tests of ability and attainment that cover the lifespan age will be needed in the future, particularly in the case of adults in those age ranges sensitive to cognitive deterioration and time-lines relevant to retirement and re-deployment. It will be prudent for adults who are constructing their difficulties as being caused by dyslexia or other types of specific learning difficulties to have review assessments of their core cognitive abilities. These should include components of fluid reasoning, crystallised intelligence, working memory and speed of information processing. Assessors will also need to be sensitive to the feelings and anxieties of their clients when apparent cognitive decline is a focus of discussion: patients' denial of their medical circumstances has been well known in the medical arena for some time (Livneh, 2009).

Cognitive decline is often the most feared aspect of aging (Deary *et al.*, 2009). Attributing difficulties in the workplace to specific learning difficulties may be psychologically acceptable to a client who is unaware of, or in denial of, cognitive decline, but this inaccurate attribution may lead to an incorrect diagnosis and delay important medical assessment and intervention such as access to memory clinics (Thompson, 2004). Re-referral to appropriate medical assessment and support will also be required in cases of identified onset of significant cognitive decline and pre-referral forms should be designed to gain useful information about physical health and reported cognitive fatigue. Contextual assessment in the workplace will need to attend carefully to those aspects of the client's work activities that load heavily on speed of processing and memory application as well as the appraisal of trend perspectives of the client's competencies over the years.

It is possible that cognitive decline in some cases may be accompanied by corresponding decline in literacy skills (Wilson *et al.*, 2009). If this is found to be the case, then the specialist assessor will probably need to appraise their theoretical preferences for assessment platforms. It should not be assumed that current models employed within the areas of evolving cognition in children and young people are the best ones. For example, given that speed of information processing has been identified as a sensitive area of cognitive decline, it is possible that it may be useful to reconsider theories such as the Double-Deficit Theory (Wolf & Bowers, 1999) with reference not to literacy acquisition, but to the impact of slower speed of processing on comprehension and other aspects of higher-order literacy skills. In addition, the research area of the elderly and literacy skills loss (Wilson et al., 2009; Thompson, 2004) might be worth exploring with a view to establishing possible links with earlier mild cognitive decline. It is possible such research might eventually lead to the phenomenon of proven and significant decline in literacy skills in mid-life to be reinterpreted. Such decline could represent a new and interesting form of acquired dyslexia, but which is part and parcel of cognitive aging.

Test Standards and the Price of Quality Assurance

Over recent years there has been a steady rise in standards in the test development industry. This is due to the changing needs and demands of assessors, emerging new techniques of statistical procedures such as IRT, theoretical advances and applied research, commercial competition, stronger legislation for special educational needs and disability, and professional protectionism. One practical consequence of such inflationary rise in standards has been the realisation that psychometric tests now have relatively short lifespans. Publishing companies are replacing or updating assessments over shorter time intervals than they did 10 years ago and this requires the specialist assessor to update regularly their training needs and purchase relatively expensive materials. A recent estimate by the authors of the start-up test purchasing costs for a consultant educational psychologist working in the private sector in the UK is approximately £6,000. Organisations that have psychometric assessment as a core part of their business or service delivery to clients will need to take care to factor in the rising costs of psychometric tests and their replacements. Such trends may reflect a basic commercial factor but there is also a valid realisation that psychometric population norms are dynamic and reflect factors such as the Flynn Effect (apparent, substantial and long-sustained increase in intelligence test scores) (Flynn, 1987). There is also the impact of cultural changes in society that influence educational standards and priorities.

Comorbidity/co-occurrence of Learning Difficulties

The rising awareness that learning difficulties have a tendency to co-occur, i.e. can be prone to comorbidity (Rose, 2009), will also lead to a growth in the availability of co-normed psychometric tests that will not only cover the lifespan but also span the education and health domains. A good example of such a trend is the DASH (Barnett *et al.*, 2007) and DASH 17+ (Barnett *et al.* 2010), tests that provide co-normed standardisation data for clients' handwriting and motor co-ordination skills. Such a focus will undoubtedly help assessing professionals become more confident in their approaches to the assessment of needs within the areas of, for example, AD(H)D, dyspraxia/developmental co-ordination disorder, etc. Use of such psychometric tests will encourage assessors to share assessment models and related conceptual language, as well as evolve a means of validly breaching traditional professional boundaries across the health and education arenas.

Electronic Scoring and Report Writing

There is already a significant trend towards assessors having the option to purchase electronic means of scoring and report writing. The advantages are clear: assessors will have an efficient means of checking their manual scoring or dispensing with it entirely. Complex statistical analyses will be available, thus preventing the assessor from having to learn and apply them manually. Options are already available for collation and statistical interrogation of data on groups of clients, and automatic report writers will provide, via data-merging facilities, the option of the automated assessment report. However the dangers are equally obvious: the assessor may find herself financially and professionally locked into relying on external systems, which could eventually disempower her and restrict the inductive, dynamic process of the diagnostic assessment. However, publishing companies are already aware of their obligations here and are keen to provide complimentary personal support for their electronic services.

Online assessment

Traditional paper-based testing could be supplemented, enhanced or replaced by web-based on-screen administration, and online scoring and reporting, with tests being delivered to the user's screen anytime, anywhere through the use of portable devices. Tests would be embedded in secure management systems that increase flexibility in all aspects of the testing, reporting and follow-up process. Publishing companies would need to be aware of access to technology, training requirements, the fast pace of technological change, security and pricing issues. Digital assessments should not replace the need for a professional's input and choice in the administration process, the capture of qualitative information and the interpretation of data.

Response to Intervention

The publication of the Rose Review, *Identifying and Teaching Children with Dyslexia and Literacy Difficulties* (Rose, 2009) in the UK and the wealth of activity surrounding IDEA (2004) and Response to Intervention models in the US will lead to improved programmes of instruction where diagnostic assessment and teaching will become truly integrated. Clinical diagnoses of specific learning difficulties will be made as a result of monitoring response to intervention but the need for in-depth clinical diagnostic assessment will still remain.

In particular, the needs of the relatively young child will be helped significantly by such a trend in that they will not be required to wait until their learning difficulties have a major impact on their learning and success before gaining access to special programmes and resources. The independent assessor will need to create systems that enable acknowledgement of such trends whereby their contribution to the contextualisation of the assessment of specific learning difficulties is clearly understood. The independent assessor will also need to prove their worth by giving added-value to the overall assessment. Absolute clarity of the reason for referral and an active engagement with adults involved in the day-to-day teaching and support of the client will be essential.

Conclusion

The implications of the above trends for the training needs of specialist teachers and psychologists are obvious. The rising sophistication of available psychometric assessment tools, the complexities of theoretical models of learning difficulties, and the higher assessment standards demanded by clients and customers will require assessors to be confident in their use and application of psychometric tests and statistical analyses. It is hoped that this book will be of practical help in this area.

Appendices

Appendices

Appendix A: Conversion Table for Standardised Scores

Z Score	T Score	Standard Score (SD 15: mean 100)	Scaled Score (SD 3: mean 10)
-3.0	20	55	1
-2.9	21	57	1
-2.8	22	58	2
-2.7	23	60	2
-2.6	24	61	2
-2.5	25	63	3
-2.4	26	64	3
-2.3	27	66	3
-2.2	28	67	3
-2.1	29	69	4
-2.0	30	70	4
-1.9	31	72	4
-1.8	32	73	5
-1.7	33	75	5
-1.6	34	76	5
-1.5	35	78	6
-1.4	36	79	6
-1.3	37	81	6
-1.2	38	82	6
-1.1	39	84	7
-1.0	40	85	7
-0.9	41	87	7
-0.8	42	88	8
-0.7	43	90	8
-0.6	44	91	8
-0.5	45	93	9
-0.4	46	94	9
-0.3	47	96	9
-0.2	48	97	9
-0.1	49	99	10
0.0	50	100	10

Appendix A: Conversion Table for Standardised Scores (continued)

Z Score	T Score	Standard Score (SD 15: mean 100)	Scaled Score (SD 3: mean 10)
0.1	51	102	10
0.2	52	103	11
0.3	53	105	11
0.4	54	106	11
0.5	55	108	12
0.6	56	109	12
0.7	57	111	12
0.8	58	112	12
0.9	59	114	13
1.0	60	115	13
1.1	61	117	13
1.2	62	118	14
1.3	63	120	14
1.4	64	121	14
1.5	65	123	15
1.6	66	124	15
1.7	67	126	15
1.8	68	127	15
1.9	69	129	16
2.0	70	130	16
2.1	71	132	16
2.2	72	133	17
2.3	73	135	17
2.4	74	136	17
2.5	75	138	18
2.6	76	139	18
2.7	77	141	18
2.8	78	142	18
2.9	79	144	19
3.0	80	145	19

Appendices

Appendix B: *Z-P* Conversion Table (Positive *Z* Scores)

z	0	0.01	0.02	0.03	0.04	0.05	0.06	0.07	0.08	0.09
0.0	0.5000	0.5040	0.5080	0.5120	0.5160	0.5199	0.5239	0.5279	0.5319	0.5359
0.1	0.5398	0.5438	0.5478	0.5517	0.5557	0.5596	0.5636	0.5675	0.5714	0.5753
0.2	0.5793	0.5832	0.5871	0.5910	0.5948	0.5987	0.6026	0.6064	0.6103	0.6141
0.3	0.6179	0.6217	0.6255	0.6293	0.6331	0.6368	0.6406	0.6443	0.6480	0.6517
0.4	0.6554	0.6591	0.6628	0.6664	0.6700	0.6736	0.6772	0.6808	0.6844	0.6879
0.5	0.6915	0.6950	0.6985	0.7019	0.7054	0.7088	0.7123	0.7157	0.7190	0.7224
0.6	0.7257	0.7291	0.7324	0.7357	0.7389	0.7422	0.7454	0.7486	0.7517	0.7549
0.7	0.7580	0.7611	0.7642	0.7673	0.7704	0.7734	0.7764	0.7794	0.7823	0.7852
0.8	0.7881	0.7910	0.7939	0.7967	0.7995	0.8023	0.8051	0.8078	0.8106	0.8133
0.9	0.8159	0.8186	0.8212	0.8238	0.8264	0.8289	0.8315	0.8340	0.8365	0.8389
1.0	0.8413	0.8438	0.8461	0.8485	0.8508	0.8531	0.8554	0.8577	0.8599	0.8621
1.1	0.8643	0.8665	0.8686	0.8708	0.8729	0.8749	0.8770	0.8790	0.8810	0.8830
1.2	0.8849	0.8869	0.8888	0.8907	0.8925	0.8944	0.8962	0.8980	0.8997	0.9015
1.3	0.9032	0.9049	0.9066	0.9082	0.9099	0.9115	0.9131	0.9147	0.9162	0.9177
1.4	0.9192	0.9207	0.9222	0.9236	0.9251	0.9265	0.9279	0.9292	0.9306	0.9319
1.5	0.9332	0.9345	0.9357	0.9370	0.9382	0.9394	0.9406	0.9418	0.9429	0.9441
1.6	0.9452	0.9463	0.9474	0.9484	0.9495	0.9505	0.9515	0.9525	0.9535	0.9545
1.7	0.9554	0.9564	0.9573	0.9582	0.9591	0.9599	0.9608	0.9616	0.9625	0.9633
1.8	0.9641	0.9649	0.9656	0.9664	0.9671	0.9678	0.9686	0.9693	0.9699	0.9706
1.9	0.9713	0.9719	0.9726	0.9732	0.9738	0.9744	0.9750	0.9756	0.9761	0.9767
2.0	0.9772	0.9778	0.9783	0.9788	0.9793	0.9798	0.9803	0.9808	0.9812	0.9817
2.1	0.9821	0.9826	0.9830	0.9834	0.9838	0.9842	0.9846	0.9850	0.9854	0.9857
2.2	0.9861	0.9864	0.9868	0.9871	0.9875	0.9878	0.9881	0.9884	0.9887	0.9890
2.3	0.9893	0.9896	0.9898	0.9901	0.9904	0.9906	0.9909	0.9911	0.9913	0.9916
2.4	0.9918	0.9920	0.9922	0.9925	0.9927	0.9929	0.9931	0.9932	0.9934	0.9936
2.5	0.9938	0.9940	0.9941	0.9943	0.9945	0.9946	0.9948	0.9949	0.9951	0.9952
2.6	0.9953	0.9955	0.9956	0.9957	0.9959	0.9960	0.9961	0.9962	0.9963	0.9964
2.7	0.9965	0.9966	0.9967	0.9968	0.9969	0.9970	0.9971	0.9972	0.9973	0.9974
2.8	0.9974	0.9975	0.9976	0.9977	0.9977	0.9978	0.9979	0.9979	0.9980	0.9981
2.9	0.9981	0.9982	0.9982	0.9983	0.9984	0.9984	0.9985	0.9985	0.9986	0.9986
3.0	0.9987	0.9987	0.9987	0.9988	0.9988	0.9989	0.9989	0.9989	0.9990	0.9990

Appendix C: *Z-P* Conversion Table (Negative *Z* Scores)

z	0.09	0.08	0.07	0.06	0.05	0.04	0.03	0.02	0.01	0
-3.0	0.0010	0.0010	0.0011	0.0011	0.0011	0.0012	0.0012	0.0013	0.0013	0.0013
-2.9	0.0014	0.0014	0.0015	0.0015	0.0016	0.0016	0.0017	0.0018	0.0018	0.0019
-2.8	0.0019	0.0020	0.0021	0.0021	0.0022	0.0023	0.0023	0.0024	0.0025	0.0026
-2.7	0.0026	0.0027	0.0028	0.0029	0.0030	0.0031	0.0032	0.0033	0.0034	0.0035
-2.6	0.0036	0.0037	0.0038	0.0039	0.0040	0.0041	0.0043	0.0044	0.0045	0.0047
-2.5	0.0048	0.0049	0.0051	0.0052	0.0054	0.0055	0.0057	0.0059	0.0060	0.0062
-2.4	0.0064	0.0066	0.0068	0.0069	0.0071	0.0073	0.0075	0.0078	0.0080	0.0082
-2.3	0.0084	0.0087	0.0089	0.0091	0.0094	0.0096	0.0099	0.0102	0.0104	0.0107
-2.2	0.0110	0.0113	0.0116	0.0119	0.0122	0.0125	0.0129	0.0132	0.0136	0.0139
-2.1	0.0143	0.0146	0.015	0.0154	0.0158	0.0162	0.0166	0.0170	0.0174	0.0179
-2.0	0.0183	0.0188	0.0192	0.0197	0.0202	0.0207	0.0212	0.0217	0.0222	0.0228
-1.9	0.0233	0.0239	0.0244	0.0250	0.0256	0.0262	0.0268	0.0274	0.0281	0.0287
-1.8	0.0294	0.0301	0.0307	0.0314	0.0322	0.0329	0.0336	0.0344	0.0351	0.0359
-1.7	0.0367	0.0375	0.0384	0.0392	0.0401	0.0409	0.0418	0.0427	0.0436	0.0446
-1.6	0.0455	0.0465	0.0475	0.0485	0.0495	0.0505	0.0516	0.0526	0.0537	0.0548
-1.5	0.0559	0.0571	0.0582	0.0594	0.0606	0.0618	0.0630	0.0643	0.0655	0.0668
-1.4	0.0681	0.0694	0.0708	0.0721	0.0735	0.0749	0.0764	0.0778	0.0793	0.0808
-1.3	0.0823	0.0838	0.0853	0.0869	0.0885	0.0901	0.0918	0.0934	0.0951	0.0968
-1.2	0.0985	0.1003	0.1020	0.1038	0.1056	0.1075	0.1093	0.1112	0.1131	0.1151
-1.1	0.1170	0.1190	0.1210	0.1230	0.1251	0.1271	0.1292	0.1314	0.1335	0.1357
-1.0	0.1379	0.1401	0.1423	0.1446	0.1469	0.1492	0.1515	0.1539	0.1562	0.1587
-0.9	0.1611	0.1635	0.1660	0.1685	0.1711	0.1736	0.1762	0.1788	0.1814	0.1841
-0.8	0.1867	0.1894	0.1922	0.1949	0.1977	0.2005	0.2033	0.2061	0.2090	0.2119
-0.7	0.2148	0.2177	0.2206	0.2236	0.2266	0.2296	0.2327	0.2358	0.2389	0.2420
-0.6	0.2451	0.2483	0.2514	0.2546	0.2578	0.2611	0.2643	0.2676	0.2709	0.2743
-0.5	0.2776	0.2810	0.2843	0.2877	0.2912	0.2946	0.2981	0.3015	0.3050	0.3085
-0.4	0.3121	0.3156	0.3192	0.3228	0.3264	0.3300	0.3336	0.3372	0.3409	0.3446
-0.3	0.3483	0.3520	0.3557	0.3594	0.3632	0.3669	0.3707	0.3745	0.3783	0.3821
-0.2	0.3829	0.3897	0.3936	0.3974	0.4013	0.4052	0.4090	0.4129	0.4168	0.4207
-0.1	0.4247	0.4286	0.4325	0.4364	0.4404	0.4443	0.4483	0.4522	0.4562	0.4602
0.0	0.4641	0.4681	0.4721	0.4761	0.4801	0.4840	0.4880	0.4920	0.4960	0.500

Appendices

Appendix D: Percentile-Z Conversion Table

Percentile	Z score	Percentile	Z score	Percentile	Z score
1	-2.326	34	-0.412	67	0.440
2	-2.054	35	-0.385	68	0.468
3	-1.881	36	-0.358	69	0.496
4	-1.751	37	-0.332	70	0.524
5	-1.645	38	-0.305	71	0.553
6	-1.555	39	-0.279	72	0.583
7	-1.476	40	-0.253	73	0.613
8	-1.405	41	-0.228	74	0.643
9	-1.341	42	-0.202	75	0.674
10	-1.282	43	-0.176	76	0.706
11	-1.227	44	-0.151	77	0.739
12	-1.175	45	-0.126	78	0.772
13	-1.126	46	-0.100	79	0.806
14	-1.080	47	-0.075	80	0.842
15	-1.036	48	-0.050	81	0.878
16	-0.994	49	-0.025	82	0.915
17	-0.954	50	0.000	83	0.954
18	-0.915	51	0.025	84	0.994
19	-0.878	52	0.050	85	1.036
20	-0.842	53	0.075	86	1.080
21	-0.806	54	0.100	87	1.126
22	-0.772	55	0.126	88	1.175
23	-0.739	56	0.151	89	1.227
24	-0.706	57	0.176	90	1.282
25	-0.674	58	0.202	91	1.341
26	-0.643	59	0.228	92	1.405
27	-0.613	60	0.253	93	1.476
28	-0.583	61	0.279	94	1.555
29	-0.553	62	0.305	95	1.645
30	-0.524	63	0.332	96	1.751
31	-0.496	64	0.358	97	1.881
32	-0.468	65	0.385	98	2.054
33	-0.440	66	0.412	99	2.326

Appendix E: Ability-Achievement Look-Up Table

Ability Standard Score	Ability-Achievement Correlation													Ability Standard Score
	0.30	0.35	0.40	0.45	0.50	0.55	0.60	0.65	0.70	0.75	0.80	0.85	0.90	
135	111	112	114	116	118	119	121	123	125	126	128	130	132	135
134	110	112	114	115	117	119	120	122	124	126	127	129	131	134
133	110	112	113	115	117	118	120	121	123	125	126	128	130	133
132	110	111	113	114	116	118	119	121	122	124	126	127	129	132
131	109	111	112	114	116	117	119	120	122	123	125	126	128	131
130	109	111	112	114	115	117	118	120	121	123	124	126	127	130
129	109	110	112	113	115	116	117	119	120	122	123	125	126	129
128	108	110	111	113	114	115	117	118	120	121	122	124	125	128
127	108	109	111	112	114	115	116	118	119	120	122	123	124	127
126	108	109	110	112	113	114	116	117	118	120	121	122	123	126
125	108	109	110	111	113	114	115	116	118	119	120	121	123	125
124	107	108	110	111	112	113	114	116	117	118	119	120	122	124
123	107	108	109	110	112	113	114	115	116	117	118	120	121	123
122	107	108	109	110	111	112	113	114	115	117	118	119	120	122
121	106	107	108	109	111	112	113	114	115	116	117	118	119	121
120	106	107	108	109	110	111	112	113	114	115	116	117	118	120
119	106	107	108	109	110	110	111	112	113	114	115	116	117	119
118	105	106	107	108	109	110	111	112	113	114	114	115	116	118
117	105	106	107	108	109	109	110	111	112	113	114	114	115	117
116	105	106	106	107	108	109	110	110	111	112	113	114	114	116
115	105	105	106	107	108	108	109	110	111	111	112	113	114	115
114	104	105	106	106	107	108	108	109	110	111	111	112	113	114
113	104	105	105	106	107	107	108	108	109	110	110	111	112	113
112	104	104	105	105	106	107	107	108	108	109	110	110	111	112
111	103	104	104	105	106	106	107	107	108	108	109	109	110	111
110	103	104	104	105	105	106	106	107	107	108	108	109	109	110
109	103	103	104	104	105	105	105	106	106	107	107	108	108	109
108	102	103	103	104	104	104	105	105	106	106	106	107	107	108
107	102	102	103	103	104	104	104	105	105	105	106	106	106	107
106	102	102	102	103	103	103	104	104	104	105	105	105	105	106
105	102	102	102	102	103	103	103	103	104	104	104	104	105	105
104	101	101	102	102	102	102	102	103	103	103	103	103	104	104
103	101	101	101	101	102	102	102	102	102	102	102	103	103	103
102	101	101	101	101	101	101	101	101	101	102	102	102	102	102
101	100	100	100	100	101	101	101	101	101	101	101	101	101	101

Appendices

Appendix E: Ability-Achievement Look-Up Table (continued)

Ability Standard Score	0.30	0.35	0.40	0.45	0.50	0.55	0.60	0.65	0.70	0.75	0.80	0.85	0.90	Ability Standard Score
					Ability-Achievement Correlation									
100	100	100	100	100	100	100	100	100	100	100	100	100	100	100
99	100	100	100	100	100	99	99	99	99	99	99	99	99	99
98	99	99	99	99	99	99	99	99	99	99	98	98	98	98
97	99	99	99	99	99	98	98	98	98	98	98	97	97	97
96	99	99	98	98	98	98	98	97	97	97	97	97	96	96
95	99	98	98	98	98	97	97	97	97	96	96	96	96	95
94	98	98	98	97	97	97	96	96	96	96	95	95	95	94
93	98	98	97	97	97	96	96	95	95	95	94	94	94	93
92	98	97	97	96	96	96	95	95	94	94	94	93	93	92
91	97	97	96	96	96	95	95	94	94	93	93	92	92	91
90	97	97	96	96	95	95	94	94	93	93	92	92	91	90
89	97	96	96	95	95	94	93	93	92	92	91	91	90	89
88	96	96	95	95	94	93	93	92	92	91	90	90	89	88
87	96	95	95	94	94	93	92	92	91	90	90	89	88	87
86	96	95	94	94	93	92	92	91	90	90	89	88	87	86
85	96	95	94	93	93	92	91	90	90	89	88	87	87	85
84	95	94	94	93	92	91	90	90	89	88	87	86	86	84
83	95	94	93	92	92	91	90	89	88	87	86	86	85	83
82	95	94	93	92	91	90	89	88	87	87	86	85	84	82
81	94	93	92	91	91	90	89	88	87	86	85	84	83	81
80	94	93	92	91	90	89	88	87	86	85	84	83	82	80
79	94	93	92	91	90	88	87	86	85	84	83	82	81	79
78	93	92	91	90	89	88	87	86	85	84	82	81	80	78
77	93	92	91	90	89	87	86	85	84	83	82	80	79	77
76	93	92	90	89	88	87	86	84	83	82	81	80	78	76
75	93	91	90	89	88	86	85	84	83	81	80	79	78	75
74	92	91	90	88	87	86	84	83	82	81	79	78	77	74
73	92	91	89	88	87	85	84	82	81	80	78	77	76	73
72	92	90	89	87	86	85	83	82	80	79	78	76	75	72
71	91	90	88	87	86	84	83	81	80	78	77	75	74	71
70	91	90	88	87	85	84	82	81	79	78	76	75	73	70
69	91	89	88	86	85	83	81	80	78	77	75	74	72	69
68	90	89	87	86	84	82	81	79	78	76	74	73	71	68
67	90	88	87	85	84	82	80	79	77	75	74	72	70	67
66	90	88	86	85	83	81	80	78	76	75	73	71	69	66
65	90	88	86	84	83	81	79	77	76	74	72	70	69	65

References

Abdi, H. (2007). The Bonferonni and Šidák corrections for multiple comparisons. In N. Salkind (Ed.) (2007). *Encyclopedia of Measurement and Statistics*. Thousand Oaks, CA: Sage.

Anastasi, A., & Urbini, S. (1997). *Psychological Testing* (7th Ed.). Upper Saddle River, NJ: Prentice Hall.

Audit Commission (2010). Evaluation of the Making Good Progress Project. Research Report DCSF-RR184. London: Audit Commission.

Audit Commission (2002). *Special Education: A Mainstream Issue*. London: Audit Commission.

Barnett, A., Henderson, S. E., Scheib, B., & Schulz, J. (2007). *Detailed Test of Speed of Handwriting*. London: Pearson.

Barnett, A., Henderson, S. E., Scheib, B., & Schulz, J. (2010). *Detailed Test of Speed of Handwriting 17+*. London: Pearson.

Bayley, N. (2006). *Bayley Scales of Infant and Toddler Development – Third Edition*. San Antonio, TX: Pearson.

Beery, K. E., Beery, N. A., & Bucktenica, N. A. (2010). *The Beery-Buktenica Developmental Test of Visual-Motor Integration, Sixth Edition*. Bloomington MA: Pearson.

Boyle, J., & Fisher, S. (2007). *Educational Testing: A Competence-Based Approach*. Oxford: BPS Blackwell.

Braverman, E. (2009). Cognitive decline and aging: Important neuroendocrinogical predictors of early cognitive decline in a clinical setting. *Anti-Aging Therapeutica, 11*, 37-46.

British Psychological Society (1999). *Dyslexia, Literacy and Psychological Assessment: Report by the Working Party of the Division of Educational and Child Psychology of the British Psychological Society*. Leicester: BPS.

Brooks, P., Everatt, J., & Fidler, R. (2004). *Adult Reading Test*. Roehampton: University of Surrey.

Bruton, A, Conway, J. H., & Holgate, S. T. (2000). Reliability: what is it and how is it measured? *Physiotherapy, 86*, 94-99.

Carlberg, C. (2011). *Statistical Analysis:* Microsoft Excel *2010*. Indiana, US: QUE.

Collins, W. A., & Goodnow, J. J. (1990). *Development According to Parents: The Nature, Sources, and Consequences of Parents' Ideas*. Hove: LEA.

Cortina, J. M. (1993). What is Coefficient Alpha? An examination of theories and applications. *Journal of Applied Psychology, 78*, 98-104.

Cronbach, L. J. (1951). Coefficient alpha and the internal structure of tests. *Psychometrika, 16*, 297-334.

Davis, F. B. (1959). Interpretation of differences among averages and individual test scores. *Journal of Educational Psychology, 50*, 4, 162-170.

Deary, I. J., Corley, J., Gow, A.J., Harris, S.E., Houlihan, L. M., Marioni, R. E., & Starr, J.M. (2009) *British Medical Bulletin, 92*, 135-152.

Deary, I. J., Egan, V., Gibson, G.J., Austin, E. J., Brand, C. R., & Kellaghan, T. (1996). Intelligence and the differentiation hypothesis. *Intelligence, 23*, 105-132.

Department for Education (2010). *Progression 2010–11: Advice on Improving Data to Raise Attainment and Maximise the Progress of Learners with Special Educational Needs*. London: DfE

References

Department for Education and Science (2001). *Special Education Needs Code of Practice (DfEs Report 0581 2001)*. London: DfES.

Department for Education and Science (2005). *SpLD Working Group 2005 Guidelines*. London: DfES.

Dodd, B., Hua, Z., Crosbie, S., Holm, A., & Ozanne, A. (2002). *Diagnostic Evaluation of Articulation and Phonolgy*. London: Pearson Assessment.

Embretson, S.E., & Reise, S.P. (2000). *Item Response Theory for Psychologists*. Mahwah, NJ: LEA.

Feldt, L. S., Steffen, M., & Gupta, N. C. (1985). A comparison of five methods for estimating the standard error of measurement at specific score levels. *Applied Psychological Measurement, 9*, 351-361.

Field, A. (2009). *Discovering statistics using SPSS* (3rd ed.). London: SAGE.

Flanagan, D. P., McGrew, K. S., & Ortiz, S. O. (2000). *The Wechsler Intelligence Scales and Gf-Gc Theory: A Contemporary Approach to Interpretation*. Boston: Allyn & Bacon.

Flanagan, D. P., Ortiz, S. O., Alfonso, V. C., & Dynda, A. M. (2006). Integration of Response to Intervention and norm-referenced tests in learning disability identification: learning from the Tower of Babel. *Psychology in the Schools, 43*, 807-825.

Flynn, J. R. (1987). Massive IQ gains in 14 nations: What IQ tests really measure. *Psychological Bulletin, 101*, 171-191.

Fuchs, L. S., Fuchs, D., & Compton, L. (2010). Rethinking Response to Intervention at Middle and High School. *School Psychology Review, 39*, 1, 22-28.

Hale, J. B. (2006). Implementing IDEA 2004 with a three-tier model that includes response to intervention and cognitive assessment methods. *School Psychology Forum: Research in Practice, 1*, 16-27.

Hale, J. B., & Fiorello, C. A. (2004). *School Neuropsychology: A Practitioner's Handbook*. New York: Guilford.

Harvill, L. M. (1991). NCME instructional module: Standard error of measurement. *Educational Measurement: Issues and Practice, 10*, 33-41.

Hedderly, R. (1996). Vernon-Warden Reading Test (Revised). *Dyslexia Review, 7, 2*.

Jaffe, L. E. (2009). Development, interpretation, and application of the W score and the relative proficiency index. Woodcock-Johnson III Assessment Services Bulletin No. 11. Rolling Meadows, IL: Riverside.

Johnson, B. E. E. (2011). Aptitude-achievement consistency analysis: An alternative to the ability-attainment discrepancy model. *Dyslexia Review, 22*, 14-16.

Kaufman, A. S., & Kaufman, N. L. (2004a). *Kaufman Assessment Battery for Children, Second Edition*. Bloomington, MN: Pearson.

Kaufman, A. S., & Kaufman, N. L. (2004b). *Kaufman Brief Intelligence Test, Second Edition*. Bloomington, MN: Pearson.

Kaufman, A. S., & Kaufman, N. L. (2004c). *Kaufman Test of Educational Achievement, Second Edition*. Bloomington, MN: Pearson.

Kavale, K. A. (2005). Identifying specific learning difficulty: Is Responsiveness to Intervention the answer? *Journal of Learning Disabilities, 38*, 553-562.

Kavale, K. A. (1987). Theoretical issues surrounding severe discrepancy. *Learning Disabilities Research, 3*, 12-20.

Kenney, J. F. & Keeping, E. S. (1951). *Mathematics of Statistics: Part 2 (2nd Ed.)*. Princeton, NJ: Van Nostrand.

Kline, P. (2000). *The Handbook of Psychological Testing: Second Edition*. New York: Routledge.

Knight, R. G. (1997). The Wechsler Adult Intelligence Scale – Revised in Clinical Neuropsychology Practice. *New Zealand Journal of Psychology, 26*, 2-18.

Knopman, D., Boland, L. L., Mosley, T., Howard, G., Liao, D., Szklo, M., McGovern, P., & Folsom, A. R. (2001). Cardiovascular risk factors and cognitive decline in middle-aged adults. *Neurology, 56*, 42-48.

Langdridge, D., & Hagger-Johnson, G. (2009). *Introduction to Research Methods and Data Analysis in Psychology*. London: Pearson Education.

Lichtenberger, E.O., & Breaux, K. C. (2010). *Essentials of WIAT-III and KTEA-II Assessment*. Hoboken, NJ: Wiley.

Lindsley, O.R. (1991) Precision Teaching's unique legacy from B.F. Skinner. *Journal of Behavioral Education, 1*, 253-266.

Livneh, H. (2009). Denial of chronic illness and disability. *Rehabilitation Counselling Bulletin, 52*, 22-5236.

Luria, A. R. (1973). *The Working Brain: An Introduction to Neuropsychology*. London: Penguin Books.

Manly, J. J., Touradji, P., Tang, M-X., & Stern, Y. (2003). Literacy and memory decline among ethnically diverse elders. *Journal of Clinical and Experimental Neuropsychology. 25*, 680–690.

Peacey, N., Lindsay, G., Brown, P., & Russell, A. (2010). *Increasing parents' confidence in the special educational needs system: Study commissioned to inform the Lamb inquiry. Interim report.* http://www.dcsf.gov.uk/lambinquiry .

Peterson, L. (2012). *The New System*. In Support and aspiration: A new approach to special educational needs and disability. Progress and Next Steps. www.nasen.org.uk

Raiford, S. E., Weiss, L. G., Rolfhus, E., & Coalson, D. (2005). Technical Report # 4. WISC-IV: Wechsler Intelligence Scale for Children – Fourth Edition: General Ability Index. London: Pearson Assessment.

Rasch, G. (1960). Probabilistic models for some intelligence and attainment tests, with a forward and afterword by B. D. Wright. Chicago: University of Chicago Press.

Raven, J. (2004). *Ravens Educational UK Coloured Progressive Matrices and Crichton Vocabulary Scale*. London: Pearson Assessment.

Raven, J. (2008). *Ravens Educational UK Standard Progressive Matrices – Plus Version and Mill Hill Vocabulary Scale*. London: Pearson Assessment.

Reynolds, C. R. (1990). Conceptual and technical problems in learning disability diagnosis. In C. R. Reynolds & R. W. Kamphaus (Eds.), *Handbook of Psychological and Educational Assessment of Children: Intelligence and Achievement* (pp. 571-592). New York: Guilford Press.

Reynolds, C.R., & Stanton, H.C. (1988). *Discrepancy Determinator 1*. Bensalem, PA: TRAIN.

Richards, M., & Deary, I. J. (2005). A life course approach to cognitive reserve: A model for cognitive aging and development. *Annals of Neurology, 58*, 617-622.

Richards, M. Shipley, B., Fuhrer, R., & Wadsworth, M .E. J. (2004). Cognitive ability in childhood and cognitive decline in mid-life: longitudinal birth cohort study. *BMJ, 328*: 552.

Roid, G.H., & Ledbetter, M.F. (2006). *Wide Range Achievement Test 4 Progress Monitoring Version*. Lutz, FL: PAR

References

Rose, J. (2009). *Identifying and Teaching Children with Dyslexia and Literacy Difficulties: An Independent Report from Sir Jim Rose to the Secretary of State for Children, Schools, and Families: June 2009.* DCSF-00659-2009. London: DCSF

Rust, J., & Golombok, S. (1999). *Modern Psychometrics: the Science of Psychological Assessment (2nd ed.).* London: Routledge.

Semel, E., Wiig, E. H., & Secord, W. A. (2006). *Clinical Evaluation of Language Fundamentals – Fourth UK Edition.* London: Pearson Assessment.

Shaywitz, B. A., Holford, T. R., Holahan, J. M., Fletcher, J. M., Stuebing, K. K., Francis, D. J., & Shaywitz, S. E. (1995). A Matthew Effect for IQ but not for reading: Results from a longitudinal study. *Reading Research Quarterly, 30,* 894-906.

Silverstein, A. B. (1982). Pattern analysis; the question of abnormality. *Journal of Consulting and Clinical Psychology, 50,* 234-240.

Singh-Manoux, A., Kivimaki, M., Glymour, M., Elbaz, A., Berr, C., Ebmeier, K. P., Ferries, J. E., & Dugravot, A. (2012). Timing of onset of cognitive decline: results from Whitehall II prospective cohort study, *BMJ,* 344:d7622.

Tabachnik, B. G., & Fidell, L. S. (2007). *Using Multivariate Statistics* (5th Pearson International Edition). Boston, MA: Pearson Education.

Thompson, R. (2004). Understanding dyslexia in the memory clinic. *Journal of Dementia Care, 12,* 35-37.

Torgesen J.K., Wagner, R.K., & Rashotte, C. A. (2011). *Test of Word Reading Efficiency – Second Edition.* Austin, TX: PRO-ED.

Wagner, R. K., Torgesen, J. K., & Rashotte, C. A. (1999). Comprehensive *Test of Phonological Processing.* Austin, TX: PRO-ED.

Wechsler, D. (1997). *Wechsler Adult Intelligence Scale – Third UK Edition.* London: Pearson Assessment.

Wechsler, D. (2004). *Wechsler Intelligence Scale for Children – Fourth UK Edition.* London: Pearson Assessment.

Wechsler, D. (2005). *Wechsler Individual Achievement Test – Second UK Edition.* London: Pearson Assessment.

Wechsler, D. (2006). *Wechsler Individual Achievement Test – Second UK Edition for Teachers.* London: Pearson Assessment.

Wechsler, D. (2009a). *Wechsler Individual Achievement Test – Third Edition.* San Antonio, TX: Pearson.

Wechsler, D. (2009b) *Wechsler Memory Scale – Fourth Edition.* San Antonio, TX: Pearson.

Wechsler, D. (2010). *Wechsler Adult Intelligence Scale – Fourth UK Edition.* London: Pearson Assessment.

Wechsler, D. (2011). *Wechsler Abbreviated Scale of Intelligence – Second Edition.* Bloomington, MN: Pearson.

Wiederholt, J. L., & Bryant, B. R. (2001). *Gray Oral Reading Tests – Fourth Edition.* Austin, TX: PRO-ED.

Willms, J. D., & Murray, T. S. (2007). *International Adult Literacy Survey: Gaining and Losing Literacy Skills over the Lifecourse.* Statistics Canada, 16.

Wilson, S.M., Brambati, S.M., Henry, R. G., Handwerker, D.A., Agosta, F., Miller, B.L., & Gorno-Tempini, M. L. (2009). The neurological basis of surface dyslexia in semantic dementia. *Brain, 132,* 71-86.

Wolf, M., & Bowers, P. (1999).The 'Double-Deficit Hypothesis' for the developmental dyslexias. *Journal of Educational Psychology, 91,* 1-24.

Woodcock, R. W., McGrew, K. S., & Mather, N. (2001). *Woodcock-Johnson III Tests of Cognitive Abilities.* Itasca, IL: Riverside.

Zenderland, L. (1998). *Measuring minds: Henry Herbert Goddard and the origins of American intelligence testing.* Cambridge, MA: Cambridge University Press.

Zimmerman, I. L., Steiner, V. G., & Pond, R. E. (2011). *Preschool Language Scales – Fifth Edition.* San Antonio, TX: Pearson.

Zimmerman, I. L., Steiner, V. G., & Pond, R. E. (2001). *Preschool Language Scales – Fourth Edition.* San Antonio, TX: Pearson.